Play Therapy with Preteens

Play Therapy with Preteens

Edited by
Eric Green
Jennifer Baggerly
Amie Myrick

ROWMAN & LITTLEFIELD
Lanham • Boulder • New York • London

Published by Rowman & Littlefield
An imprint of The Rowman & Littlefield Publishing Group, Inc.
4501 Forbes Boulevard, Suite 200, Lanham, Maryland 20706
www.rowman.com

Unit A, Whitacre Mews, 26-34 Stannary Street, London SE11 4AB

British Library Cataloguing in Publication Information Available

Library of Congress Cataloging-in-Publication Data

Names: Green, Eric, 1974- editor. | Baggerly, Jennifer, editor. | Myrick, Amie, editor.
Title: Play therapy with preteens / edited by Eric Green, Jennifer Baggerly, Amie Myrick.
Description: Lanham, Maryland : Rowman & Littlefield, 2018. | Includes bibliographical references and index.
Identifiers: LCCN 2018013693 (print) | LCCN 2018014773 (ebook) | ISBN 9781538108628 (electronic) | ISBN 9781538108604 (cloth : alk. paper) | ISBN 9781538108611 (pbk. : alk. paper)
Subjects: LCSH: Play therapy. | Adolescent psychotherapy.
Classification: LCC RJ505.P6 (ebook) | LCC RJ505.P6 P574 2018 (print) | DDC 618.92/891653—dc23
LC record available at https://lccn.loc.gov/2018013693

∞™ The paper used in this publication meets the minimum requirements of American National Standard for Information Sciences Permanence of Paper for Printed Library Materials, ANSI/NISO Z39.48-1992.

Printed in the United States of America

Eric—To my twinkling stars Izabel and Lily, and JonRoss: thanks for reminding your doting uncle that merry-go-round dreams are still made, on the love parade.

Jennifer—To my playful and loving pre-teen daughter, Katelyn: thanks for reminding your mom to play with you daily so we can enjoy your childhood together, forever and always.

Amie—To the very special little people in my life: whether I go by Mommy, Mimi, Amie, or some other variation, you each light up my life in a way that only you can.

Contents

Preface

Eric Green

> "This issue of love I am struck more by our similarities than our differences. With discernment we see not shadows lurking in closets or the stereotypes of what was once believed; rather, we see families committed to the common purpose of love, devotion, and service to the greater community. Let us look less to the sky to see what might fall; rather, let us look to each other and rise."—Michael McShane (2014)

Play therapy with preadolescents is a relatively unstudied paradigm in the current literature, as much of the research focuses on play therapy with elementary school–aged children. However, play therapy is often utilized by school counselors, child psychologists, social workers, and other mental health professionals to meet preadolescents' unmet mental health needs. Preadolescence, the general time frame between ten and thirteen years old, is a unique developmental epoch, deserving of treatment modalities and play therapy interventions specific to the psychosocial challenges that this age group encounters. Therefore, this book aims to present integrative models of play therapy that incorporate expressive arts and evidence-informed interventions when working with preadolescents from a play-based context. The current research demonstrates treatment efficacy when incorporating creative, dynamic interventions in work with preadolescents and their families.

My initial thoughts about writing this book came to me one day as I noticed most of my private practice work, however unwittingly, had shifted to patients with a median age of about ten, or the middle school years. I found that they were quite sophisticated and almost resistant to completing typical nondirective play in the playroom, yet not quite mature enough to do purely integrative or directive activity–based therapy as we sometimes employ with adolescents. So, I developed a treatment plan based on their learning and developmental style, each one being disparate from the one before.

Therefore, I began to search the literature to find resources to assist me with employing play therapy in a private practice setting with this fairly unstudied middle group in childhood, perhaps with a consistent or manualized focus. And, to my surprise, there was a paucity of literature specific to play therapy treatment with middle school students. It is then I realized that perhaps a volume addressing this population specific in the play therapy context may be of some benefit to other clinicians who see this demographic population, whether in schools or in private practice work. I then reached out to two of the most competent play therapists and researchers I know, Jennifer Baggerly and Amie Myrick, who also work regularly with this unique population. They both agreed to come on board, so next was the task of finding colleagues, researchers, clinicians, and educators who have nationally recognized specialization with this population and would be able to assist us in fulfilling the mission of this text, mainly to provide a guidebook of play therapy with children who are not quite teenagers but perhaps too mature to engage in typically early childhood play in the consulting room. And so the book began.

What makes this book unique is that there has not yet been a book written specifically on play therapy with preadolescents. *Play Therapy with Preteens* adds to the body of current literature in that it presents a comprehensive yet practical feel covering play therapy with preadolescents, one that integrates expressive arts like music, movement, play, sand, and poetry into treatment, along with familial involvement. This material is aimed at you, the reader, to be a helpful resource for master's and doctoral level mental health clinicians from social work, counseling, psychology, and the expressive arts, who seek to become more integrative within their preadolescent psychotherapy emphasis/practice. The intended audience is the typical master's level (and doctoral) practitioner market in the mental health field:

a. child-focused counselors in the American Counseling Association
b. family counselors who work with children and are involved in the International Association of Marriage and Family Counselors
c. elementary school counselors in the American School Counselor Association
d. play therapists in the Association of Play Therapy
e. child psychologists and school psychologists who are members of APA Division 53–Society of Clinical Child and Adolescent Psychology
f. child psychiatrists
g. clinical social workers

What makes me especially proud of this volume is the way in which it was written—mainly in a less academic, more accessible tone. We invited our contributors to write as casually and as accessibly as possible, thereby harnessing a conversational tone to speak directly to the reader. We did not want an artificial barrier of statistics and research to unnecessarily cloud the salience of the warm, nonjudgmental, humanistic relationship that is central to any effective work with preadolescents. We also included robust case studies with each chapter to give the reader illustrative examples of how these approaches may be employed in the consulting room. We also incorporated closing sections in each chapter with heartfelt reflections, many of which include the pitfalls of this work and mistakes we sometimes make along the way. As with any other psychotherapy book, reading this volume alone does not necessarily provide the reader the skills to ethically engage in new approaches without the proper mental health license, training, education, and relevant supervised practice. It is just one piece of the entire complex puzzle as we meet preadolescents where they are and attempt to build a relationship with them where they develop the tools, along with their families, to self-heal.

This volume starts with an introductory chapter by David Crenshaw and Sarah Caprioli, which provides the reader with an up-to-date synthesis of the most current developmental literature available when treating preteens. Next, the book delves into different theoretical approaches, such as cognitive behavioral therapy, written by the preeminent play therapist and researcher Janine Shelby. Clair Mellenthin goes on to apply her working knowledge of attachment-based theory to middle school students in a highly accessible, easy-to-understand style in chapter 3. Chapter 4, by Kristin Meany-Walen, is specific to Adlerian play therapy, and chapter 5, by Anne Stewart, Ariel Marrero, and Joseph Pellegrino, is dedicated to family therapy. Dee Ray and Cody Lankford explicate relational transformation and child-centered theory with this population in chapter 6; their case study is superbly written, heartfelt, full of discussion of unforeseen difficulties, and worth the purchase of the book alone. Next, Sang Min Shin, a former student and supervisee of mine from Johns Hopkins University and now a university professor in her own right, alongside Jacqueline Swank, wrote an imaginative take on incorporating nature in play with children. I remember when Sang Min moved here from her native country to study and the seminal importance that nature and Earth was to her and still is. In chapter 8, Robert Jason Grant takes us into his developed model of play therapy with children affected by autism. His approach is genius in its simplicity as he has dedicated much of his professional career to this population. Pam Dyson in chapter 9 provides multiple practical techniques clinicians can augment their tool kit with in the consulting room, a topic she presents on often to play therapists in the Dallas/Ft. Worth area and beyond. In chapter 10, Audrey Punnett writes a sumptuous narrative of sand play, and how to incorporate sand play with preteens within the context of play therapy. This chapter is one of the shining highlights of the entire volume as Audrey takes such complex, dense, Jungian material and makes it easily understandable and accessible to the reader. In my opinion, it's a striking chapter. The book concludes with two practical chapters: chapter 11, by Laura Fazio-Griffith, is on middle school counseling and social skills. The last chapter—ethics/self care—is written by Jodi Crane and Amie Myrick. We all need to continue learning about ethical challenges that we might encounter in this very technological and modernized society.

Finally, and most important, I graciously acknowledge you, the reader, as you are most likely working in the trenches with preteens day after day. Or perhaps you're a graduate student, or maybe even an educator, looking for new ideas and inspiration. We believe the critical reflectivity sections in each chapter, written with honesty and care by the contributors, as well as the casual tone of narrative employed throughout this book and when explicating case material, will help ignite new ways of being with children and playing with them toward self-healing. *Play Therapy with Preteens* was a two-year labor of love in the making, and I, along with my coeditors and contributors, am eager to share our passions and play-based humanism with you as you take the journey into the heart of play with preteens.

REFERENCE

McShane, M. (2014, May). *Case No. 6:13-cv-01834-MC*. Retrieved from: media.oregonlive.com/politics_impact/other/OPINION.pdf.

Acknowledgments

Eric Green

I want to thank the viscerally honest, vulnerable, and ultimately triumphant preteen patients I have the privilege of working with week after week, and their families, who place their trust in me throughout the process. We learn more from them than they ever learn from us. I also want to thank my family, who survived my own tumultuous adolescence, including Mom and Dad, my sister Jana and brother-in-law Ross, my grandmother Edith, my sister-in-law Paige Benoit, and my uncle/mentor Rev. Paul Metrejean. Sending appreciation to dear friends Muriel Dyson, Jose Ortiz, Ilene Pearce, Cordell Robinson, Melissa Kahn-Grey, and especially Laurie Barnes, for allowing me to nurture you and be nurtured in return. I also want to thank my clinical work family, who inspire me with their humility and grace, including Joni Orazio, Lisa Strauss, Jimmy Reaux, and Monica Daigle. Deep gratitude to Luke Elliot, Jimmy Chance, Art Kleiner, Brenda Bryant, and the courageous Katie Mitchell (DCFS), for giving me an unexpected Act 3 of a career through the nonprofit Better Options Initiative. To sandplay colleagues Audrey Punnett, Rosalind Heiko, Jackie Kelly, and Harriet Friedman, thanks for opening my heart to the power of Kalffian sandplay. Finally, I want to acknowledge the play therapists who kindle hope through their selfless work in the trenches, including Melissa Austin, Gregory Barden, the late Mistie Barnes, Robin Bell, Kendra Benesch, Norma Bonet, Patty Boylen, Christina G. Collins, Linda Dench, Barbara Fishgrab, Theresa Fraser, Erin Golden, Theresa Hill-Berting, Arnzie Johnson, Sueanne Kenney-Noziska, Liz Kong, Kris Marowski, Josephine Martin, Sarah McDermott, Rachel Parker-Stephens, Phyllis Post, beloved friend Jennifer Baggerly, and especially Amie Myrick, for standing by me but, more important, children in need, time and time again.

Jennifer Baggerly

With much love and gratitude, I thank my mother, Jean Baggerly, who turns ninety this year. I have fond memories of my preteen years when we played board games, rode a tandem bike along the Trinity River, and traveled internationally. I thank my father, Leo Baggerly, who also turns ninety this year. I have fond memories of my preteen years hiking together in the mountains with Carole, Philip, Keith, Derek, and Christine. I am so grateful for my daughter, Katelyn Jean Baggerly, as I watch how play, imagination, games, going to the park, and being a Ninja Warrior renews your creative and enthusiastic spirit during your preteen years. Thank you to Beth Kelly for the ongoing support and fun adventures to England and France with Katelyn, Natalie, and Cadence. I express deep appreciation for my play therapy mentors, Garry Landreth and Sue Bratton, for guiding me in the field of play therapy. I am grateful for the next generation of play therapists who took my classes at the University of North Texas at Dallas. Thank you to Kay Trotter for the opportunity to provide play therapy at Kaleidoscope Behavioral Health. Finally, thank you to the visionary and enthusiastic Eric Green and Amie Myrick, for your ongoing dedication to healing children through play therapy.

Amie Myrick

Where to start? I often reflect on my childhood, and I realize now more than ever what love, support, and acceptance I received, without exception from my mom and dad. Thank you both for putting up with me during my preteen and teen years and seeing me through to the other side! To my little boy, I am privileged and blessed to be your mommy. Thank you for letting me be a part of your adventures so far. I cannot wait to see what your preteen years (and beyond) hold for you! To my family and friends, who have been by my side during, arguably, the most challenging two years of my life, I am grateful every single day for every single one of you. Your unwavering support and love have made me strong; because of you, my cup is full. To my mentors and colleagues, especially Bethany Brand, Victor Welzant, and Eric Green, all I know about being a clinician, researcher, and contributor to this field, I have learned from you. You each saw something in me that I did not see in myself, and for that I will always be in your debt. Eric, you and Jennifer Baggerly, once again, have allowed me the opportunity to combine my love of writing and counseling into a beautiful book of which I am so proud. We did it! Last, but certainly not least, to the teens and families who come through my office every week, I am honored and humbled to be permitted into your worlds. Thank you.

Chapter One

Play Therapy with Preadolescents

A Developmental Overview

David A. Crenshaw and Sarah Caprioli

PREADOLESCENT STRUGGLES

The preteen stage of development is a vivid example of a "perfect storm." Ambiguity, confusion, and conflicting biological and social demands are rampant during this period. The internal rapid changes are occurring in the context of a fast changing social and cultural environment. I (David Crenshaw) wonder how many readers would want to be growing up in the world that previous generations, including all of us, have created and handed to today's youth. Many of us agonize over how to raise children and grandchildren who will be able to master the challenges of youth who are frequently referred to as tweens, not to mention the teen years to follow.

Several recent experiences opened my eyes to the toll that our current high performance and increased velocity world exact of our youth. I was invited to speak at a conference for administrators, social workers, and guidance counselors in the Mid-Hudson Valley (upstate New York). There was a strong consensus among these administrators and school counselors that in recent school years there has been a dramatic increase in anxiety and panic disorders. There was also a strong belief among these school officials that social media has drastically changed the exposure to risk and vulnerability of our impressionable youth. Another takeaway point from the conference, after listening to many school officials as well as a middle school youth who was on a panel that I moderated that day, is that the impact of social media is profoundly affecting the social anxiety of youth at all age levels with the peak occurring in middle school or early high school years.

In preparation for the conference, I asked my four undergraduate field placement students in psychology and four graduate interns in mental health counseling about their experiences in middle school and high school. They (all women; six Caucasian; two racial minority students) were quite willing to share their own stories of extreme competitive pressures throughout middle school and high school. I was astonished because the students are accomplished students and the undergraduates are all committed to pursuing graduate school. The students described not only the pressure of taking as many honor and advanced placement classes as possible but also strengthening their vita with as many impressive extracurricular activities as they could squeeze into an already crammed schedule. Some indicated that such heavy demands virtually nullified a social life or opportunities for play and fun.

What was especially striking was the concern they expressed for younger siblings currently in high school or middle school, who they believe are under even more pressure than they were at the time. Some of their siblings are suffering currently with symptoms of anxiety and depression. Some samples of the student descriptions of the life of a tween are contained below, included with the permission of the students.

Shaelynn, Marist undergraduate, junior, psychology major, social work minor

"Preadolescence is a time where children are going through significant life changes including puberty, entering high school, and figuring out their self-identity. I remember this stage as being full of confusion and sometimes feeling uncomfortable in my own skin. These milestones and emotions are already stressful enough for any preteen. Adding the rise in social media usage to the equation can potentially cause further distress and complications. My younger brother is thirteen and for years his classmates have had a social media presence. Their excessive use of sites like Instagram, Twitter, and Snapchat worries me as these sites can contain mature material that can accidentally or intentionally be accessed. In this way, social media can negatively impact their safety and self-esteem."

Caitlin, graduate student in clinical psychology, Columbia University

"At a time in [preteens'] lives when they are already struggling to 'fit in' and to find their niche in their peer group, social media can create unrealistic and unnecessary expectations. I can imagine my brother's female friends on Instagram comparing their bodies, clothes, hair, and even makeup to celebrities' and older girls' pictures. This constant comparing and conforming can significantly deplete their sense of self-worth. These girls are posting suggestive pictures on Instagram thinking that this is a healthy way to get attention from their peers. Overall, with the rise of social media it seems that both girls and boys are growing up 'too fast' due to the material that they are constantly being exposed to every day. Children of this age should be outside having fun with their friends, care free. Instead, their faces are glued to screens in an endless cycle of overstimulation. Without careful parental monitoring, I fear that social media use can damage the healthy development of preadolescence."

Tara, senior psychology major, SUNY-New Paltz

"Over the last decade, the rise of social media has been particularly prevalent amongst adolescents. Social media aims to connect people through the sharing of news, pictures, videos, and other content. Adolescents feel pressure to get likes, shares, and views. The fear of missing out is forcing adolescents to adhere to a new set of societal norms, and this, coupled with academic and life responsibilities, is producing a higher sense of disconnectedness and leading to negative health implications. Increased anxiety, depression, and other mental illness can even be damaging to the physical health of individuals.

As an adolescent living through the social media era, I have directly been impacted by the social pressures of needing to be included in the conversation. In middle school, my classmates and I were the first to join new social media sites and apps. The pressure to get likes and followers was overwhelming. We would do anything to get the attention that we needed from our peers to feel socially accepted.

I experienced the pressure and anxiety of trying to fit into the social norms. Spending hours trying to take the perfect selfie, or come up with clever posts to get likes seemed to be equivalent to picking out an outfit for school. Often, I would wonder why other girls had more likes, followers, and comments on their pictures and would then try to model them to get the same feedback. I pressured myself into believing I was ranked according to my likes and followers, and those who had more than I did were better. I often felt the fear of missing out, which is more common now due to the ubiquity of social media. I would go through the pictures and posts of what looked to be a fun night everyone else had and would wallow in self-pity because I was not invited. Being ranked, self-conscious, and feeling left out are often feelings adolescents experience, but the rise of social media exacerbates these conditions for adolescents, much more now, than in past generations."

Stephanie, senior psychology major, Marist College

"On the social media platform Instagram, there are always pictures of gorgeous, skinny, fit girls. They all have the perfect bodies, flowing hair, and the lives everyone desires. They all have a lot of friends, attend all different types of events and parties, and go on luxurious vacations. As a preadolescent, these are the girls they look up to. They follow their Instagram accounts and like and comment on all their pictures explaining how pretty and amazing they look. These preadolescents all sit together on their phones looking through these accounts wishing and dreaming that they could be just like them. The problem with social media posts like this is that it only shows one side of the story. All you see is the pictures on Instagram, but not the girls' lives behind the pictures. No one knows about the imperfections, but instead, only sees what is perfect about their lives."

These students capture some of the complexity, confusion, and conflict endemic to growing up in today's world in Western culture, which makes preadolescence a particularly treacherous passage for some and highly stressful for most. Preadolescents catch a glimpse of what awaits them in the adult world and some recoil from taking the baton adults are eager to hand off to them. It is a sobering reflection that perhaps we have created a world that our youth are not eager to inhabit as adults.

BRIEF LITERATURE REVIEW

The preadolescent years demand that the emerging youth gradually relinquish some of the joys, excitement, and shelter of childhood to begin to explore the world of adolescence with changing hormones and increased expectations of independence and growth toward adult roles (Purswell, 2016). Preadolescents are growing in their reasoning ability and most preadolescents are capable of decision making in which reasoning dominates emotion (Siegel & Paine Bryson, 2011). At the same time, these children (10–13 years old) are a long way from having adult reasoning powers. We now know that specialization and pruning in the brain continues into adult life. Physically, growth in multiple domains occurs during the onset of puberty, including improved gross and fine motor coordination; growth and maturity in their physical bodies; and increased hormones resulting in interest and curiosity about sex and romance.

As if preadolescence is not confusing enough as a developmental stage, advertisers spend millions to pitch ads to preteens, particularly girls, with messages that foster contempt toward their bodies unless they conform to the Western cultural ideal of thinness and hypersexualization (Bosacki, Elliott, Bajovic, & Akseer, 2009; Daniels, Layh, & Porzelius, 2016; Varies & Jackson, 2015). Preadolescents and adolescents are focused to a large extent on mastering their social world and finding acceptance among their peers. Complicating these efforts are perceptions of peer acceptance and rejection that can be distorted in depressed or aggressive preadolescents (Morrow, Hubbard, Sallee, et al., 2016). These researchers found that preadolescents with higher depression scores were more likely to underestimate their peer acceptance and friendship. Conversely, preadolescents with higher aggression were more likely to overestimate their peer acceptance and friendship especially when they experienced low levels of peer victimization.

The impact of social media on today's preadolescents is profound (Tiggemann & Slater, 2014; Varies & Jackson, 2015). Research shows that 40 to 50 percent of preadolescent girls report body dissatisfaction and wished they were thinner (Wertheim, Paxton, & Blaney, 2008). Such concerns make these young girls at-risk for eating disorders (Wertheim, Paxton, & Blaney, 2008).

Western culture grooms our youth, especially preadolescent and adolescent girls, to feel contempt for their own bodies if their bodies do not conform to the unrealistic ideal of the female body displayed on the cover of teen magazines. In addition, preadolescence is a critical developmental stage for another form of grooming of our youth by Western culture in terms of early sexualization, especially of girls (American Psychological Association Task Force on the Sexualization of Girls, 2007). These cultural pressures that groom young girls to believe that their value as persons hinge on looking sexy or "hot" for boys has been called the "shadow abuser" (Caprioli & Crenshaw, 2017). These authors explain the concept of the shadow abuser:

> For child victims of sexual abuse, the culture of sexual violence can feel like a living, breathing entity; a kind of "shadow abuser" that behaves and affects them in ways that mimic those abusers who take human form. The culture both grooms them and coerces them into silence. It creates shame about their bodies and their worth. It whispers to them that they deserved what happened to them and destroys their credibility with the people who might otherwise have helped them. The culture of sexual violence works in tandem with sexual aggressors, and in fact one would not be able to survive without the other. (p. 177)

While victims of child sexual abuse are particularly targeted for the insidious grooming of early sexualization, the influence is pervasive and seen frequently in middle schools in the United States where girls (and boys to a lesser degree) seek popularity and acceptance through provocative clothing. The APA task force report (American Psychological Association Task Force on the Sexualization of Girls, 2007) noted an indicator of how early retailers market sexualized and provocative clothing to young children. The report explained:

> Given that girls may be developing their identity in part through the clothing they choose, it is of concern when girls at increasingly younger ages are invited to try on and wear teen clothes designed to highlight female sexuality. Wearing such clothing may make it more difficult for girls to see their own worth and value in any way other than sexually. (p.13)

PRACTICAL INTERVENTIONS

Developmentally, preadolescence presents unique challenges to therapists. In my (David Crenshaw) private clinical practice over a thirty-six-year period, I often saw the same children at different developmental stages as new challenges arose over the course of their development. The child who at age seven loved the sessions, enjoying playing with puppets and drawing pictures, shows up in my office at age twelve wanting no part of therapy and resentful that he or she was coerced into coming by parents or as a result of pressures from school to seek help. I would sometimes wonder, "Is this the same child who at a younger age looked forward to the sessions and was reluctant to leave at the end? Could this be a case of mistaken identity?" No, this was a case of the profound impact of the "between stage" of development where identity is confused and shaken and leaning on adults—whether parents, teachers, or therapists—is experienced as a threat to their emerging autonomy. Usually the reluctance of the preadolescent returning to therapy or the new preadolescent client can be overcome, but the experience is remarkably different from the younger school-age child who typically welcomes the interest and presence of a listening and concerned adult. There are always exceptions, however, but preadolescents typically find the therapy space to be awkward and unnatural, and they are self-conscious about engaging in a process of self-reflection at a time when the ground underneath them no longer seems solid and dependable.

Beverly James (1994), in a presentation to the New York Association for Play Therapy, explained that preadolescents and adolescents feel a heightened sense of vulnerability and exposure when they come into a therapist's office. She elaborated that it is almost like these young preteens and teens believe that the therapist has "x-ray vision and can see right through their skin." Younger children are known for starting a story in the middle and assuming that the therapist knows the beginning, but with little sense of self-consciousness or exposure. Meeting the challenge of the awkward, unnatural, and vulnerable sense experienced by the typical preadolescent requires that therapy be offered in a face-saving package. One of the primary tools that assists the preadolescent to participate in therapy in a more comfortable, natural, and face-saving way is expressive arts interventions (Bratton, Ceballos, & Ferebee, 2009; Erath, Tu, & El-Sheikh, 2012). Expressive activities in therapy, like play itself, activate the right hemisphere of the brain, which taps the emotional, holistic, and creative functioning of the person (Schore, 2012). Among the expressive arts that elicit the creative and artistic energy and talent of the preadolescent are sandplay, writing, poetry, drawing, painting, sculpting, music, dance, movement, dramatic play, fantasy activities, phototherapy, puppetry, wood burning, collages, and, as illustrated in the case study of Abby below, animal-assisted therapy (Bratton, Ceballos, & Ferebee, 2009; Malchiodi & Crenshaw, 2017). The use of creative, expressive interventions with preadolescents enables them to engage in therapy in a less exposed and threatening way that verbally expressive approaches often entail, and in a developmentally appropriate way (Malchiodi, 2017).

CASE STUDY: ABBY

Sometimes professional growth has a way of sneaking up on you. Like physical growth, we often expect it to happen predictably over long periods of time, but in fact it is much more likely to occur in surges and spurts of intense and sometimes difficult development. When I (Sarah Caprioli) met Abby (pseudonym) in 2013 I had no idea that she would become the catalyst for one of the most substantial professional growth spurts of my career. Abby was eleven, just starting middle school, and about as defiant as they come. At least that's how her family, teachers, and most other adults in her life described her. She showed up to our first session in an oversized black sweatshirt, the hood of which she kept cinched tightly around her face so that only her eyes, nose, and mouth were visible. She spoke only to tell me that she was bored and to ask when the session would be over.

Until recently, Abby had been carrying a secret. When she was six years old her uncle, who watched her after school most days during the week, had begun to sexually abuse her. Confused and unable to find a trusted adult to whom she could disclose, the abuse progressed and worsened over time. Abby began to withdraw, putting up walls and acting out to cover up the deep shame and loneliness she carried inside. She got into fistfights at school and earned a reputation as a "bad kid" from school personnel and students alike. The abuse was discovered shortly before Abby's eleventh birthday, when she broke down after watching a film about sexual abuse in school and disclosed to her teacher. I met her a few months later.

Crenshaw and Mordock (2005) used the phrase "fawns in gorilla suits" to describe children who develop thick walls of anger and detachment to protect the vulnerable core selves that have been so damaged by experiences of trauma, betrayal, and rejection. Abby's gorilla suit was so convincing that she had persuaded nearly everyone in her life not to see the hurt and terrified fawn hiding beneath the surface. Our early conversations consisted mostly of lists of the "bad" deeds she had done and the other kids she had fought. She wanted no part of the play therapy room, glancing briefly inside one day and immediately declaring the whole space was "stupid." She wasn't just a preadolescent, with all the requisite aloof behavior and eye rolling that comes with the territory, she was a preadolescent with a profoundly wounded spirit, and she had built a fortress around herself to protect it.

Help came first in the form of art. For all of her tough exterior, I couldn't help but notice the way Abby's eyes would drift to the crayon wax art on my wall or the pile of paper and markers left by an earlier child. The day she asked me if I would help her make her own melted crayon art, I knew I had found a way in. Abby's aunt, one of the few consistently stable and caring adults in her life, had a penchant for crafting that she had passed on to Abby. It was innately comforting to her in a way even her gorilla suit could not disguise. Expressive arts therapy in this way became a common language between us. It created an opening: a space in which trust could grow and a place to test out small moments of vulnerability. The act of creating art itself also had a deeply regulating effect on Abby. Because she was living with extensive developmental trauma and used aggression as a protective mechanism, she often came to session quite dysregulated. During these periods of hyperarousal, she had tremendous difficulty focusing, processing information, and modulating emotion. But she was able to attend to art, and the sensory soothing combination of texture, color, and rhythm allowed her entire body to relax. Painting was particularly effective for this purpose. Abby used paint in a uniquely tactile way, layering thick brushstrokes of color over and over each other. She became perfectly silent and focused under the rhythm of mixing, brushing, and blending, and I could almost see the frenetic activity in her brainstem begin to calm. Also essential in our use of art to promote self-regulation was the opportunity it provided for relational engagement. By allowing me this window into her inner world, Abby was also developing the ability to trust and rely on me in more and more important ways. The connection meant that I was becoming a trustworthy adult in her eyes; one who could be counted on to provide consistent safety and support. It was a position I was and still am honored to hold.

Engaging Abby using expressive arts also allowed her to add some flexibility to the very rigid framework she had developed to contain her wounds. She grew a little softer, and began to tell me stories about defending other kids against bullies instead of doing the bullying herself. We met regularly in the playroom now, as that space contained a larger table to work at, and she took to running her hands through the sand tray when she needed a break. Much like the fluid texture of the paint, the flow of sand through her fingers calmed her in a way that created openings for emotion and vulnerability to pass through. I introduced her to the sand tray miniatures. Where just a few months earlier she had rolled her eyes sarcastically at the mention of "play," she now scanned my shelves intently, looking amused but interested. She stopped on a grotesquely disfigured ogre wielding two large axes, easily the scariest figure in the bunch. Plucking him from the shelf, she dug a hole and buried him, piling all the sand in the tray on top of that spot. "It's my uncle" she told me. "But he's even uglier."

From that point on we incorporated sand trays into most of our sessions, and the work continued to deepen. It was also around that time that we learned Abby's case was likely going to trial. The sand tray became a staple then, as Abby re-created the courtroom setup in the sand repeatedly to try to gain some mastery over the terrifying realization that she would be expected to testify in open court, in the presence of her uncle. She selected figures for each of the players in the courtroom, including army men to represent court officers, which she amassed in the sand and moved in endless variations in an attempt to come up with a configuration that made her feel safe. Although I also did my best to maintain a safe space for Abby to explore her fears, the development of a deep and visceral sense of safety remained elusive until I had the rare opportunity to bring in a co-therapist highly skilled at healing deep wounds to the spirit: a three-year-old service dog named Bosch.

Bosch was very generously on loan to us from the Torrington-based service dog agency, Educated Canines Assisting with Disabilities (ECAD), for the purpose of providing comfort to Abby before, during, and after her trial. Thanks to a landmark case in 2011 where a service dog named Rosie (Bosch's great grandmother!) was allowed to accompany a young girl onto the witness stand, New York State now had solid legal precedent to allow this accommodation for other vulnerable witnesses testifying in open court (Crenshaw, 2011, 2014). The addition of Bosch to our sessions erased the last of Abby's resistance to play. Since Abby and Bosch needed to develop a strong bond for him to do his job most effectively, we were encouraged to play games with him in addition to using him in our regular session work. Abby's play with Bosch was joyful and spontaneous, and it wasn't long before he became an integral part of our more structured play therapy work too.

In the playroom, Abby worked with Bosch the way a younger child might work with dolls. She took care of him, gently brushing his fur or making "food" for him to eat. She put him to bed for naps, and even used the doctor's kit to take his blood pressure or give him a shot. Abused children often remind us of what many of us take for granted—the joy of giving love to others. Abused children often are deprived of safe persons to give love to and consequently of the joy of giving and loving. Highly trained dogs like Bosch fill that emptiness in the soul of the abused child exceedingly well because far more than any person, they are safe to care for, to give to, and to love wholeheartedly. The extent of the therapeutic impact cannot be overstated. As she cared for him, Abby also talked to him, first in whispers and later loud enough to include me in the conversation. She told him about being angry and fighting at school, and about the shame she felt over what had happened to her. With Bosch's help, Abby completed her first hopeful piece of art. It took months to finish, partly because the "help" Bosch provided often ended with me and Abby diligently scrubbing a paw or snout that had somehow or other ended up covered in paint.

When it was done, the painting depicted an enormous green hill under a deep blue night sky, filled with stars. On the hillside were written the words, "Never give up. Keep going," with arrows pointing up to the sky. She presented it to me unceremoniously one day, and told me that I could have it if I would hang it in my office for other kids to see. I replied that not only would I hang it in my office, but that I would hang it in *every* office I ever practiced in for the duration of my career, and that when I retired I would hang it in my house. I have moved offices three times since then, and the painting has come with me to each one.

Like the stories of most of the children who pass through our offices, I don't yet know how Abby's story ends. Her case did indeed go to trial, but her incredible courage and readiness to take the stand so panicked her abuser that he pleaded guilty the day before she was slated to testify and is currently serving a long-term prison sentence. After having worked so closely with the district attorney's office to get Abby and Bosch ready for court, we all decided that we needed Bosch around on a more permanent basis. So, with the help of a number of dedicated agencies and individuals, the Dutchess County Courthouse Facility Dog Program was born. The program is housed at our local district attorney's office and gives crime victims of all ages access to Bosch in forensic interviews, court, and during counseling sessions. It is only the third of its kind in New York State. I have never seen Abby so genuinely overcome with emotion as I did the day she found out that she (along with the equally courageous child who testified with Rosie's help in 2011) was the inspiration for the program. Her ability to express such pure joy in that moment will, for me, always be the best marker of success.

INCORPORATION OF FAMILY

Research supports the benefit of including parents in the child therapy process. The participation and support of parents increases the efficacy of play therapy and child/adolescent therapy (Ray, 2015). The challenge is including the parents of the preadolescent without alienating or causing mistrust in the youthful therapy client. This may require some fancy footwork on the part of a therapist in order to prevent a premature ending to the therapy. One important consideration is genuineness and honesty on the part of the therapist. It is critical to be open and transparent with preadolescents and to consider their input and feedback in the process. Sometimes it works to have the parents participate in at least a portion of the preadolescent's session on some regular interval (such as every six weeks) and for the client and therapist to share their ideas of how the therapy is going and if the parents can be doing anything different to support and enhance the therapy. If the therapist meets with the parents in a separate feedback session because the preadolescent doesn't feel comfortable participating, then in subsequent sessions the preadolescent should always be invited and have the choice to participate. If they elect to not be present, it still can be helpful in maintaining trust to review with the preadolescent ahead of the session what the therapist plans to share with the parents about the progress of therapy and if there are specific things that the preadolescent would not want the therapist to share. Of course, when informed consent is given at the beginning of the therapy, the client would be clearly informed of any exceptions to confidentiality such as imminent danger to the client or another person.

Family therapy can avoid some of the worries and mistrust the preadolescent might entertain when the therapist meets separately with the parents. Family therapy, however, may conflict with the developmental needs of the preteen who may back away from anything that threatens their independence or by even the appearance of turning back to their parents for emotional support. Bringing the family together to address the problems might even be contraindicated for a preteen who is overly dependent and emotionally enmeshed in the family. In enmeshed families, the family therapist would work with the family to create more space and clearer boundaries between the family members, but another way to establish the needed boundaries would be to meet separately with the child and the parents.

In contrast to the enmeshed family, some families are disengaged, with too much space between the family members, and in this case the goal of the family therapist would be to create more closeness and intimacy between family members. A feature of preadolescents that psychoanalytic writers have focused on is a phase of severe fault finding of their parents. The parents are harshly criticized for virtually anything they do, even such minor transgressions as the way they stir their iced tea. The severe fault finding serves the developmental need to put distance between the preteen and their parents but in a manner that creates tension and hurt in family relationships (Fussner & Crenshaw, 2008). In this case, the play therapist can engage the family through playful methods such as puppet play, sand tray, or other creative arts activities to work on increasing proximity and improving communication skills especially on emotional issues.

CONCLUSION

Preadolescence under the best of contextual conditions is a bewildering and confusing time for our youth. This phase of development is exasperated by the rapid social and technological changes occurring in this historical moment in time, which mirrors preadolescents' rapid and intense hormonal changes within their bodies. No wonder the schools are facing a crisis dealing with anxiety problems among students especially in middle school and high school. Added to these baseline conditions are the exposure to adversity faced by youth, especially those who are referred for clinical services.

It is a sad commentary regarding contemporary Western culture that preadolescents face so many challenges. They experience confusion and angst that is endemic to the "tweenager" developmental stage. They have rapid physiological, especially hormonal, changes and growth spurts. Preadolescents also confront a rapidly changing social and technological world with insidious influences such as the impact of social media promoting unhealthy body images and cultural sexualization of our youth. In addition, preadolescents live with the overarching importance of finding acceptance and belonging among peers at a time when bullying and peer victimization reaches a peak. Due to the complex challenges of treating preadolescents, therapists need to be well versed in a wide range of play therapy and expressive arts strategies to engage the "betweeners" in a meaningful and helpful way.

REFERENCES

American Psychological Association Task Force on the Sexualization of Girls. (2007). Report of the APA Task Force on the Sexualization of Girls. Retrieved from http://www.apa.org/pi/women/programs/girls/report-full.pdf.

Bosacki, S., Elliott, A., Bajovic, M., & Akseer, S. (2009). Preadolescents' self-concept and magazine preferences. *Journal of Research in Childhood Education, 23*(3), 340–350.

Bratton, S., Ceballos, P., & Ferebee, K. W. (2009). Integration of expressive activities within a Humanistic play therapy format for preadolescents. *The Journal for Specialists in Group Work, 34* (3), 251–275.

Caprioli, S., & Crenshaw, D. A. (2017). Silencing and the culture of sexual violence: The "shadow abuser." In Malchiodi, C. A., & Crenshaw, D. A. (Eds.) (2017). *What to do when children clam up in psychotherapy: Interventions to facilitate communication* (pp. 176–196). New York: Guilford Press.

Crenshaw, D. A. (2011). The play therapist as advocate for children in the court system. *Play Therapy, 6,* (Dec.) 6–9.

Crenshaw, D. A. (2014). Advocacy for vulnerable children. Play Therapy, 9, 20–23.

Crenshaw, D., & Mordock, J. (2005). *Understanding and treating the aggression and violence of children: Fawns in gorilla suits.* New York: Jason Aronson.

Daniels, E. A., Layh, M. C., & Porzelius, L. K. (2016). Grooming ten-year-olds with gender stereotypes? A content analysis of preteen and teen magazines. *Body Image, 19*, 57–67.

Erath, S. A., Tu, K. M., & El-Sheikh, M. (2012). Socially anxious and peer-victimized preadolescents: "Doubly primed" for distress? *Journal of Abnormal Child Psychology, 40,* 837–848.

Fussner, A., & Crenshaw, D. A. (2008). Healing the wounds of children in a family context. In D. A. Crenshaw (Ed.). *Child and adolescent psychotherapy: Wounded spirits and healing paths* (pp. 31–48). Lanham, MD: Rowman & Littlefield.

James, B. (1994). *Handbook for treatment of attachment-trauma problems in children.* New York: Lexington Books.

Malchiodi, C. A. (2017). Art therapy approaches to facilitate verbal expression: Getting past the impasse. In Malchiodi, C. A., & Crenshaw, D. A. (Eds.) (2017). *What to do when children clam up in psychotherapy: Interventions to facilitate communication* (pp. 198–216). New York: Guilford Press.

Malchiodi, C. A., & Crenshaw, D. A. (Eds.) (2017). *What to do when children clam up in psychotherapy: Interventions to facilitate communication.* New York: Guilford Press.

Morrow, M. T., Hubbard, J. A., Sallee, M. L., Barhight, L. R., Lines, M. M., & Rubin, R. M. (2016). Dyadic accuracy and bias in preadolescents' perceived peer relations: Associations with aggression, depression, and peer victimization. *Journal of Social and Personal Relationships, 33*(7), 892–916.

Purswell, K. (2016). The extraordinary 11-year-old. In D. C. Ray (Ed.), *A therapist guide to child development: The extraordinary normal years* (pp.152–164). New York: Routledge.

Ray, D. (2015). Empirical support for practice. In D. A. Crenshaw and A. L. Stewart (Eds.), *Play therapy: A comprehensive guide to theory and practice* (pp. 467–482). New York: Guilford Press.

Schore, A. N. (2012). *The science of the art of psychotherapy.* New York: Norton.

Siegel, D. J., & Paine Bryson, T. (2011). *The whole-brain child.* New York: Delacort.

Tiggemann, M., & Slater, A. (2014). NetTweens: The internet and body image concerns in preteenage girls. *Journal of Early Adolescence, 34*(5), 606–620.

Varies, T., & Jackson, S. (2015). Preteen girls, magazines, and the negotiation of young sexual femininity. *Gender and Education, 27*(6), 700–713.

Wertheim, E. H., Paxton, S. J., & Blaney, S. (2008). Body image in girls. In L. Smolak & J. K. Thompson (Eds.), *Body image, eating disorders, and obesity in youth* (pp. 47–76). Washington, DC: American Psychological Association.

Chapter Two

Cognitive Behavior Therapy with Preadolescents

Using Academic Curricula Standards to Guide Treatment Interventions

Janine Shelby

> Two men look out through the same bars.
> One sees the mud, and one the stars.—(Langbridge, 1896, p. 27)

The period between childhood and adolescence is a time of striking change as children's bodies begin to take on adult characteristics, their linguistic styles reflect peer influences, and their cognitive abilities advance. Cognitive behavior therapies (CBTs) have the strongest research base of any class of psychotherapy, but may pose cognitive challenges for some preadolescents, whose complex abstract thinking skills may not be sufficiently formed to meet the demands of all aspects of the treatment. However, preadolescents are uniquely positioned to benefit from CBTs because middle school academic curricula include modules designed to build many skills also required for participation in CBT. In sixth-grade English language arts (ELA), mathematics, and science curricula, as in CBT, preadolescents are taught to differentiate facts from opinions, examine the evidence for conclusions, hypothesize outcomes, identify the perspectives of others, estimate probabilities, and understand basic scientific methodology. This shared content with CBT has the potential to mutually reinforce knowledge and skills acquired in each setting, and bolster abstract thinking competencies. The overlap between school- and CBT-related abstract thinking skills is also beneficial to CBT practitioners, who can draw on academic curricula standards to become familiar with common academic trajectories for exposure to these concepts.

Knowledgeable clinicians are better able to evaluate preadolescents' suitability for CBTs, and individually tailor treatments based on each preadolescent's academic exposure and proficiencies. In this chapter, I present an overview of CBT theory, components, and common techniques, as well as a case example of CBT with a preadolescent girl. I describe not only how CBTs can be used effectively with preadolescents, but also ways in which the unique overlay between preadolescents' academic and therapy content can be tapped to optimize their CBT outcomes.

LITERATURE REVIEW

CBT Overview

CBT, pioneered by Aaron T. Beck and Albert Ellis in the 1960s and 1970s, is not a single therapy but a class of similar therapies that share a common theoretical base and often include similar interventions. CBT is centered on the belief that cognitions (i.e., thoughts and beliefs), behaviors, and affect (i.e., feelings) are interrelated and influence each other. Despite this connection, it is difficult for someone to alter mood directly by simply choosing to feel better. CBT theory contends that feelings change when people alter their thoughts or behaviors. For example, a girl who is immobilized with anxiety about taking a test at school can decrease her distress by behaving differently (e.g., doing something she enjoys, using relaxation techniques, talking about her feelings with a trusted adult, or engaging in physical exercise) or altering her thoughts (e.g., saying to herself, "this is stressful, but I will get through it"). This interdependent process is known as the cognitive triangle, because it is often depicted as a triangle or a diagram similar to figure 2.1.

Changing any part of the cognitive triangle can result in changes to other components of the triangle. As the girl alters her behavior, her thoughts are likely to change. This, in turn, influences her mood. For instance, exercising before school might result in an increased sense of physical well-being, which is likely to lead to more hopeful thoughts and elevated mood.

CBT modules vary somewhat based upon the specific disorder they were designed to treat, but all CBTs include a cognitive triangle component and emphasize the client's ability to recognize, evaluate, and change thoughts and/or behaviors. In CBT, clients are instructed to use cognitive techniques, such as examining the evidence for thoughts and beliefs, identifying the pros and cons of specific thoughts or behaviors, and reframing cognitions to think of situations, experiences, or attributions differently. CBT emphasizes the use of both *accurate **and** helpful* cognitions. So, an *untrue* thought (e.g., "I always fail at everything") is replaced with a true and helpful cognition (e.g., "I do a good job in a lot of areas" or "I worked hard to learn a lot of things for this test"). A true but *unhelpful* thought (e.g., "I didn't study very much; I'm

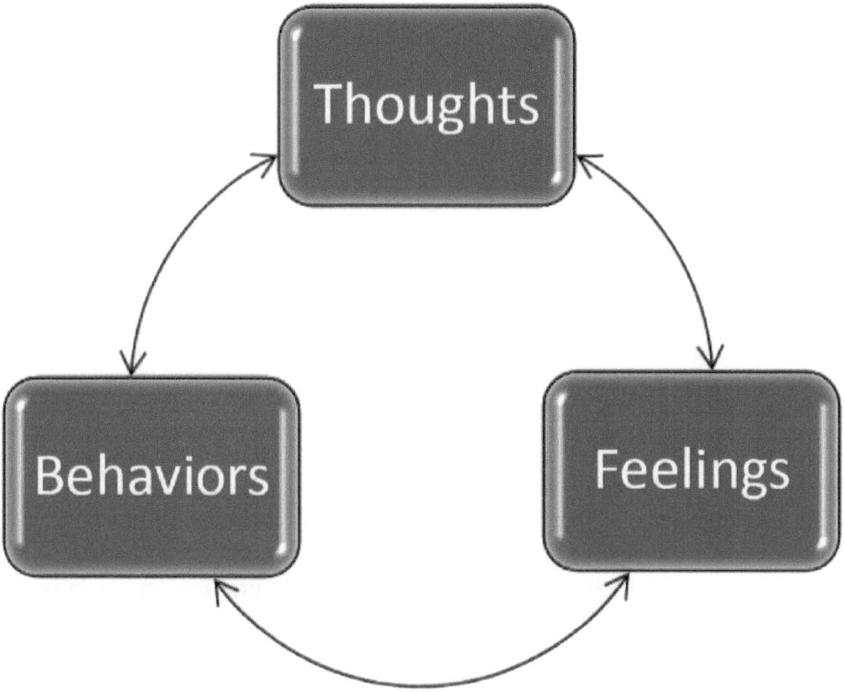

Figure 2.1. The Cognitive Triangle. Created by Janine Shelby

totally going to fail!") is also exchanged for a true and helpful thought (e.g., "I didn't study very much, but the test is in fifteen minutes so at this point I'll just focus on doing my best"). Unrealistic thoughts (e.g., "Everything will be fine even if I don't study") are not likely to achieve desired outcomes. Therefore, they are substituted with realistic cognitions (see figure 2.2). In addition to their cognitive focus, most CBTs incorporate behavioral activation, wherein clients are taught to change emotions through overt behavioral action (i.e., increasing activity level to engage in more positive experiences, such as taking a walk or attending a social event, while also decreasing negative behaviors like oversleeping or isolating oneself). Other common CBT modules are psychoeducation, enhancement of coping skills, and in vivo or imaginal exposure to feared or avoided stimuli. Training to enhance relaxation and problem-solving or social skills, as well as anticipatory guidance for future problem situations, are also included in many protocols (see also Friedberg and McClure [2015] for an overview of cognitive therapy modules for children and adolescents).

CBTs have been widely demonstrated to be effective for youth with a wide range of psychological disorders and are consistently categorized as

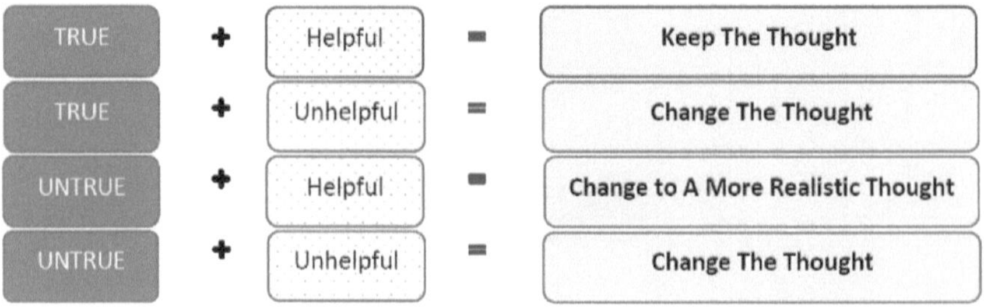

Figure 2.2. Helpful and Unhelpful Thoughts. Created by Janine Shelby

evidence-based among the many organizations and databases that evaluate and classify various therapies' scientific support levels. In addition to their effectiveness with clinical populations, CBTs and related interventions have been found to be beneficial in nonclinical settings, such as academic achievement, athletic performance, and the improvement of health issues (e.g., diabetes, pain, and obesity).

CBTs are goal focused and designed to achieve progress in a relatively short period of time. To do this, CBTs rely upon collaboration between the therapist and client as they discuss and target specific, highly detailed goals, symptoms, or problems. At the beginning of treatment, CBT therapists conduct thorough psychodiagnostic assessments using multiple sources of information, including standardized, normed assessment instruments, as well as clinical interviews with clients, their caregivers, and, when appropriate, their teachers. After the diagnosis has been determined, a corresponding CBT protocol is selected based upon a match between the diagnosis and rigorous scientific research demonstrating the effectiveness of a treatment with similar youth who have the same disorder. One difference between CBT and many other therapies is the use of metrics and data-driven decisions. The baseline presence, severity, and/or frequency of clinical concerns is measured in quantifiable ways (i.e., usually client affect ratings or symptom frequency/intensity). For example, using a scale such as the one shown in figure 2.3, clients measure their initial mood or distress level, and they contrast this baseline rating with later measurements to track progress over the course of treatment. The use of quantifiable data allows clients to use relatively objective indicators of therapeutic success and symptom reduction. Particularly for those with disorders that make it difficult to self-monitor positive changes, this data-driven approach helps clients recognize their therapeutic gains.

Many CBTs follow a similar sequence during each session to help ensure that treatment targets are systematically addressed and progress is steady. Sessions typically begin with assessment of symptoms from questionnaires

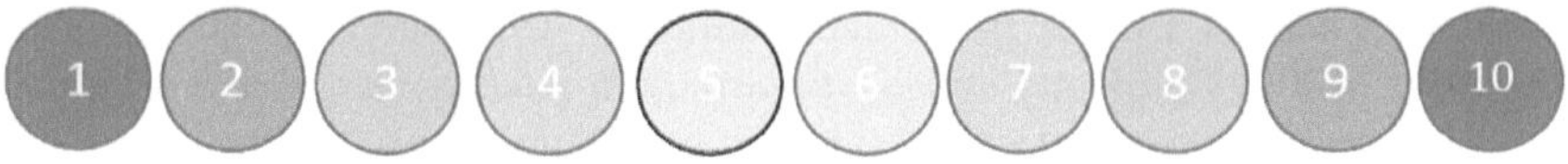

Figure 2.3. 10-Point Mood Rating. Created by Janine Shelby

and/or numerical ratings of affect. Next, youth provide brief updates about their week. Therapy homework is reviewed early in the session and is considered an essential part of the treatment because most change occurs outside the therapy setting as clients develop and practice skills in their natural environments. If youth arrive at sessions with uncompleted or incomplete homework, it is often finished during the session. When they have difficulty completing their assignments, therapists help them identify and reduce barriers to future homework completion. Also, relatively early in the session, therapists link the current session to the prior session by asking clients what they remember from the last meeting and summarizing the prior session. Then, both therapists and clients collaboratively set and address the items on the session agenda. Before the conclusion of the session, homework assignments related to the agenda are developed with preadolescents' input. The appointment ends with clients' feedback about helpful and unhelpful parts of the session.

CBTs emphasize the teaching and learning of new skills, but clients are regarded as valued collaborators rather than passive recipients of therapists' instruction. Therapists do not dictate which thoughts and behaviors are helpful. Rather, they explore the outcomes of clients' specific cognitions and behaviors, and promote the use of true and helpful cognitions. To do this, therapists often use the Socratic questioning technique, in which they ask clarifying questions to help clients discover for themselves the cognitions and behaviors likely to lead to positive results.

Preadolescent Development and CBTs

During the past two decades, the child and adolescent psychotherapy field has shifted toward greater use of evidence-based treatments (EBTs), and clinicians' decisions are now often informed by therapy outcome research. However, clinical reasoning should also be guided by child development research, given that some EBTs, particularly CBTs, require cognitive abilities that may not yet have been acquired by some children and preadolescents. So, therapists must evaluate whether and how specific treatments or techniques should be implemented with youth of various cognitive and developmental levels. In evaluating developmental readiness for CBT or particular techniques embedded within CBT, Garber, Frankel, and Herrington's

(2016) points are helpful to consider: (a) Which particular cognitive skills are needed to benefit from a particular treatment?; (b) When do the required cognitive abilities typically appear in normative development?; and (c) How can the cognitive capacities required to benefit from a treatment be assessed? In addition, it is important to remember that even among preadolescent youth cognitively capable of participating in adult-oriented treatments, methods/ techniques that are engaging, enjoyable, and interactive are almost always preferred.

Next, I will describe several cognitive abilities required in CBTs, and the corresponding cognitive capacities of typically developing preadolescents. This section ends with a brief discussion of assessment issues and use of appealing, play-based techniques. CBT participation generally requires the ability to engage in cognitive processes described by Inhelder and Piaget (1958) as *formal operational thought*. Though now understood to be a more fluid and experience-based developmental process than a fixed stage (Siegler & Richards, 1979), formal operational thought involves the acquisition of abstract thinking skills, such as metacognition (i.e., thinking about the content and processes of one's own thoughts), hypothetical thought, deductive reasoning, and the ability to hold multiple pieces of information in working memory during problem-solving efforts. Pre- and early adolescents are increasingly—though not necessarily fully—able to engage in the complex abstract thinking tasks required in CBT. In terms of metacognition, most youth begin to contemplate their own thoughts and systems of thinking during mid- to late elementary school. So, preadolescents can usually recognize their own cognitions and differentiate helpful from unhelpful thoughts.

Preadolescents are also developing the ability to formulate ideas about hypothetical events rather than using the techniques of younger children (i.e., trial-and-error or observational learning) to guide decisions. However, combining their newly acquired skill to think hypothetically with metacognition (e.g., forming prospective hypotheses about their own future thoughts) may be difficult for many youth of this era. For example, when asked by his therapist to name some helpful things he could say to himself if he were bullied at school, an eleven-year-old boy may interpret the question in an overly concrete manner, replying "It's summer so I'm not at school." Even though he is capable of complex abstract thinking skills that would allow him to generate several possible cognitions in the scenario presented to him, he does not yet recognize that a hypothetical premise calls for a hypothetical response. When prompted, he may be able to either generate potentially helpful thoughts, or use prospective hypothetical thought to identify possible future behavioral responses in the scenario. However, combining metacognition with prospective hypothetical reasoning about optimal future thoughts may be challenging for him without visual aids or other concrete cognitive anchors to help him simultaneously access these abilities. Regarding abstract reasoning, preadolescents' emerging deductive reasoning skills allow them to evaluate their behaviors, solutions to problems, and the evidence for thoughts/beliefs. Yet, adolescent egocentrism, a developmentally normative form of intense self-focus, may prompt those in pre- and early adolescence to discount relevant facts in favor of egocentristic beliefs. As Elkind (1967) observed, adolescents' personal fables involving the belief in their sense of uniqueness, invincibility, and centrality (i.e., that everyone is as focused on the preadolescent as he or she is) may persist despite strong evidence to the contrary. So, although they may have the cognitive capacity to use deductive reasoning, preadolescents may form firm beliefs based upon hypothetical thoughts (e.g., "everyone hates me" or "they are all staring at me") rather than reality or evidence. A twelve-year-old girl may insist that everyone at school stared disapprovingly at her when she tripped, though she may also accurately recount that most of her peers were engrossed in their own activities and did not look in her direction when she stumbled.

Other CBT-related abilities involve imagining thoughts, feelings, and experiences from another person's perspective (i.e., perspective-taking), estimating and quantifying experiences, identifying affect, and comprehending/expressing language. Preadolescents often have the rudimentary cognitive skills to take the perspective of another in simple or familiar situations, particularly when prompted, though empathy and other complex skills continue to evolve through adolescence and are never attained by some adults. At times, preadolescent egocentrism and the belief in his or her centrality compete with perspective-taking skills, as the young person has difficulty overcoming the tendency to regard his or her own cognitions/experience as the correct or only perspective. Also, youth capable of perspective-taking may not routinely apply this skill in situations where it would be helpful to do so. In contrast, estimation and data-reporting capacities are well developed during preadolescence, as the simplistic reports of younger children (e.g., based on a single, usually the most recent or salient, criterion) yield to preadolescent abilities to retrospectively report on thoughts, behaviors, and experiences using multiple criteria over discrete time frames. CBTs require the ability to accurately depict emotion states. Because this skill develops slowly across childhood and adolescence, preadolescents may have initial difficulty differentiating their thoughts from their feelings.

With practice, most preadolescents learn to distinguish thoughts from feelings sufficiently to benefit from CBT. The development of verbal skills has a rapid upward trajectory in late infancy and early childhood and is sufficiently developed in normative preadolescents to participate in CBTs. However, preadolescents' vocabularies are somewhat more limited than adults, and they commonly use linguistic innovations that conform to their peers but sometimes bewilder adults (e.g., the overuse of "like" or "be" or the use of new, abbreviated, or euphemistic words that may be unfamiliar to some adults, such as "TBH [to be honest]," "9 [a parent is watching]," or "ship" for relationship).

Assessment of the cognitive skills required for CBT participation is helpful during preadolescence because of the wide variation in cognitive development among youth this age. However, informative, formal psychological assessment of intelligence and achievement is not practical in many settings. A pragmatic, though less precise, method of estimating preadolescent cognitive preparedness for CBT is to consider the youth's academic exposure to CBT-related skills. Therapists knowledgeable about commonly used academic curricula can gauge when preadolescents are typically exposed to CBT-related skills in their academic trajectories. For example, by the end of the sixth grade, most skills that overlap with CBT modules have been taught to preadolescents, but some of these topics reappear in the seventh- and eighth-grade curricula in more sophisticated forms consistent with the skills needed to grasp complex CBT techniques (e.g., use of Socratic questioning) for adults. To assess a child's ability and/or motivation to use these skills, therapists can also do the following: (a) review the child's grades or teacher reports for subjects or modules with high CBT overlap; (b) review the preadolescent's performance on relevant subscales of standardized achievement tests administered at school; (c) explore the young person's likes and dislikes regarding ELA, mathematics, and science; and (d) ask clients whether they have learned specific content that overlaps with CBT requirements at school yet. When youth identify or their records show difficulty, lack of exposure, or negative opinions of the content shared between CBT and their academic curricula, therapists can use this information to evaluate the fit between the protocol and the young person's CBT readiness. Clinicians can also use this information to adapt the treatment to match the preadolescent's current cognitive abilities (e.g., omitting or modifying specific techniques or concepts), or to build competencies in the underdeveloped areas by providing extensive exposure to challenging concepts through engaging, play-based, developmentally sensitive intervention techniques until the necessary skills are acquired to participate in the full CBT protocol.

Apart from the developmental challenges CBT poses for young children, there is rising agreement that active-learning and/or play-based interventions enhance therapeutic engagement, motivation, and enjoyment of therapy sessions for youth of all ages. Whereas CBT has traditionally relied upon adult-oriented methods (e.g., verbal teaching, list-making activities, and data tracking in journals), there is now widespread recognition that CBTs should be developmentally sensitive. Consequently, numerous authors have proposed techniques to blend CBT modules with play-based, developmentally sensitive techniques (see also Drewes, 2009; Cavett & Drewes, 2012; Lowenstein, 2014; Shelby & Berk, 2009).

In summary, the beginning of adolescence marks the time in which most developmentally normative youth have acquired the cognitive capacities necessary to participate fully in CBT. Because these skills are developing and accumulating during preadolescence, youth in this age range usually show individual variations in their respective cognitive capacities and skill proficiencies. Their academic curricula provide exposure to most concepts that underlie CBT modules/techniques, but exposure does not always indicate mastery. Delayed skill development, limited experience using newly acquired skills, difficulty applying cognitive abilities to real-world situations, and uneven skill development may pose challenges during the implementation of some CBT techniques. Yet, this overlap can be leveraged to optimize CBTs' developmental sensitivity for preadolescents.

PRACTICAL INTERVENTIONS

To improve preadolescents' acquisition of CBT skills, interventions that link academic and CBT content are proposed. I will describe several interventions designed to be both developmentally sensitive and informed by academic curricula standards for sixth-grade learners based upon the Common Core Standards Initiative (National Governors Association Center for Best Practices, Council of Chief State School Officers, 2010) and Next Generation Science Standards (NGSS Lead States, 2013). In table 2.1, CBT modules or related skills appear in the first column; sixth-grade ELA, math, and science standards are listed in the middle column; and the third column contains intervention strategies that map onto both CBT and academic concepts.

In the CBT psychoeducation module, youth learn facts about their mental health conditions, diagnoses, or problems. Youth who have learned to differentiate fact from fiction can use their skills in the Psychoeducational Flashcards technique. Preadolescents are given index cards with either a true or untrue statement written on each card. Providing illustrations on the cards makes them more engaging and easier for youth with lingering reading difficulties. The preadolescent is asked to sort the cards into three categories. First, cards with true statements (e.g., "Depression happens for many people because brain chemicals get out of balance," or "There are many things people can do to feel better") are placed in a specially decorated box. Next, cards with false statements (e.g., "Only losers go to therapy") are placed in the trash, and cards about which the child is unsure (e.g., "Kids are to blame when their parents don't get along well") are given to the therapist to discuss later. After all the cards are sorted, the therapist reviews any inaccurate card placements, provides supplemental information related to each point, and explores the areas in which the preadolescent is uncertain. This technique gives preadolescents the opportunity to use their burgeoning skills to evalu-

Table 2.1. Active Learning Techniques Based on CBT and Educational Modules

CBT Module	Educational Core Curriculum Standard	Academic-CBT Integrated Technique
Psycho-education	Differentiate between fact and fiction	• Psychoeducation flashcards • Self-initiated sticky note search
Cognitive triangle	Understand cause and effect relationships	• Chemically reactive thoughts • Domino cognitive triangle
Analyze and alter thoughts	Distinguish fact from opinion; Use reasons/evidence to support an opinion Distinguish fact from fiction; Develop arguments to support a claim	• Thought trial
Coping skills	Understand cause and effect relationships; Use problem-solving strategies	• Coping box
Behavioral experiments	Learn the meaning of scientific method and independent and dependent variables; Identify the experimental question	• Planned activities designed to test the accuracy of beliefs, or to discern the effect of independent variables (e.g., pleasant activities) on dependent variables (e.g., mood levels)
Problem-solving and social skills	Use problem-solving strategies and estimate; Identify the perspectives of literary authors and characters	• Best-worst thing to do

ate and discern fact from fiction in psychoeducational materials, instead of solely receiving information from the therapist. In a related intervention, the Self-Initiated Sticky Note Search, the therapist places sticky notes in a conspicuous place, such as his or her office wall or on a swiveling chair. Each note contains a common question about preadolescents' difficulties, disorders, or typical trajectories for recovery (e.g., "Will I ever feel better?" or "Can therapists explain to parents that depression causes kids to act grumpy?"). Young people then select the items that contain questions of interest to them, and therapists provide the requested information via verbal explanations, written materials, or online resources. Blank notes are also available to allow youth to write their own questions on the cards. This activity is made more engaging if the chair rotates as children scramble to find questions salient to them or if they try to pull a selected note off the wall while their eyes are closed.

To comprehend the cognitive triangle, understanding of cause-and-effect relationships is necessary. Although many adolescents can comprehend this concept without manipulative or visual aids, techniques that provide visible evidence of cause and effect relationships help youth as they transition from concrete operational thought to a more abstract view of this concept. In the Chemically Reactive Thoughts technique, chemistry principles are used to demonstrate the role of cognitions in the cognitive triangle. The therapist and client build a tower or volcano using the cardboard inside a paper towel or toilet paper roll. If desired, they then place edible or interesting materials (e.g., chocolate kisses, small objects, or sand) at the base of the structure. The therapist asks the preadolescent to identify a potentially stressful situation while the client fills the roll with baking soda to depict the stressor. After the situation has been specified, the therapist asks the youth to identify an unhelpful cognition, and the preadolescent pours vinegar in the roll to represent the thought. Observing the subsequent eruption, the therapist and client discuss how chemical reactions occur when ingredients do not mix well. The therapist extrapolates that combining unhelpful thoughts with difficult situations can also cause feelings to "explode." The ruined chocolates or marred objects at the base of the structure demonstrate how these eruptions can harm other things in their path. Next, this activity is repeated, replacing the vinegar with altered ingredients. Baking soda again represents the situation and is placed in the container, but this time the youth identifies a helpful thought or thoughts while cornstarch, water, and a small amount of oil are added to the container. Because this makes play dough instead of an explosive chemical reaction, the preadolescent discovers positive outcomes from the new combination of ingredients. The youth can play with the play dough or eat the chocolates, as the therapist describes how using helpful thoughts can create something good from a situation, or preserve the objects in the path of the eruption. The youth and therapist then discuss how to apply helpful thinking to the young person's current or future situations. In another intervention technique, the cognitive triangle is demonstrated with dominos (Shelby & Berk, 2009) aligned in the shape of a triangle and placed upright. After naming a challenging situation, a thought, behavior, and the resulting feeling is written on a small note at each apex. After all three elements of the cognitive triangle have been identified, the young person pushes the initial domino and watches as each domino successively topples the next, landing on the labels at each point of the triangle and continuing to fall until the triangle collapses. Thus, the interconnectedness of thoughts, behaviors, and feelings via the fallen dominos is visually demonstrated.

In CBT, preadolescents are taught to recognize and evaluate thoughts and systems for thinking. This can be cognitively taxing for some preadolescents, despite their exposure to similar academic modules in ELA and science where they are taught to list evidence to support a claim, and use evidence to draw conclusions. Using the metaphor of a court proceeding, the Thought Trial technique places the accuracy of an identified cognition "on trial," where it will be considered from both sides of the case. First, the therapist reviews the role of a judge, whose job is to be sure the rules are followed and each side is represented well. Next, the therapist ensures that the preadolescent understands the role of attorneys, who must represent their respective sides of the case by presenting their best evidence and refuting the evidence of the other side. Then, either the therapist or preadolescent selects one of the youth's cognitions that leads to negative feelings or behaviors (e.g., "My teacher hates me" or "I'm the biggest loser at my school"). Finally, the youth assumes the role of the attorney arguing in favor of the untrue/unhelpful cognition, and presents all the evidence for this side of the case. It is helpful for the therapist to write the points of evidence on a dry erase board or flip chart so the client can refer to these items later. After all of the evidence in favor of the targeted cognition has been presented, the youth is reminded that both sides of a case must be presented well or the judge rules a mistrial. The young person is then asked to play the role of the opposing counsel, presenting contrary evidence and refuting the evidence rendered earlier. These opposing points are also written on the board or chart to make it easy for the preadolescent to address and contrast each item of evidence previously presented. The client concludes with closing arguments, reversing roles as necessary so that each side is summarized. Then, the case begins the deliberation process in which the jury decides the verdict based upon only the evidence presented. The preadolescent is asked to speak as the jury foreman and announce which side has prevailed. Most youth conclude that the evidence does not support his or her initial negative cognition. In this case, the preadolescent selects a more accurate/helpful cognition. If the young person maintains that his or her initial cognition is correct despite the evidence to the contrary, the youth has nevertheless learned a valuable process for evaluating the accuracy of a thought and considering alternate points of evidence. This can be used in future situations to give the youth a framework for analyzing his or her cognitions.

CBTs commonly include a module on coping skills, and familiarity with cause and effect relationships from school curricula assist youth as they recognize the ways in which thoughts and behaviors influence outcomes. Despite their familiarity with the concept of cause and effect, preadolescents often require tangible prompts, such as a Coping Box, to apply coping behaviors to real-world settings. To create Coping Boxes, shoe-box-sized boxes are filled with items designed to tap into all the sensory experiences (e.g., a funny or comforting picture to see, lyrics of a favorite uplifting song to sing aloud or to repeat mentally as silent musical imagery, a favorite scent or scratch-and-sniff sticker to smell, something small to taste, and a comforting item to touch, such as cotton balls, a miniature furry stuffed animal, or a stress ball). An encouraging note from a friend, favorite adult, and/or the preadolescent him- or herself is also helpful to assist the youth during times of low mood, distress, or hopelessness. In a similar intervention, suicidal adolescents benefitted from creating Hope Boxes (Asarnow et al., 2015) that reminded them of both coping techniques and reasons to live.

Behavioral experiments are commonly used in CBT for depression or anxiety, and preadolescents' study of scientific methods in science curricula help prepare them to participate in this portion of therapy. In these experiments, youth test the accuracy of their cognitions. For example, a preadolescent who insists nothing would work to make him feel happier is asked to rate his current mood. Using the scientific method often taught in sixth-grade science classes, the therapist invites the boy to participate in an experiment, to test whether anything could elevate his mood. Consistent with scientific methodology, the result is not known until the end of the experiment when the evidence is examined (i.e., the hypothesis that nothing that can be done to improve mood may or may not be accurate, but this can be determined only by isolating and testing the hypothesis in the experiment). When he understands the basis of a scientific experiment, the therapist engages the youth in one or more activities that are extremely likely to result in elevated mood. For instance, they might leave the therapy office to play tag outside, throw water balloons on the parking lot pavement, or visit an ice cream shop for a snack. After engaging in the activity, the therapist asks the youth to provide another mood rating. This mood rating is contrasted with the earlier one to discover whether the youth's activity elevated his mood. Even if the boy reports only a slight elevation, the experiment demonstrates that something can help, thereby disproving the hypothesis that "nothing" can be done. Future sessions are devoted to combining this highly pleasurable activity with other activities or thoughts that are likely to produce even greater elevations in mood. In the unlikely event that the youth reports no mood elevation or a decrease in mood, the therapist explores the reasons for this outcome, ensures that future experiments involve activities the youth is likely to find enjoyable, and tests alternate activities during subsequent sessions.

For CBT problem-solving and social skills modules, preadolescents' cognitive capacities allow them to identify problems, both retrospectively and prospectively. In school, they have had ample exposure to problem-solving and estimating tasks in math and science, as well as analyzing perspectives in ELA literary content. Yet, preadolescents may not be skilled at finding solutions to their own problems. The Best and Worst Thing intervention relies upon preadolescents' ability to use problem-solving and perspective-taking skills to generate, differentiate, and evaluate helpful and unhelpful courses of action. After a problem has been identified by the client, the chart is used to name various ways the preadolescent and people important to the client would advise him or her to solve the problem (see figure 2.4). For example, twelve-year-old Ashlynne comes to therapy saying that she has a terrible report card, and she plans to hide it from her parents. Then, the therapist asks Ashlynne to name the worst thing she could do in this situation. After writing this in the corresponding cell, she is asked to name the best thing she could do. Next, the therapist queries Ashlynne about the perspectives of other people important to her, and writes the "best" and "worst" courses of action each of these people would tell her she could take. The activity compels Ashlynne to generate options that might not have been obvious to her from her own perspective but occur to her when she is asked to think from another person's perspective. Extra rows are made available for the youth to identify perspectives of additional people, and the list continues until Ashlynne supplies several solutions likely to be effective.

Next, the therapist asks Ashlynne to notice patterns from her responses (e.g., she was the only one who believed withholding the report card was a good idea, and almost everyone suggested increasing her communication with her parents when showing them the report card). This intervention not only helps youth generate solutions and develop problem-solving skills but also gives them practice taking another person's perspective.

CASE STUDY

The blond hair covering the twelve-year-old girl's face did not conceal her scowl. Audrey had come to this, her first session, at her mother's insistence and her displeasure was clear. Audrey's mother, Ms. Summers, hoped that I could help Audrey with her daily irritability, sporadic anger outbursts at

Problem: Bad Report Card	**Worst Thing I Can Do**	**Best Thing I Can Do**
Client	"Tell my parents about it."	"Hide it from my parents."
Client's Best Friend	"Make a fake report card."	"Be super nice to your parents. Then, tell them about your report card and say you are sorry."
Client's Parents	"Not show us"	"Show us so we can help."
Client's Favorite Teacher	"Ignore the problem."	"Give it to them and tell them that you will do your homework more regularly next semester."
Client's Favorite Responsible Adult	"Hide it."	"Show them and ask them for advice about how to do better."
Other Person		

Figure 2.4. Best and Worst I Can Do. Created by Janine Shelby

school, troubled peer relationships, excessive fatigue, and "bad attitude" at home. Earlier, Ms. Summers revealed that she and Audrey's father had divorced when Audrey was nine years old. Shortly thereafter, Audrey's father moved to another state and had infrequent contact with his daughter. After the divorce, Ms. Summers struggled financially, and was often away from home working long hours and attending night school. Despite these hardships, Audrey's academic performance flourished. However, a few months ago her grades and peer relationships began to fluctuate. In addition to the changes she experienced at school, Audrey's physical appearance and social experience also underwent rapid changes. She towered over the boys in her class and felt painfully conscious of this and the minor blemishes that speckled her face. To make matters worse, Audrey's feet had grown quickly over the past few months, and the disproportionality of these appendages relative to her thin frame left her feeling clumsy and awkward as she negotiated her way through life in her favorite rainbow-colored, high-top sneakers.

After she settled into my office during our initial session, Audrey looked at me quickly through a partition in the hair that covered most of her face. Her glance told me that if I asked her questions, she would respond with monosyllabic utterances, such as "mm," or approximations of phrases, such as "ay-o-oh," the preadolescent protestation form of "I don't know." "It must be tough to be here when you really didn't want to come," I said gently. A shrug of her shoulders momentarily caused an unintended part in her hair, which gave her the chance to briefly take stock of me. She saw that I was wearing neither ripped jeggings nor trendy high-tops. No tats, no interesting piercings, no bedazzling hair dye. We became mutually aware that a shared sense of vogue would not be the bridge that connected us. Given her preadolescent sense of conspicuousness, I decided not to comment on her visual inspection of me. Drawing attention to the fact that I was noticing *her* noticing *me* would likely augment the embarrassment, self-consciousness, and uneasiness she dreaded. Instead, I offered the more validating, "I am sure you have important reasons for feeling the way you do." She agreed with the silent nod of her blond head. I continued, "I don't know your reasons yet, but when you are ready to tell me, I'll listen and do my best to understand your side of things." I waited as her preadolescent cognitive skills went to work, contrasting her anticipated experience of awkwardness, pressure, and scrutiny with her actual experience of respect and encouragement. I allowed her time to silently hypothesize about the varied possible outcomes of our meeting, and to use her deductive reasoning skills to determine whether therapy might hold some benefit for her. For a brief moment, Audrey's eye contact with me implied that she thought this therapy thing might not be *entirely* bad. In an attempt to help Audrey feel as comfortable as possible, I told her that her thoughts and feelings were welcome here, even those about not wanting to come to therapy. "O.K., O.K.," she conceded, and repeated almost inaudibly, "O.K., Cool Beans." Audrey's cognitive abilities and physical development made clear that she was no longer a child. Yet, her behaviors and demeanor simultaneously revealed that she was not yet *not* a child.

I placed a small box of kinetic sand between us, and let it fall through my fingers. She put her hair behind her ears, and joined me in rearranging the sand. After a couple minutes, she said that she liked the sand, but also that she was "totally fine" and did not need therapy, carefully articulating "no offense" at the end of her sentence to sound polite. I reflected her point of view, normalized her therapy reluctance, but also asked if I could find out more about how she viewed the irritable mood and other symptoms her mother reported about her. After Audrey agreed and endorsed several depression symptoms, I offered her the chance to find out more about her depression level so that she could make a fully informed decision about therapy. Audrey liked this idea, saying that adults usually just told her what to do without asking her to decide for herself. Audrey promised to respond accurately to norm-based questionnaires, so she could learn how her depression and anxiety levels compared to same age peers. When I showed Audrey the results, she was surprised to learn that the depression symptoms to which she had become accustomed placed her in the clinically significant range relative to other youth. Seeing the data for herself was important, given her blooming sense of independence. Also, because she had learned in school how to distinguish facts from opinions and to use evidence to support a claim, she responded to the objective nature of the data I presented to her. Audrey then listed the pros and cons of attending therapy and determined that she had more to gain (e.g., "My mom will finally stop talking about me going to therapy" and "It might help") than she had to lose (e.g., "It might be a waste of time" and "It would make me miss good TV shows"). So, Audrey agreed to continue therapy on a trial basis for one month "just to find out" whether therapy could help her feel better. During this time, the diagnosis of mild major depressive disorder was made based on multiple methods and sources of data, and a CBT protocol was chosen. One of Audrey's first tasks was to complete a schedule of her weekly activities and discover the points of the day in which she had the lowest and highest mood ratings. She also identified variables that were related to low ratings (e.g., being alone or tired), as well as high or higher ratings (e.g., spending time with friends, watching funny cat media clips, or going out with her mother). In the first few weeks of therapy, Audrey used the information from both her schedule and behavioral experiments to discover activities that substantially elevated her mood. Outside the session, she increased the amount of time she spent engaging in these pleasant activities. Audrey also reduced the amount of time she was alone in her apartment by joining afterschool clubs, doing errands with her mother on weekends, and engaging in two special activities with her mother each week. This use of behavioral activation to decrease unhelpful activities and increase helpful ones quickly resulted in moderate treatment gains, though some depression symptoms persisted. After the initial month of treatment, Audrey agreed to continue CBT to make further gains. She received more in-depth psychoeducation about depression and learned about the cognitive triangle. Audrey developed a miniature coping box for use at school when she faced upsetting situations, and practiced using it to help her modulate her intense emotions. Audrey also learned to identify and alter cognitions that contributed to her depression symptoms. The Thought Trial technique helped her examine the veracity and helpfulness of some of her untrue/unhelpful cognitions. When she mastered these concepts, her school-related angry outbursts were targeted. Using a piece of butcher paper that covered the length of my office, she drew and labeled the chain of events preceding targeted angry outbursts. Audrey discovered that the antecedents for her outbursts were related to her interpretation that she had been slighted (e.g., friends spending time together without her) or her appraisal that her belongings had been damaged (e.g., someone stepping on her shoes during the afternoon rush at the end of the school day). One repeated cognition she identified following these triggering events was "They hate me." When asked about the first time she recalled having a similar thought, Audrey recognized that the current experiences were connected to her of feelings of abandonment and rejection by her father. She also realized that the experience with her father formed the basis of a more pervasive cognition about herself (e.g., "I am not lovable"). Audrey used this information to separate her past from current experiences, and to challenge and alter the belief that her father's departure proved she was unlovable. Over the course of several sessions, Audrey diagrammed the triggers, cognitions, behavioral responses, feelings, and external consequences that related to her outbursts. Audrey's chart helped her understand how her interpretations and reactive behaviors led to problematic outcomes with her peers. She then used stickers, paints, and markers to add alternate cognitions and behaviors likely to result in more positive outcomes. For example, in thought bubbles where she had identified unhelpful cognitions (i.e., "They hate me" or "I'm gonna get her back for stepping on my shoes!"), she drew a peace sign to illustrate her new plan to tell herself to "Peace out until I find out if they meant to disrespect me," and "Wait until I'm calm to react." She also drew a picture of her cat, which she said reminded her to think, "This will pass and I'll be home with Fluffy soon." Audrey drew her Coping Box in the diagram, which symbolized her plan to substitute it for her former unhelpful behaviors (i.e., saying mean things and pulling classmates' backpacks off their school locker hooks). The therapist and Audrey engaged in role-playing activities in which Audrey practiced applying her new cognitions and behaviors in simulated school-based scenarios. Audrey also practiced using her new cognitions and behaviors at school as therapy homework assignments and adjusted her cognitions and behaviors as necessary to make them effective. Meanwhile, in collateral sessions Audrey's mother learned to distinguish Audrey's irritability and other symptoms of depression from misbehaviors. Also, Ms. Summers was taught the importance of ensuring that Audrey had enough pleasant experiences in her schedule to combat her depressed mood. Positive mother–daughter time was increased, and they engaged in special outings twice a week. Ms. Summers was coached to communicate with her daughter by using more reflective listening and praise and less advice and criticism. Mother and daughter also engaged in role-playing activities in which they focused on increasing positive verbalizations toward each other. Within five months, Audrey's symptoms remitted and her scores on self-, parent-, and teacher-report questionnaires fell to nonclinically significant levels. Audrey agreed that she no longer felt depressed and was ready to terminate the treatment. Audrey was taught to recognize signs and symptoms of depression in case she had a future episode, and she was invited to attend a booster session in a couple of months to maintain the gains she had made during treatment.

INCORPORATION OF FAMILY

Although early CBT studies involving preadolescents did not typically include caregiver components in their protocols, most contemporary CBTs focus on the importance of caregiver involvement in the children's CBT (c.f. Shelby, 2015). However, the level of adult involvement in child CBT sessions varies across protocols; some treatments require caregiver participation each week, and others include less frequent contact. Most CBT collateral sessions for caregivers include psychoeducation regarding the child's symptoms, diagnosis, and treatment techniques. In many CBT protocols, adult caregivers also learn CBT skills similar to those their children are learning so they can practice and model CBT skills at home. Friedberg and McClure (2015) identify the following additional common modules when working with parents of CBT clients: cultural context issues, establishing realistic expectations, helping parents define problems, helping parents increase their child's desirable behaviors, helping parents deal with their child's undesirable behaviors, giving commands and directions, linking child behaviors to parental consequences through contingency management, improving parent-child communication skills, and enhancing positive parent-youth interactions.

REFLECTION AND CONCLUSION

CBTs are empirically demonstrated psychotherapy approaches that benefit youth with a variety of mental health concerns. CBTs align well with most adolescents' ability to engage in complex abstract thinking tasks. For preadolescents, however, some cognitive skills important for participation in CBT may not be fully developed, evenly developed across situations or problems, or consistently applied in real-world settings. In these cases, there is little guidance in the literature as to how to adapt CBTs based upon specific cognitive capacity levels or grades. This chapter is intended to contribute to the literature on CBT applications for youth, and optimize therapy outcomes for preadolescents. By drawing attention to the overlap between academic curricula and CBT concepts, I hope to help CBT therapists become more aware of their preadolescent clients' school exposure to CBT-related skills to enrich intervention strategies and frame clinical decisions with knowledge from child development, pedagogy, and therapy outcome research.

REFERENCES

Asarnow, J. R., Berk, M., Hughes, J. L., & Anderson, N. L. (2015). The SAFETY Program: A treatment-development trial of a cognitive-behavioral family treatment for adolescent suicide attempters. *Journal of Clinical Child and Adolescent Psychology, 44*(1), 194–203. http://doi.org/10.1080/15374416.2014.940624

Cavett, A. M., & Drewes, A. A. (2012). Play applications and trauma-specific components. In J. A. Cohen, A. P. Mannarino, & E. Deblinger (Eds.), *Trauma-focused CBT for children and adolescents: Treatment applications* (pp.124–148). New York, NY: Guilford Press.

Drewes, A. (2009). *Blending play therapy with CBT.* Hoboken, NJ: John Wiley & Sons.

Elkind, D. (1967). Egocentrism and adolescence. *Child Development, 38*(4), 1025–1034. doi: 10.2307/1127100

Friedberg, R. D., & McClure, J. M. (2015). *Clinical practice of cognitive therapy with children and adolescents: The nuts and bolts* (2nd ed.). New York, NY: Guilford Press.

Garber, J., Frankel, S. A., & Herrington, C. G. (2016). Developmental demands of cognitive behavioral therapy for depression in children and adolescents: Cognitive, social, and emotional processes. *Annual Review of Clinical Psychology, 12*, 181–216. http://doi.org/10.1146/annurev-clinpsy-032814-112836

Inhelder, B., & Piaget, J. (1958). *The growth of logical thinking from childhood to adolescence: An essay on the construction of formal operational structures.* Abingdon, United Kingdom: Routledge.

Langbridge, F. (1896). *A cluster of quiet thoughts* (p. 27). London, Great Britain: The Religious Tract Society.

Lowenstein, L. (2014). *Cory helps kids cope with sexual abuse: Playful activities for traumatized children.* Ontario, Canada: Champion Press.

National Governors Association Center for Best Practices, Council of Chief State School Officers (2010). Common core state standards. Washington, DC: National Governors Association Center for Best Practices, Council of Chief State School Officers.

NGSS Lead States (2013). Next generation science standards: For states, by states. Washington, DC: The National Academies Press.

Shelby, J. S. (2015). Family-based cognitive behavioral therapy. In E. J. Green, J. N. Baggerly, & A. C. Myrick (Eds.), *Counseling families: Play-based treatment* (pp. 3–20). Lanham, MD: Rowman & Littlefield.

Shelby, J. S., & Berk, M. J. (2009). Play therapy, pedagogy, and CBT: An argument for interdisciplinary synthesis. In A. Drewes (Ed.), *Blending play therapy with CBT* (pp. 17–40). Hoboken, NJ: John Wiley & Sons.

Siegler, R. S., & Richards, D. (1979). Development of time, speed and distance concepts. *Developmental Psychology, 15*, 288–298.

Chapter Three

Attachment-Centered Play Therapy with Middle School Students

Clair Mellenthin

> Attachments lie at the heart of family life. They create bonds that can provide care and protection across the life cycle, and can evoke the most intense emotions—joy in the making, anguish in the breaking—or create problems if they become insecure.—J. Bing-Hall

Middle school can be a time of difficult transition in family life. The preadolescent child is entering into a new phase of development and experiencing new kinds of engagement with their peers, family members, and other adults in their life. With the current education trend in the United States of including sixth grade in middle school, many latency-age children are experiencing higher levels of pressure to grow up faster and rush through this last critical year of development. For many children entering middle school, this is the first time without a consistent adult caretaker figure, as they shuffle from class to class and experience multiple teachers throughout the day. This can bring about a sense of insecurity and anxiety until the child is able to adjust to these changes effectively. These changes mirror the uncertainty and insecurity they may feel within their home environments and primary relationships, which may compound already insecure attachment behaviors.

Attachment behaviors are children's method of seeking to meet their attachment needs (Ainsworth & Bowlby, 1965). In infancy, these behaviors include differential crying, smiling, vocalizations, concern for mother's whereabouts, and joy in reunion after a separation. In a secure attachment, a parent is able to respond appropriately to these behaviors and reciprocates love and affection (Ainsworth, Blehar, Waters, & Wall, 1978). Their caregiving and nurturing is consistent and predictable. As the child grows, his or her behaviors may change, but basic attachment needs remain the same. For example, a securely attached child can seek out a parent for comfort when feeling anxious or scared and, in high-functioning children, can express their feelings openly and honestly. A child may say, "Mom, I need you right now. I am feeling so worried about my math test," and the parent who responds with a hug and words of comfort or reassurance helps to soothe the child's worries and anxieties, resulting in a shared moment of attunement and security. This child grows up knowing that he or she is loved, important, and valued.

A child who grows up in a home with a lack of consistent nurture and caregiving has a much bleaker experience. This same child upon entering middle school for the first time, when feeling upset, scared, or anxious may learn to lash out aggressively or isolate him- or herself from others (Ainsworth et al., 1978). When they use these behaviors it may be the only time when they receive attention from their parents, even though it is negative attention. The child may learn that his or her thoughts and feelings seem not to matter to their parent and that it is better to not ask for help for fear of risking rejection, ridicule, or harsh punishment. They may experience the challenges of middle school with much more difficulty, as they repeat these learned responses in the school environment. Many of the behavioral referrals that clinicians receive may be manifestations of a poor attachment (Ainsworth et al., 1978). It is critical for clinicians and school counselors to do an in-depth attachment interview with their middle school age clients to rule out an attachment issue, and not solely focus on the superficial behavioral presenting issues (Green, Myrick, & Crenshaw, 2013; Mellenthin, 2018).

LITERATURE REVIEW

It is pertinent to offer a brief overview of attachment theory in this chapter. Attachment refers to the bonds of connection typically developed in early childhood and infancy through the relationship between parent and child (Ainsworth & Bowlby, 1965). These early relationships pave the way for an individual's ability to form connections outside of the family systems and throughout his or her lifetime. These primary relationship patterns are also referred to as attachment patterns or styles (Ainsworth et al., 1978). There are four main patterns of attachment that exist in relationships: *secure, insecure, avoidant,* and *chaotic/disorganized*. Instead of being neat, well-defined categories, these attachment patterns are developed into a spectrum of levels of security.

Secure attachment is characterized by the parent providing consistent, predictable caregiving and nurture (Ainsworth et al., 1978). In the parent–child relationship, the child (and parent) can manifest appropriate levels of distress when separated and tolerate separations from their attachment figure, resulting in the child easily experiencing soothing upon reunification. The development of a secure attachment enables children to develop core relationship competencies, including the ability to seek out and accept proximity and comfort from their caregiver, modulate psychophysiological arousal, and experience and trust the caregiver to be a secure base (Shapiro, 2011). Securely attached parents and caregivers are able to offer consistency, reliability, and emotional availability to their children, which allows for attunement and affect regulation to occur.

Insecure attachment develops through inconsistent caregiving and nurture, which results in the child feeling unsure as to if and when parents will be able to meet his or her emotional and physical needs (Ainsworth et al., 1978). This attachment pattern is characterized by the child experiencing high levels of distress upon separation, due to the innate fear that a parent may not return. Upon reunion, the child may behave in a clingy or angry manner and is often very difficult to soothe. Insecure attachment patterns do not support the developmental goals of felt security and regulation of affect, and they offer diminished opportunities for exploration and autonomy (Shapiro, 2011).

Avoidant attachment develops because of an insecure attachment and is characterized by avoidant, withdrawn, closed off behaviors (Ainsworth et al., 1978). The child has learned to expect that caregiving is inconsistent, leaving him or her unsure as to whether their emotional (and sometimes) physical needs will be met. In avoidant attachment, there is an attempt to "deactivate" the attachment system and suppress the attachment needs of the individual (Johnson, 2004). This is often achieved through family members' excessive focusing on work or tasks, limited engagement in emotional or intimate encounters with one another, and a lack of permission to express one's feelings or self.

Disorganized and/or chaotic attachment is created through a traumatic upbringing and relationship (Ainsworth et al., 1978). The child learns through experience that a parent or caregiver is frightening, fearful, and unreliable. The parent lacks an ability to provide organized caregiving and may severely neglect the child. In extreme situations, the parent(s) may fail to protect infants and children from danger, including physical and sexual abuse, as they are unable to offer protection from their own negative affective states (Shapiro, 2011). The child then engages in attachment strategies that both seek out closeness and simultaneously avoid closeness when it is offered, resulting in a chaotic emotional existence (Johnson, 2004).

These early life experiences in parent–child relationships enable children to develop an internal working model of self and relationships (Goodman, 2009). When positively reinforced, this internal working model teaches a child that he or she is worthy and that the world is a predictable and positive place if a secure attachment has been developed and nurtured (Ainsworth et al., 1978; Green et al., 2013). If the child has learned that the opposite of this is true and has developed an insecure or disorganized attachment to a parent or caregiver, this results in a belief that he or she is *not* worthy of love and the internal working model changes to a belief that the world and others are unsafe, untrustworthy, and unpredictable. The model that a child has internalized greatly impacts his or her ability to navigate this new phase of adolescent development and to tolerate the changes and nuances of the tween years in an adaptive, healthy manner.

PRACTICAL INTERVENTIONS

The dynamics of play therapy change as a child grows older (Green et al., 2013; Mellenthin, 2018). Often middle school clients become slightly resistant to go into the playroom and will say, "That's for little kids." They may stop playing with the typical play therapy toys, such as puppets, dolls, or medical or school-based toys, that they had gravitated towards in their earlier treatment and/or developmental stages. The nature of play also begins to change developmentally, as the child is readying him- or herself to go into adolescence and developing abstract thinking capacities. Sand tray, expressive arts, and music offer the middle schooler a new way to gain personal insight, improve relationships, and learn healthy social and emotional coping skills (Green et al., 2013). As the child develops more insight and awareness into self and others, he or she can begin to self-motivate behavioral changes and gain a greater ability for connections and self-expression. This in turn can create much more positive interactions between parent and child, especially if the parent is self-aware or working on developing this insight and self-regulation in tandem with the child.

Including the parents into the play therapy process when addressing attachment-related injuries or issues is crucial to the long-term healing and growth of the client (Gil, 2015). Research has demonstrated that attachment-based interventions and programs that focus on relationships, either with the parents themselves or with the therapist as a symbolic representation of them, can help to begin resolving the underlying dysfunction and hurt within the parent–child relationship (Goodman, 2009). It is critical for the child to experience a trusting relationship with an attachment figure who can help reframe or modify their frightening or insecure representations of others. When a child can experience vulnerability, and explore feelings of uncertainty or fear of being unlovable and the parent is able to soothe and comfort the child in that moment, a new pattern of interaction can develop, paving the way for repairing and reconnection, strengthening the attachment between them (Gil, 2015). The following interventions are helpful in repairing attachment wounds and ruptures, as well as creating a sense of safety in the parent–child relationship. It should be noted that these interventions are focused on the *non-offending parent* and child, as it is important to maximize the parent's role in creating safety and security for the child.

Two Hands Intervention

In preadolescence, expressive arts can be a creative, fun, and powerful way to explore a child's thoughts and emotions. In family play therapy, expressive arts can also help give words to the unspeakable and open up new ways of dialogue and communication between parent and child (Gil, 2015). In my practice, I have found that hands carry a very powerful symbolism and metaphor. Hands can offer comfort or initiate pain. A hand to hold is something for which most humans yearn. In attachment-centered play therapy, hands (both literal and figurative) are used extensively as we teach and enhance a parent's ability to give nurture and reassurance, resulting in the child learning to seek out their parent in a healthy way and the parent to reciprocate this reaching out by creating a holding space of safety (Mellenthin, 2018). This play therapy intervention was developed to strengthen the parent–child attachment system. In this intervention, both parent and child engage in expressive arts and create simultaneous collages representing one another's strengths and value. This intervention can enhance the parent–child relationship by focusing on positive attributes, engagement of creativity, and working on creating a project side by side together.

Supplies Needed

Blank card stock
Scissors
Glue
Markers
Multiple magazines

Directions

Instruct your clients to trace one another's hands on the blank cardstock and then cut out the handprints. Offer multiple magazines to your client to use for collage work. Instruct your clients to cut out different pictures, images, or words that describe or represent the positive strengths or traits of one another. The child will create the parent's hand, and the parent will create the child's. Once they have found their collage images, instruct them to glue them onto the hand cutout, filling up the entire hand. When both the parent and child are finished, the clinician will explore with their clients what hands can do. For example, sometimes hands can hurt, they can help lift someone up, and hands can comfort or create beautiful things. Hands can dig in the dirt or pot a plant. Hands can hold another hand. Hands can lift heavy things or soothe someone's hurt. Think of all the things hands can do and write them down.

You may want to process the following questions with your clients:

1. What are the differences and similarities between the two hands you have created?
2. How can two hands create holding or strength? (Think about this literally for a moment, is there a difference between what one hand can hold versus two?)
3. What small things can you identify that can help strengthen your relationship using your two hands together?

At the end of the therapy session, the parent and child are then instructed to find some way to connect the hands together on a larger piece of card stock or poster board. You may want to frame it with them in session or encourage them to buy a frame together and hang this artwork in a place where they can see it on a regular basis and remember one another's positive attributes.

Stars and Dots

This family-based play therapy activity focuses on increasing the child's self-esteem and self-worth, which are key to establishing a more secure attachment. The child needs to believe that he or she is lovable and loved in order for long-lasting growth and change to occur within the parent–child relationship. This intervention helps to identify and decrease negative self-talk and the child's internal belief that a parent is disappointed *because of who he or she is*, not just because of unwanted or "bad" behavior. Also, the parent/caretaker is able to reaffirm his or her love and acceptance of the whole child. This intervention is adapted from my technique found in *Play Therapy Engaging and Powerful Techniques for the Treatment of Childhood Disorders* (Mellenthin, 2018).

Supplies Needed

You Are Special, a book by Max Lucado (1997)
Star stickers
Gray dot stickers
Washable markers
My Blanco™ doll

Directions

1. Ask your clients to sit either on the floor or in a comfortable position. Ask the parent to read the book *You Are Special* by Max Lucado to the child if possible. If this causes discomfort for any reason, the therapist can read the book to parent and child. Explore what the dots and stars in the story mean to the child, as well as what it means when the woodcarver says, "You are special because I made you, and I don't make mistakes." Does the child believe it is possible to be special and not a mistake?
2. Instruct the child to draw each of their gray dots (symbolizing negative thoughts or beliefs about themselves) on the My Blanco™ doll (if the doll is unavailable, you can also use a blank piece of paper cut in the shape of a gingerbread man). Gray circle stickers can also be used.
3. Instruct the parent/caretaker to think of their child's stars (symbolizing positive attributes, characteristics, and personality traits) that they love or honor about the child and then draw a star or place a star sticker for each of these onto the doll.
4. Explore together the stars and dots that each person has drawn and how they think and feel about each dot and star.
5. Turn the doll around. On the other side, write down and reframe each gray dot with an opposite, positive thought. An example of a negative thought could be, "I don't have any friends at school," which could be reframed as, "Tommy sits by me at lunch. He likes me," or, "I can play with my next door neighbor, and she is my friend."

CASE STUDIES

Case Study 1

Zara (pseudonym) is an eleven-year-old girl who has recently been referred to therapy for high levels of anxiety and sleeping disturbance. Upon review of her developmental history in the parent consultation, her mother reports that she and her ex-husband divorced when Zara was a toddler and have been in a custody dispute and in various legal proceedings against one another since this time. Zara has experienced multiple extended separations with her father due to this, as well as his frequent travel overseas, which took him away from the country for weeks at a time. Her mother reports that since the last sabbatical her father took (which lasted several months), Zara has struggled significantly in school, with friends, and with sleeping. She refuses to sleep alone at night in her own bed and will wake often throughout the night and panic if her mother is not in bed next to her. She has been moody and verbally aggressive to others, especially towards her friends, which has

Figure 3.1. Stars and Dots Intervention. Created by Clair Mellenthin

caused them to begin distancing themselves from her. Her mother reports feeling trapped and guilty for both resenting and enjoying this amount of intense one-on-one time together with her child. She says that although she knows it is in her daughter's best interest to sleep alone, this also offers her a sense of companionship and comfort to have another body in her bed.

During the initial phase of play therapy, several themes of enmeshment and fear of abandonment were present in Zara's expressive art projects. She would create various sand trays in which there would be a series of traps or entanglements that a small elephant would have to resolve to find safety. Once the elephant freed itself and went to "the safe place," there would be

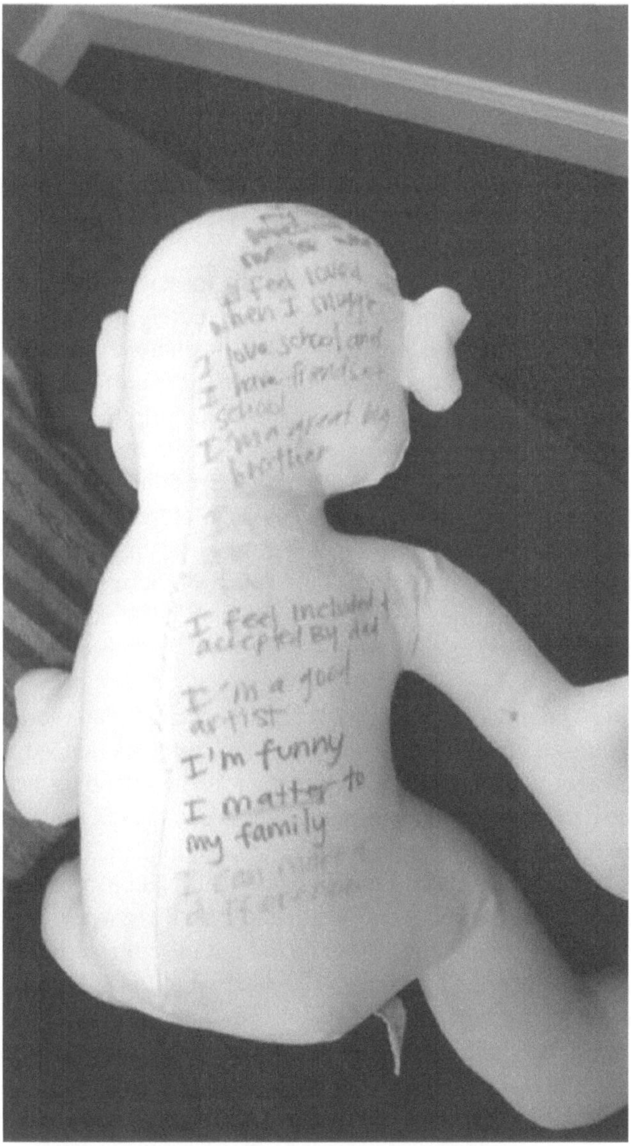

Figure 3.2. Stars and Dots Intervention. Created by Clair Mellenthin

another trap waiting. This played out over and over for several weeks. Zara's mother was present for many of the therapy sessions and, at times, could appropriately offer words of encouragement to the elephant figurine or comfort to her daughter when she became tearful or dysregulated. There appeared to be a sense of felt safety and nurture in their relationship that Zara would respond to, as she was able to accept comfort easily (she would move closer and rest her head on her mother's shoulder) and internally regulate her affect. On other occasions, Zara's mother needed constant redirection, as she would attempt to manipulate her daughter's sand trays to encourage distance or fear of her father, making statements such as, "This is how you feel when he doesn't show up or puts his travel ahead of you in his lack of twisted priorities" or "This snake is just like Dad. You can't trust it, and if you let down your guard, he will bite you."

It became clear that Zara experienced an insecure attachment to both parents. She manifested a more enmeshed insecurely attached relationship with her mother and an insecure-ambivalent attachment towards her father. In time, it was determined that Zara would benefit from family play therapy with her father to work on strengthening and repairing their relationship, as well as ongoing individual therapy, and therapy with her mother to work on healthy boundaries and coping skills. Initially, her father was very enthusiastic about this, reporting he had been desiring a closer connection with his daughter and was very worried about her level of anxiety, as well as her enmeshed relationship with her mother, which he described as "toxic and unhealthy." However, after a few sessions, her father stopped scheduling appointments or returning calls from the therapist and, shortly after, left the country again.

Zara and her mother continued attachment-centered play therapy to work through the abandonment, grief, and loss that Zara experienced in the ruptured attachment with her father. Her mother began attending her own personal therapy to address the enmeshment between herself and daughter, as well as to work on healthy coping skills in managing her own emotions and distress resulting from watching her daughter's hurt and pain. Zara gravitated towards the sand tray throughout her therapy, as this gave her a means of self-expression and processing when she did not have the verbal language to articulate her thoughts and feelings. The sand would also help regulate her affect; she could run her fingers through the sand until her breathing was calm and regulated, and as she put it, "My brain clears up, so I can think again."

As play therapy progressed, Zara's sand trays also progressed. She began constructing bridges and access points for the elephant, who learned about the hidden dangers in the sand and was able to seek and find true safety. As Zara developed a healthier relationship with her mother, one that had clear boundaries and limits, she began making and keeping friends, being able to concentrate and excel in school, as well as develop a sense of worth and self-esteem that had not been present before.

Case Study 2

Elijah (pseudonym) and Nicholas (pseudonym) are brothers who were referred to counseling following the death of their father, who had died by suicide the week prior. It is believed to have been an accidental suicide as there were no indications that he had been suicidal previously; however, he had an extensive substance abuse problem. Elijah and Nicholas's parents had never married but had been together for several years and were high school sweethearts. Their mother reports that substance abuse had been an issue for both parents since their teenage years, but as she had become pregnant and began to be a mother, she decided to become sober. This had caused contention in their relationship, as she was no longer tolerant of drinking or drug use in the home. She described her relationship with her partner as "passionate" and said, "We loved and fought passionately every day of our lives since we were fourteen years old." Throughout the intake, the boys would take turns trying to comfort their mother, who would vacillate between sobbing and laughing. At times she would hug them tightly, then just as fast, she pushed them away.

In play therapy, the boys described a chaotic home life that was filled with boisterous laughter that would shift to violent fighting regularly. They had witnessed their mother and father fight each other on a regular basis, with both initiating physical violence towards the other throughout their childhood. Once the fighting had stopped, they would find their parents holding one another while kissing and crying together. Their parents would embrace the boys and apologize for scaring them and for fighting. There would be temporary peace for a few days filled with dinners out, surprise gifts, loving gestures, and laughter-filled conversations until the violent cycle returned.

Elijah was in sixth grade and was a high-achieving student who was regularly on the honor roll. He was well liked by both peers and his teachers, but did not have any close friendships. He presented as a quiet intellectual. Nicholas was in seventh grade and had been held back a grade. He was repeating seventh grade due to failing grades and excessive absences from school. He also did not have any close friendships and was not reported to be especially likeable. In fact, the school counselor reported that he was regularly referred for disrespectful and acting-out behavior in the classroom.

Nicholas was a gifted artist, and although he did not share this talent with many people, in his therapy sessions, art was used frequently to express his grief, anger, resentment, and fear. He was able to use his art to show his feelings and experience a sense of validation and acceptance from his therapist. In time, he was able to share these feelings with his mother, who was also in individual counseling to address the grief and trauma she had experienced.

Elijah struggled with fully engaging in play therapy. Initially, he was very enthusiastic about the process and would bounce into the play therapy room and engage in child-centered play until he experienced a moment of vulnerability and acknowledged his grief and anger at his father for "leaving" the family. Following this session, for several weeks he would only play board games or card games with his therapist and refused to attend family therapy sessions, crying and at times screaming in the waiting room that he hated therapy, hated his family, and hated his life. With time, Elijah gradually began engaging in more meaningful play and was able to begin addressing the trauma to which he had been exposed.

After several months of counseling, the boy's mother called the therapist and informed her that they were moving to live with relatives in another state and would no longer be able to attend therapy. This decision had been made on the spur of the moment, and she had decided to move over the coming weekend, giving her children thirty-six hours' notice of the drastic family and lifestyle changes that were to take place. The therapist encouraged her to allow for time and permission for closure for the boys with their school, peers, and therapist. She refused, as she could not understand how the boys would need anything "special" to say goodbye.

INCORPORATION OF FAMILY

As demonstrated by the two different case studies, attachment wounds can manifest in a myriad of ways in behavior, emotions, affect, and engagement. In attachment-centered play therapy, the involvement of the parent is crucial to long-term change and successful resolution of the presenting issues (as well as the underlying concerns) a child is experiencing. The family system becomes the client, rather than just focusing on the individual child. Research (Ainsworth et al., 1978; Goodman, 2009; Shapiro, 2011) has well documented that attachment wounds impact the family system, rather than an individualized pain only one person feels. By including the parents (and other family members when appropriate), lasting change and healing is possible. This is a top-down approach to family counseling, as it is believed that the parent holds the key to lasting change and healing in the relationship. Depending upon the nature of the existing attachment pattern and current level of wounding in the relationship, it may take some time for healing to take place. The more dysfunctional the attachment patterns have been, the longer it may take to repair and create a healthier way of getting the child's attachment needs met.

Play therapy gives the family permission to practice seeking vulnerability and allows for the family's defense mechanisms to be put back in place, as the natural flow of therapy becomes a sort of dance between family members

(Gil, 2015). Through laughter, engagement, touch, and permission for silliness, the family deepens their connections to one another, resulting in a sense of trust that can allow for deeper processing and vulnerability. As the child learns to trust a parent's ability to hold "the yucky stuff" (i.e., fears, worries, uncomfortable emotions, thoughts, and feelings), their attachment deepens and strengthens. As a clinician, allowing for this ebb and flow to happen is crucial in teaching how to tolerate affect as well as teaching valuable parenting skills of pacing, mirroring, and modulating affective states. Giving your clients permission to take a break from processing and allowing for laughter and play to resume is also important to long-lasting progress to enhance and repair familial relationships.

Gil (2015) writes, "The fields of family therapy and play therapy have a great deal in common: They are both creative ways of working, designed to shake things up, initiate novel solutions, and reorient family member to each other, thereby reestablishing or deepening emotional connections and empathy" (p. ix). Incorporating an integrated, flexible approach in family play therapy can model healthy, adaptive engagement as well as offer the family novel ways of simply experiencing being with one another.

REFLECTION AND CONCLUSION

Middle school can be a time of rapid transition in family life. Suddenly, a child who laughed and played with toys not so long ago is entering puberty, wearing makeup, playing sports, and choosing to spend more time with friends than with family. For many parents, this time of transition can be a confusing and sometimes emotionally painful period, especially if the strain of their child's blossoming independence impacts their own feelings of control, connection, and rejection. The parent–child relationship and attachment patterns that have been developed over the course of childhood may ebb and flow during this phase of development.

Addressing the underlying attachment needs underneath the problem behaviors is critical throughout ages and stages, but particularly within this developmental phase. Preadolescents need physical touch and nurture even as they may rebuff or reject a parent's attempts to offer this, in their attempt to be more "grown up." Working with both parent and child to work through the challenges associated with this developmental period is critical for a healthy and secure attachment in the coming adolescent period. Finding ways to have meaningful connection, both physically as well as emotionally, is crucial in developing a coherent sense of self and self-worth. Attachment-centered play therapy uses an integrative, flexible, developmentally sensitive model to teach and enhance the parent–child relationship.

REFERENCES

Ainsworth, M., and Bowlby, J. (1965). *Child care and the growth of love*. London: Penguin Books.

Ainsworth, M., Blehar, M., Waters, E., & Wall, S. (1978). *Patterns of attachment*. Hillsdale, NJ: Erlbaum.

Gil, E. (2015). *Play in family therapy* (2nd ed.). New York, NY: Guildford Press.

Goodman, G. (2009). The impact of parent, child, and therapist mental representations on attachment-based intervention with prepubertal children. *Clinical Social Work Journal 38*, 73–84. doi: 10.1007/s10615-009-0238-9

Green, E. J., Myrick, A. C., & Crenshaw, D. A. (2013). Toward secure attachment in adolescent relational development: Advancements from sand play and expressive play-based interventions. *International Journal of Play Therapy (22), 2*, 90–102.

Johnson, S. M. (2004). *The practice of emotionally focused couple therapy* (2nd ed.). New York, NY: Brunner-Routledge.

Lucado, M. (1997). *You are special*. Wheaton, IL: Crossway Books.

Mellenthin, C. (2018). *Play therapy. Engaging and powerful techniques for the treatment of childhood disorders*. Eau Claire, WI: Pesi Publishing & Media.

Shapiro, J. (2011) *Attachment in the family context: Insights from development and clinical work*. In S. Bennett and J. Nelson (eds.), *Adult attachment in clinical social work*. Essential Clinical Social Work Series. New York, NY: Springer.

Chapter Four

Adlerian Play Therapy with Preadolescents

Kristin Meany-Walen

A unique component to working with preadolescents is their consistent swaying between child-like and adolescent-like behaviors, desires, and cognitions. At the same time as their cognitive abilities change, they experience physical and social milestones that disrupt their functioning in the world. Few adults look back on their preadolescent experiences with fond memories. I find working with preadolescents an enjoyable challenge as I attempt to stay with the client as he or she swings back and forth like an unregulated pendulum in an earthquake. Adlerian theory helps me to understand this population and work with them using effective and responsive interventions.

LI TERATURE REVIEW

Adlerian therapy, also known as individual psychology, was founded by Alfred Adler (1998/1927) and emphasizes people's creative and unique ways of interpreting life experiences and finding belonging. According to Adlerian theory, people are born socially embedded, with their first social experience being that with their family. Their experiences within their family and their perceptions of those experiences build the foundation of their *lifestyles*. The lifestyle is a person's unique way of being in the world and contributes to a person's belief about self, others, and the world. Adler believed the developed lifestyle becomes relatively stable around the age of eight years. Birth order, family dynamics and atmosphere, culture, and parental expectations—specifically, the perceptions of these factors—provide a framework for how a child believes he or she belongs and gains significance (Kottman & Meany-Walen, 2016). Adler suggested that unless a person experienced a significant psychological disruption, the developed lifestyle would be a set of patterns of beliefs, attitudes, emotional responses, and behaviors that carry over throughout an individual's life. Significant psychological disruptions are experiences that challenge one's core beliefs and create opportunities or the necessity for a change in one's lifestyle. Experiences such as going on mission trips, experiencing trauma, pursuing higher education, or engaging in therapy can be the impetus for a psychological disruption and change in lifestyle.

Adlerian play therapy was developed by Terry Kottman in the late 1980s as a result of not finding an approach to play therapy that matched her beliefs about how people develop and what they need in order to change (T. Kottman, personal communication, January 2006). In her work with adult clients, she used Adlerian theory. However, during her doctoral studies she was learning play therapy as a nondirective approach. She valued play and the developmentally responsive necessity of play with children. Yet, she felt inauthentic being solely nondirective and had an experience with a child client who challenged who she was in the playroom as compared to who she was outside of the playroom (T. Kottman, personal communication, January 2006). This experience contributed to Kottman's development of Adlerian play therapy. She structured Adlerian play therapy by merging play therapy skills and concepts with the therapeutic framework of Adler's individual psychology.

Adlerian play therapy follows the same four phases of therapy as that of Adlerian therapy with adults: building an egalitarian relationship between client and counselor, investigating the client's lifestyle, helping the client gain insight, and reorienting/reeducating the client (Kottman & Meany-Walen, 2016; Mosak & Maniacci, 1999). Specific interventions and activities within the phases vary dependent upon the client, his or her developmental age, presenting concerns, culture, and individual needs or interests. Because this book is focused on working with preadolescents, the following descriptions will include potential strategies for this age group assuming typical developmental progression (i.e., a chronologically aged eleven-year-old operates from a maturity level of an eleven-year-old).

In the first phase, the play therapist works to create an egalitarian relationship with the client (Kottman & Meany-Walen, 2016). The counselor will, at times, direct the session activities and at other times allow the client to lead the session or portion of the session in an effort to emphasize collaboration and shared partnership.

Investigating the client's lifestyle is the second phase of Adlerian play therapy (Kottman & Meany-Walen, 2016). It is in this phase that the therapist works as a detective to gather information about the client's unique lifestyle. The counselor is open to using play, activities, questions and answers, and information from other people in the client's life such as parents or teachers to draw hypotheses about how the client interprets the world (emotions, thoughts, and attitudes) and behaves. The Adlerian play therapist is particularly interested in preadolescents' private logic, mistaken beliefs, goals of misbehaviors, personality priorities, functioning at life tasks, feelings of inferiority and compensation, Crucial Cs (i.e., feeling connected, capable, that they count, and courage), assets, and talents. Since details about each of these is beyond the scope of this chapter, you are encouraged to read *Partners in Play: An Adlerian Approach to Play Therapy*, 3rd ed. (Kottman & Meany-Walen, 2016) for more information.

In the third phase, helping the client gain insight, the Adlerian play therapist uses directed activities and discussion to help the client develop awareness into his or her patterns of beliefs, emotions, and behaviors (Kottman & Meany-Walen, 2016). Essentially, the therapist's goal in this phase is for the client to have a greater level of understanding into his or her lifestyle in order to make educated and informed changes in the next phase. Therapists can use any number of activities such as drawing and art, sand tray, music, movement, storytelling, puppets, and role-play to help the client gain insight. A skill unique to Adlerian theory is *spitting in the client's soup.* In using this technique, the therapist points out patterns the client is employing that are not working in the client's favor. For example, a preadolescent girl who procrastinates doing her homework, earns poor grades, and then is ineligible for school sports may complain about her parents' or school's rules. If I were to spit in her soup, I might say, "Hmmm, I guess if you don't get the grades you need in order to play in the game, you also don't have to deal with the pressure you feel from your parents to be a good player." This strategy points out to the client the secondary gains of her behavior of which she may or may not be aware. You may also notice that while this is presented with empathy, it could come off a bit abrasive, which is why a relationship must be established before the counselor uses this technique.

In the last phase, reorienting/reeducating the client, the Adlerian play therapist looks for examples and opportunities for when the client thinks, feels, or responds more constructively than previously. The therapist can use interviewing and consulting with other people in the client's life, questioning the client, setting up opportunities for the client to demonstrate change, observing the client in different situations (e.g., waiting room, classroom, recess or lunch room, counseling room), and doing activities with the client in the therapy room to assess client change and readiness for termination.

Adlerian play therapy is a popular and effective treatment approach to working with children. In the most recent study of play therapists' preferred theory, Adlerian play therapy was identified as the third most used theory of play therapy (Lambert et al., 2007). Because of its popularity, Meany-Walen, Bratton, and Kottman (2014) conducted a randomized control trial using Adlerian play therapy as the independent variable. This was the first known

Adlerian play therapy study. This study was later used to achieve evidence-based treatment status for reducing disruptive disorders in school-aged children by the Substance Abuse and Mental Health Services Administration (SAMSHA; 2017). As of today, no research has been published that accounts for Adlerian play therapy's effectiveness with preadolescents or adolescents. However, anecdotal evidence and the natural fit between preadolescents' developmental milestones and Adlerian concepts suggests Adlerian play therapy with this population can be an advantageous treatment.

PRACTICAL INTERVENTIONS

The following descriptions of practical interventions are suggestions that therapists might find fitting for their clients. I recommend tailoring any of the following in order to best meet the needs of your clients. The descriptions I have provided are intentionally vague, which allows you to custom design your processing questions or other components of the intervention. I have organized them through the phases of Adlerian play therapy so readers can see how similar interventions can be used with different goals in mind.

Building the Relationship

The goal of this phase is to build a relationship of trust and collaboration. The therapist is wise to match the tone of the client while communicating care, concern, and understanding. The therapist avoids placing judgment on the client or trying to "fix" any problems identified by the client. Understanding and agreement are not synonymous; there have been many times when I understand the client even when I don't agree with him or her. Reflective listening skills such as restating content, paraphrasing, reflecting feelings, asking and answering questions, and engaging actively with the preadolescent are used by the therapist.

Investigating the Lifestyle

Each of the following activities is aimed at helping the therapist learn about the client's unique lifestyle. Specific processing questions can be tailored to gather specific information such as a client's personality priority, goals of misbehavior, role in the family, and so on.

Sand Tray

The counselor can give a general prompt such as "Create your world" or specific prompts such as the following:

> Show me how you feel when your mom doesn't come home at night.

What are your strengths and talents?
Create a picture of your role within your friendships/sport team/church/family/etc.
Pick three miniatures that represent different parts of you.
What is something you wish other people knew about you?

Drawing/Art

Draw a picture of your family.
Create a collage about yourself.
Using clay, create your spirit animal. Create an environment for him or her to live.

Music

Bring in a song that describes how you feel about yourself/family/friends/future/past. (This can be lyrics and/or genre and tempo of music.)
Make up a song that expresses how you feel about [your body, your family, your recent move, your new school, your breakup, etc.].

Movement/Dance

Without using words or sounds, show me how it feels to be you at home/school with family/friends.
Pretend you're a mime. How would you communicate what it feels like/felt like when . . .
Make up a dance from your mom's/dad's/sister's/teacher's/friend's perspective about how they feel about you or what they think of you.

Storytelling

Pretend you can write the script for the rest of your life. How would it go?
If a movie was made about your life, who would play you? Describe the movie with a beginning, middle, and end.

Helping the Client Gain Insight

The goal in this phase is for the client to develop increased awareness into his or her patterns of feeling, thinking, and behaving. Interventions and the processing that occurs during and after an activity are used as the vehicle for the increased insight.

Sand Tray

If all your problems were gone tomorrow, what would your world look like?

The therapist can create a tray for the client that depicts particular patterns of the client or other areas the therapist thinks the client could benefit from seeing.

Create a tray of your current problems from mom's/dad's/friend's/etc. perspective.

Drawing/Art

This is about the masks we wear. Using a blank masquerade mask (either on paper or an actual mask), instruct the client to create the outside as what he or she presents to the world and the inside as parts he or she hides from others.

Create a "security or insecurity" blanket. On a large piece of fleece or other material write words or draw pictures of the client's strengths or assets (e.g., family, talents, accomplishments, goals, characteristics) on one side, and on the other side write negative characteristics the client feels or believes about his- or herself (these are not necessarily true but the client believes they are true). The client can choose to wrap him- or herself in security or insecurity. The therapist can create this with the client or the client can create it alone.

Music

Cocreate a song or dance with a client. The therapist can interject particular lines or movements into the song or dance to help ignite opportunities for client insight.

Using instruments, the client can play music from other people's perspectives. For example, "Pick an instrument to represent your mom. Make sounds that would resemble how your mom feels about you." Do the same thing with dad, siblings, teachers, friends, your future or past self, etc.

Movement/Dance

Invite the client to take the perspective of different animals. (This might or might not be connected to other activities you've done with your client in which he or she identified with a particular animal.) The client can walk and move like the animal, talk about advantages and struggles of that animal, or share how that animal contributes to the world. The therapist can use the client's responses to draw connections between the animal and the client. For example, a client describes a bird and moves through the room flapping his wings. The client and therapist discuss advantages, disadvantages, talents, and gifts of birds. The therapist might make comments like, "In some ways, you're like a bird. You really like being independent and having freedom *and* you'd really like when you can flock together with your family. If you were in the V formation with your family, which bird would you be? What about when you're with your friends?" The counselor might also make comments about how the bird moves such as, "You seem exhausted flapping your wings all over the room. I wonder if you ever take a break and if so, where do you rest?"

Storytelling

Cocreate a story with the client. The therapist starts the story and shares one or two sentences. The client continues with the story, adding one or two sentences. The therapist and client continue this until the story comes to a conclusion. While the client has freedom to add whatever he or she wants, the therapist intentionally directs the story in ways that helps the client gain insight into particular life patterns. This can be done with parents or family members in session as well.

I show a picture of something I have found online or from somewhere else and ask the client, "What happened before or after this?" I ask the client to describe what happened before or what happened after the picture took place.

Reorienting/Reeducating

Interventions during this phase are designed to teach and create opportunities for the client to practice or demonstrate new ways of thinking or behaving. I assess the client's changed feelings, thoughts, attitudes, and behaviors through my experiences with him or her, through observation of the client, and through reports from the client and/or other people in the client's life (e.g., parents, family member, teachers, etc.). The following interventions are some I have used with preadolescents.

Sand Tray

The client creates two trays—one that depicts the client at the beginning of therapy and one at the current time.

What strategies, skills, or relationships do you have that can help you overcome challenges?

Create your world.

Drawing/Art

Create something that can be taken with the client in his or her everyday life. This "thing" represents concepts you want the client to remember during distressing moments. The client can create worry stones (stones the client rubs when he or she feels sad, worried, anxious, etc.) to keep in his or her pocket and rubs when feeling distressed. The client can create pocket friends, which are miniature figures (made of clothespins or other small materials able to be kept in the client's pocket) that can remind the client that he or she is loved and cared about.

Because most all preadolescents I have worked with have smartphones, I ask them to take pictures of something that represents how they see the world (or I take a picture of an object based on the goals of counseling) and bring it to our next session. We use the image as a metaphor to talk about how the client sees him- or herself, others, the world, or a specific situation. If the client leans toward self-defeating thoughts, I directly or indirectly include assets of the client. For example, the client brings a picture of a park slide. She talks about the curvy slide and how it makes people dizzy. I agree that this could happen *and* that it has lots of benefits such as it is fun, it is different from ordinary slides, it is colorful, lots of people think it's cool and different, and it is one part of many pieces of equipment on the playground and how lonely the playground would feel without the slide.

Have several flat rocks or stones available. Using paint or markers on one side, draw images that represent current problems or struggles. On the other side draw solutions to those problems.

Movement/Dance

Show me your feelings Provide a list of feeling words and ask the client to show one of their feelings by movement or dance. Randomly pick a feeling and ask the client to act out that feeling, pretend they experience that feeling and express it to another person, or describe times in which they feel that feeling.

Modeling Although this is not usually a specific intervention that is planned and placed in a therapy session, I use modeling with clients often. If I want clients to practice being imperfect, I model being imperfect. If I want to model sharing power, I share power. If I want to model recovering from or social skills of being wrong, losing, winning, being disappointed, feeling sad, or being embarrassed, I do those things. I may verbally process this with the client or I may do it and let it sit with the client while I observe his or her reactions.

"As if" movement Ask the client to move "as if" he or she was someone he or she respects or wants to emulate. You can also ask your client to act "as if" he or she has the skills, thoughts, feelings, or other qualities he or she desires. You can do this in session and/or have the client do this in other situations such as school or home.

Music

I choose a few songs that I believe represent different parts of the client. I play the songs and have the lyrics available for the client to read. The client chooses parts of each of the songs that he or she believes are accurate representations of how he or she sees him- or herself.

The client starts with an instrument of his or her choosing (e.g., drums, harmonica, cymbals, bells, etc.) and I instruct the client to keep a steady beat. After several seconds, I introduce a scenario or a feeling and ask the client to pick up or slow down the tempo that represents how he or she feels or thinks about the scenario. Then, the client returns the tempo to baseline and talks about how he or she can return to baseline. For example, after the client establishes a steady beat, I introduce feeling alone in a crowd during lunch. The client beats the drum faster and louder. Upon my cue, the client returns the tempo to the original beat and talks about taking deep breaths, starting small talk with another person at lunch, or reading a book while eating.

Storytelling

Ask a client to tell a story or write snippets of a negative experience, thought, or feeling, and then find a way to let it go. We might write it on balloons filled with helium and let it into the sky, scraps of paper that are crumpled and thrown away, toilet paper that is flushed, eggs that are smashed outside, or other things that can be discarded.

Ask the client to pretend he or she has just won a major award. (I tailor this award to something he or she is interested in such as movies, race car driving, sports, or music.) The client gives thanks to people who have helped him or her to make changes and gives advice to other people that will help them be the best they can be.

CASE STUDY

Sydney (pseudonym) was an eleven-year-old European American female who was intelligent and athletic. She lived with her biological parents until she was ten years old, at which time her mother moved out. She had no siblings. For the past year, Sydney lived with her father and has had periodic and inconsistent visits with her mother.

Prior to meeting Sydney, I met with her father to discuss his concerns about Sydney and his goals for her counseling. He described that Sydney had symptoms of anxiety and had stopped spending time with friends and leaving the house except for scheduled events. My goal with meeting Sydney's father was to start to build a relationship with him, and to help him understand the therapeutic process and goals for counseling.

In my first session with Sydney, she was kind and polite. She succinctly answered questions and appeared to be cautiously assessing me and trying to gauge the therapy process. I described what I anticipated of our time together (e.g., doing activities, getting to know each other, helping her to make some counseling goals, and working toward those goals). Her demeanor relaxed a bit as she felt more at ease with the process. I noted that she valued predictability and felt more comfortable when she knew what to expect. (Process note: Even during the first session where my primary goal is to build a collaborative relationship, I am learning about the client's lifestyle.) I presented her with three different games and she chose Jenga®. My intention for playing a game was to create a safe environment for us to be together, talk, and for her to not feel overwhelmed or interrogated by our discussion. I was also interested to observe how she took turns, how she handled winning and losing, and her reactions to the process of doing activities.

Throughout our first three sessions, Sydney began to feel more comfortable and grew to trust the routine that we established. She entered the session and we engaged in some small talk about her week. I gave her limited choices about an activity. Because she was quite anxious and had a desire to please me, I thought giving her free reign of choosing an activity would be too overwhelming for her. Limited choices provided her an opportunity to get to make a choice without hyperextending her anxiety. I always gave a choice of three things: a game, an art activity, and a sand tray. Each of the first three weeks she chose a game; I believe for her this felt the safest and most familiar of the options. Halfway through the third session she asked about the other activities and what she would be expected to do. In addition to verbally answering her questions, I showed her the materials with the intention of making them seem more relatable and safe.

I started session 4 much in the same way I started each of the previous sessions. This time, she chose to do a sand tray. Because I believed our relationship was well established, and I wanted to explore more of her lifestyle, I prompted the tray with "Create a tray of your family." In her tray she included miniatures to represent herself, her father, their pets, and how they spent their time. She did not include a miniature to represent her mother. When I verbalized this, she appeared thoughtful and said, "I don't really know how my mom fits in our family anymore." She decided to include a small witch figure and placed it in a corner, to represent her relationship with her mom. I also noticed that Sydney and her father did not spend a lot of time interacting with one another, although he tended to her needs. For example, he made sure she completed her homework, got to volleyball practice, went to school, and so forth.

Over the course of our next several sessions, Sydney became more amenable to doing other types of activities. She chose art activities, sand trays (sometimes I gave a prompt and sometimes she came up with the prompts ranging from family scenes, friend scenes, and school scenes), and storytelling. This led me to believe that when she felt safe, she was willing to take risks and extend beyond her comfort level. She did maintain an air of uncertainty as demonstrated by her looking at me for approval or permission to engage in an activity; her consistent changing, erasing, or starting over of activities; and her indecisiveness. Because I wanted to stretch her willingness to take risks (and then encourage her efforts), I didn't attempt to ease her discomfort in making choices. [Process note: This is more in line with phase four of Adlerian play therapy and demonstrates the cyclical nature of Adlerian therapy as compared to rigid adherence to stages.]

At this point, I had worked with Sydney for seven sessions. She and I had cocreated a mutual relationship in which she trusted me and we shared power within the sessions (i.e., phase 1). Through engagement, the processing and the product of the activities, I learned a great deal about her lifestyle (i.e., phase 2). Before moving to phase 3, in which my goal was to help her gain insight into her unique lifestyle, I developed a conceptualization of the client. This helped me to create a cognitive image of her lifestyle and to fashion interventions that were meaningful and useful for her to gain insight and make changes. Kottman and Meany-Walen (2016) provide a conceptualization outline and treatment planning guide consistent with Adlerian play therapy. Table 4.1 shows an example of a condensed outline and treatment plan for Sydney.

During phase three, I wanted Sydney to gain insight into how she viewed herself and the meaning she made of her past experiences and relationships. I specifically created interventions designed to meet her treatment goals that capitalized on her assets and interests. One such intervention utilized her interest in storytelling. I instructed her to choose two puppets—one that represented a sad animal (she chose a turtle) and one that represented a happy animal (she chose a rabbit). She was then asked to tell a story with those two being the main characters. In her story the turtle was slow and cautious. It could hide in its shell when it was sad and then others didn't have to see it cry. The rabbit was quick and bouncy; it had a lot of energy and was liked by everyone and had big families that burrowed together to share food and stay warm. Through prompts, questions, and added story lines from me, Sydney discovered that she had both parts to herself. She stated that when she was a young child she felt more like a rabbit and has recently felt more like a turtle. We talked about strengths and limitations to both animals and how each animal could be misunderstood.

In the next session, I instructed her to create an environment in which each of the two puppets could live happily. Because she felt connected to the puppets and the story she created, she readily got to work using various craft materials to create an environment in which the two animals could live harmoniously and both enjoy themselves. In addition to the physical creation

Table 4.1. Lifestyle conceptualization concepts, client descriptions, and treatment planning

Lifestyle conceptualization concepts, client descriptions, and treatment planning			
Family constellation	Only child Single father	Sydney is accustomed to having her needs met without competition from other siblings. She interacts mostly with adults and functions at a level more mature than others her age. Until she was 10, she grew up with two loving parents, who loved each other and loved her. Her mother moved out, and she has lived with her father for the past year.	
Family atmosphere	Calm; stable Disengaged	Sydney's physical and social needs are met by her father. For the past year, she receives relatively little emotional interaction with her father.	Tx goal/intervention: Increase parent-child emotional interaction and relationship. Dad and Sydney can find mutual interests and spend time together interacting.
Personality priority	Control of self	Sydney strives to remain in control of her emotions and emotional expression. She believes that if she is out of control, her world will unravel. She engages in activities and relationships in which she believes she can predict the outcome, therefore remain in control.	Tx goal/intervention: Demonstrate making mistakes and recovering. Help Sydney gain insight into her need for control and how that can create problems at times.

Goals of misbehavior	Power	Although her behaviors are not disruptive or cause great problems for others in her life, Sydney's behavioral goals are to remain in power, thus satisfying her personality priority of control.	Tx goal/intervention: Create opportunities in which Sydney is not solely in power and metacommunicate about Sydney's success at handling sharing power. Dad will develop understanding for how being in power is a safety mechanism for Sydney and will learn strategies for sharing power with his daughter.
Functioning at life tasks	School, family, friendship, self, spirituality	She functions at a high level in school and functions relatively well at the friendship life tasks. She has a few close friends; she does not spend time with them outside of school. Although her family life task is stable, it feels empty and lonely to her. Her self and spirituality life tasks are developmentally on par as she is in the process of defining who she is and what she believes about the meaning of the world.	Tx goals/interventions: Increase parent-child emotional interaction & improve parent-child relationship. Improve relationship quality with friends.
Mistaken beliefs	I am; Others are; The world is;	*I am* alone, not good enough, responsible for myself. *Others* are temporary, are expendable, and are selfish; leave, don't really care about me. *The world is* unpredictable, cruel, distrustful, empty, and meaningless. Therefore my behaviors must be controlled and I must not engage in relationships because they are not lasting and honest. If I do not create problems, people will not become upset and leave, and I can predict my life.	Tx goals/interventions: Increase parent-child emotional interaction & improve parent-child relationship. Help Sydney identify areas of support in her life. Assess for changes or shifts in her mistaken beliefs to be more realistic and constructive.

Crucial Cs	Capable Courage Connect Count	*Capable* – believes she is capable of accomplishing tasks and meeting her own needs. *Courage* – fears making mistakes and thus does not easily engage in challenges. *Connect* – is likeable and people want to connect with her. She does not perceive this to be true of herself and reluctantly engages with others. *Count* – does not believe she matters to others or the world.	Tx goal/intervention: Therapist will demonstrate making mistakes and recovering. Increase parent-child emotional interaction & improve parent-child relationship. Improve self-concept related to belonging and connecting.
Assets	Includes talents, interests, and other areas that can contribute to success and/ or resiliency	Athletic – participates in athletic teams; particularly likes volleyball. She is a valued member of the team. Intelligent – does well in school. She is smart and a valued member of her classes. Teachers and students appreciate her contributions to class and assignments. Creative – has an interest in music and storytelling. Supportive father – her father wants the best for her and is willing to make changes that contribute to Sydney's wellbeing.	Tx goal/interventions: Incorporate Sydney's interests in volleyball and music/storytelling into interventions.

Note: Similar goals and interventions can be used to address multiple lifestyle concepts. Different goals for each concept are not necessary and often are not an efficient use of therapists' or clients' time and energy.

of the environment, I asked about other animals who might live there or visit them. I asked who took care of the animals and how they got their needs met. We created scenarios about how they show various feelings. By the end of our session, she had created a community that supported each other.

I instructed her to do a few more activities with the goal of increasing her insight. I gave her freedom to choose elements of the activities, and encouraged her willingness to attempt new things and complete activities that were new to her, which strengthened her Crucial C of courage, and helped to gain balance of her control-of-self personality priority. One of the activities that seemed to be especially meaningful to Sydney was mashing songs (i.e., blending two prerecorded songs by overlaying the vocal track of one song seamlessly over the instrumental track of another) about her relationship with her mom. She was quite a bit more versed in technology than I and she enjoyed playing around with her computer. This allowed her to (a) teach me (and I could encourage her Crucial Cs of count and connect), (b) use her creativity and interests in music, and (c) explore her feelings about her mom with distance. She chose three songs from three different genres (hard rock, country, and alternative) and with three different emotional tones about mothers (anger, love, and longing). For her, the process of creating the mash-up as well as the product and processing of the song was powerful. She described her various feelings about her mother, which was new to her as she hadn't considered having the ability to have so many conflicting feelings of the same person at the same time. She also verbalized what she wished she had from her mom and the realization that she probably would never get it again. This prompted us into phase 4 activities of writing letters to her mom (she didn't send them but kept them in case she one day decided to mail them) and creating poems to herself from her mom's perspective.

From here, we merged into phase 4. She recognized that many of the things she wanted from her mother (expressed during our puppet stories) she was able to get from others (neighbors, relatives, friends' mothers, me, teachers, dad, etc.). Additionally, she and her dad started spending relationship time together. They went to the gym to practice her volleyball serve. This was a significant shift in their relationship; it was one of the first times in the past year that they interacted together in a way that required eye contact, cooperation, and prolonged time spent together. Prompted by dad and agreed upon by Sydney, dinner routines changed so that at least three nights a week they cooked and ate dinner together without interruption from the TV, computers, or cell phones. Sydney's father also reported that she was spending more time with friends outside of school. She was going to movies, having friends over, and going to friends' homes. Although her anxiety was not directly addressed outside of session, both Sydney and her father reported she had reduced anxiety in all areas of her life. She also reported finding a new hobby in writing her own lyrics and mashing music. She described the process as cathartic and an effective way for her to "let go of bottled-up emotions."

Sydney had met the therapy goals and was feeling more confident and less anxious in many areas of her life. After discussion, we decided that we would move from weekly sessions to biweekly sessions for three more sessions. Over the six weeks, our counseling interventions and discussions seemed to naturally move into typical preadolescent concerns (i.e., popularity, friendship complications, and a budding interest in romantic relationships), none of which were major problems or concerns for her. In our last session, she did a timeline activity about the changes she made over the previous few months and I initiated a brief conversation about being available if she wanted to check in or needed something more in the future.

INCORPORATION OF FAMILY

Adlerian theory emphasizes the significant role of the family in the development of personality, and the family becomes a regular part of the Adlerian play therapy process (Kottman & Meany-Walen, 2016). At times, the entire family or subsets of the family join some or all sessions. With regard to parent consultations, I typically practice a transparent relationship with the parent because preadolescents can shift between wanting support and openness from parents (much like a younger child) to other times wanting privacy (much like an adolescent). Thus, the preadolescent is aware that I communicate with parent(s) and, to the degree possible, is present in my meetings with parents. Importantly, while I attempt to maintain the preadolescent's confidentiality, I always follow therapeutic judgment and client safety in determining what I share with the parent.

In this case, Sydney's father consulted with me prior to my meeting Sydney. I communicated with him my expectations and plans for his involvement in the process. He and I also met every two or three weeks in the presence of Sydney. Because Sydney had an overall demeanor of anxiety and distrust, it was important to me that communication between her father and I was open and that she be aware of discussions we had. The consultation with Sydney's father took many forms. Sometimes, it was a check-in, in which I asked him and Sydney if they had anything specific they wanted to discuss, and of their perceptions of progress or setbacks. A few times, Sydney and I had discussed her desire to have specific conversations with her father (e.g., her wanting more relationship time with him) and our sessions included her having this discussion with him, with my support. Sydney's father played more of a supporting role and less of a main figure in our time together; he followed through with suggestions, met with us in session when asked, and expressed his support and concerns for his daughter during our sessions.

REFLECTION AND CONCLUSION

Working with preadolescents poses unique challenges. They become more able to use abstract reasoning, allowing more "talk" to enter the sessions, yet they are still more fluid in the language of play and activity. As I worked with Sydney (and with all preadolescents), I paid close attention to how she engaged in activities and the consistency between what she articulated and what she shared through her activity process.

Throughout my time with Sydney I was keenly aware of the potential for transference. I am close to the same age as her mother and was offering her emotional support that she needed. I don't necessarily find transference a problem but I wanted to be sure that she was able to transfer the emotional support she was receiving from me to other people in her life (i.e., neighbors, relatives, teachers, etc.). One of the things Sydney, her father, and I talked about was how to get support from others and who might be best suited for different things such as talking about upcoming physical changes, purchasing feminine hygiene products and undergarments, dealing with friendship and relationship issues, and helping with other needs that would emerge.

Overall, therapy with Sydney was successful. She was able to understand herself and make changes to better meet her needs and desires. Her relationship with her father improved and they were able to communicate in a more open fashion. Sydney's anxiety symptoms reduced as she felt more connected and valued and had courage to be imperfect. Although we successfully terminated therapy after successful completion of therapy goals, it was also likely that she would experience additional stressors as she matured and her relationship with her mother, or her understanding of that relationship, changed.

REFERENCES

Adler, A. (1998). *Understanding human nature*. England: Oneworld Oxford. (Original work published in 1927.)

Kottman, T., & Meany-Walen, K. K. (2016). *Partners in play: An Adlerian approach to play therapy* (3rd ed.). Alexandria, VA: American Counseling Association.

Lambert, S. F., LeBlanc, M., Mullen, J. A., Ray, D., Baggerly, J., White, J., & Kaplan, D. (2007). Learning more about those who play in session: The national play therapy in counseling practices project (phase 1). *Journal of Counseling & Development, 85*, 42–46. doi:10.1002/j.1556-6678.2007.tb00442.x

Meany-Walen, K. K., Bratton, S. C., & Kottman, T. (2014). Effects of Adlerian play therapy on reducing students' disruptive behaviors. *Journal of Counseling & Development, 92,* 47–56. doi: 10.1002/j.1556-6676.2014.00129.x

Mosak. H., & Maniacci, M. (1999). *A primer of Adlerian psychology*. Philadelphia, PA: Brunner/Mazel.

Substance Abuse and Mental Health Services Administration (SAMHSA; 2017). *Adlerian play therapy*. Retrieved from http://nrepp.samhsa.gov/ProgramProfile.aspx?id=160

Chapter Five

Family Play Therapy with Preteens

Anne L. Stewart, Ariel D. Marrero, and Joseph F. Pellegrino

There is no development without relationships.—Jack P. Shonkoff, MD

The family that plays together, stays together. —*Parents* magazine

In this chapter we will describe the evolving field of family play therapy (FPT), including a discussion of the contributions of play and family therapy to FPT, a rationale for its use, and the evidence base for its effectiveness. We will share findings from neuroscience with a developmental and attachment framework to explore using family play therapy with preadolescents to enhance skills of emotional regulation, perspective taking, and understanding the self. We will share techniques that engage tweens and their families in playful therapeutic activities. The activities are inclusive for diverse family configurations and congruent with the key social and biological changes occurring during this dynamic stage of development. Last, we will illustrate an integrated approach to intervention with a tween and her family.

LITERATURE REVIEW

Family play therapy, broadly conceived, is a therapeutic approach that intentionally engages children in therapy in the context of their family system. FPT may be practiced by clinicians trained in play therapy who purposefully broaden their intervention from a focus on the child to including parents[1] and/or family members. Alternatively, FPT may be used by clinicians trained in the field of family therapy who consciously attend to the age-appropriateness of their strategies and interventions to ensure participation of children in sessions. FPT was created by practioners, researchers, and consumers appreciating the unique and complementary constructs that promote change from both play and family systems theory.

Contributions from Play and Systemic Family Therapy

Play is a ubiquitous phenomenon observed in nearly all cultures and takes many forms. Physical or rough-and-tumble play, social play, language play, object play, creative play, expressive arts, and pretend play are a few examples. Throughout the life span, play and play therapy afford people opportunites to communicate their needs and wishes, transmit values and beliefs, engage in creative problem-solving, and symbolically explore crises, developmental challenges, and frightening or taboo topics or experiences. Play stimulates conjunctive emotions that connect us with others, creating bonds that strengthen relationships. Children view people who are fun to be with (i.e., playful) as more trustworthy, caring, and approachable. The delight sparked by play can invigorate and help repair relationships. The healing power of play has been advanced across numerous theoretical approaches from child-centered to Adlerian to cognitive-behavioral play therapy. For children, play is an essential component of a therapeutic relationship.

Systemic therapy constructs are at play (so to speak) in families and offer therapists inventive tools to promote connection, understanding, and change. Foundational to systemic theories are these two ideas: the whole (the family) is different than the sum of the parts (the family members) and all the parts of a system (the family members in the family) exert reciprocal influence on each other. Thus, when one family member is in crisis, the whole family system will experience a level of disturbance. A hopeful possible outcome of this perspective is that the "child's problem" can be newly understood as a shared "family problem" with each family member being affected and affecting one another in particular ways. I often illustrate this idea to families with a mobile (see figure 5.1). We select one object on the mobile to represent the child with the identified problem. Then, I lightly tap that object to show the impact of the problem. When the whole mobile starts to wave, with some parts moving more wildly than others, family members quickly understand the phenomenon.

Another important consideration is that families function within the context of other systems of care. So, an important aspect of your intervention may be to connect the family to other organizations with resources that can help address their needs, such as schools, social services, and medical offices. Of course, this means that you will be in communication with the organization's providers to constitute an interprofessional team of support for you and the family.

Figure 5.1. Mobile to Illustrate Reciprocal Influences in Family Relationships. Courtesy of the authors

Rationale and Evidence Base for Family Play Therapy

The rationale for using FPT is informed by the fields of play therapy and family therapy. Leaders and practitioners of play therapy have long recognized the importance of thoughtfully and deliberately including family members, specifically parents, in child treatment (Schaefer & Carey, 1994; Gil, 2015). Likewise, leaders in family therapy promoted the active participation of children in family therapy sessions. Bratton et al. (2005) conducted a meta-analysis of more than ninety studies exploring the effectiveness of play therapy. A significant finding was that incorporating parents in play therapy resulted in larger treatment effects than when the intervention was solely individual play therapy. Researchers surveying family therapists reported that clinicians related using family therapy techniques such as storytelling, drawing, puppet play, games, and family mural drawing in therapy (Sori & Sprenkle, 2004). As family members play together, therapists can identify the patterned ways the family members interrelate. Family play therapists, for example, can observe who helps whom and whether the help is easily offered and easily accepted, who leads/who follows, how decisions are made, what emotions are expressed, and how conflict is addressed.

Studies supporting the efficacy of play therapy and family therapy treatments from a wide variety of theoretical perspectives continue to mean accumulate. The Substance Abuse and Mental Health Services Administration's National Registry of Evidence-based Programs and Practices (NREPP) catalogs affirmative outcomes associated with child-centered play therapy and Adlerian play therapy. Especially relevant to the focus of this chapter, NREPP lists treatments that involve parents, such as filial therapy, Theraplay, and Child Parent Relationship Therapy. Additionally, there is convincing depth and breath in the family therapy studies listed on the NREPP site. Positive findings are noted across many family therapy theoretical orientations, including significant outcomes for family behavior therapy, multidimensional family therapy, and attachment-based family therapy.

The field of FPT is in an exciting "under construction" stage. Eliana Gil, the undisputed leader in advocating for family play therapy, notes that researchers are generating innovative integrations of play and family therapy, such as incorporating play therapy techniques in emotion-focused family therapy and parent coaching models (Gil, 2015). As investigations demonstrating specific applications of integrated approaches emerge, we encourage readers to work in concert with the American Psychological Association's definition of evidence-based practice.[2] Namely, we encourage you to integrate available research findings in play therapy, family therapy and family play therapy with your knowledge of tween development and, importantly, your own clinical expertise in the context of the family's characteristics, culture, and preferences. In this way, we can promote effective mental health practice by applying empirically supported principles of building authentic, therapeutic relationships and generating sound case conceptualizations to inform our interventions.

Although training programs and licensure for play therapy and family therapy follow discrete and separate trajectories, currently there is considerable interest in family play therapy from practioners and graduate students. Indeed, a survey of Association for Play Therapy (APT) members conducted by Haslam and Harris (2011) stated that over 80 percent of the participants endorsed that it was "possible to integrate family and play therapy approaches" (p. 60). A related, and rather worrying, finding from their report was that the respondents did not believe their graduate programs prepared them well for practice in play or family therapy. We believe this finding calls for us all to thoughtfully reflect on our knowledge and skills in play and family therapy and, likely, gain requisite training so that we can practice effectively and ethically in the scope of our abilities and talents.

PRACTICAL INTERVENTIONS: INFORMED BY TWEEN DEVELOPMENT, NEUROSCIENCE, AND ATTACHMENT THEORY

Tween development signifies remarkable growth across all maturational domains. Tweens are primarily in Piaget's cognitive period of "concrete operations," characterized by an enhanced ability to organize their thoughts and anticipate consequences through deductive reasoning, use more abstract thinking, and maintain their attention for longer periods of time. In the context of family interactions and family play therapy, this means that tweens are better able to conceive of and share their opinions with parents and siblings (and the therapist).

The techniques we share are informed by findings from neuroscience and attachment theory. Research results from these fields indicate that daily interactions and relationships continue to influence the structure of the brain during tween years and beyond. The quality of interpersonal interactions, and corresponding attachment relationships, actually shapes brain circuits and lays the foundation for future developmental outcomes, from school performance to mental health and interpersonal skills (Cozolino, 2010; Siegel, 2013). Moreover, neuroscience research demonstrates play, as an improvisational, emotionally engaging experience, increases levels of oxytocin and stimulates feelings of emotional well-being and trust. While engaged in playful interactions, our mirror neurons are activated, helping us accurately understand and respond to one another's feelings and form new neural patterns (Cozolino, 2010). Thus, the experience of play can be harnessed to create therapeutic encounters in the family.

The developmental changes being navigated by tweens are often manifested in challenges in their ability to regulate their emotions, to take the perspective of others, and to understand themselves and their emerging identity exploration. Techniques are grouped under these three dimensions. The selection and timing of what technique to use should be determined considering your comfort level, the client's age and presenting issue(s), the family's values and culture, and the therapeutic goals. Most techniques can serve to assess family strengths and challenges or be targeted to address specific concerns.

Emotional Regulation

Tweens with secure attachment relationships demonstrate greater social competence and self-regulation while those with insecure attachments display problems in emotional regulation, including exhibiting more aggressive, anxious, and withdrawn behavior (Bosmans & Kerns, 2015). These activities offer opportunities for families to offer support and delight in each other and acknowledge the importance of relying on each other for coregulation.

Bouncing Back

In this activity, family members use a "super ball" to illustrate who in the family helps them bounce back. Family members sit in a circle and the person holding the super ball states a problem. The person then bounces the ball to the family member who helped them "bounce back" and briefly describes what the person did that was beneficial. This can be modified so the person names a current problem and bounces the ball to the person(s) in the family they would like to ask for help in resolving the issue.

Rock On!

Many families enter therapy with their fund of positive interactions severely depleted. The "Rock On!" activity invites each family member to think of a trait or activity they "rock" (do well). Parents are invited to identify a trait or activity that they excelled in as a tween—and still rock. Family members each decorate a rock with the name or a symbol of their talent. In a circle, family members share their talent and then end with a distinctive dab.[3] The activity can be modified so each person also says and shows their skill and then finishes with a dab flourish. Alternatively, family members could name what they see as a trait another family member rocks at.

Family Speedball

This game provides practice in managing heightened emotions and staying engaged with family members, all in a ball toss game. The family is instructed that the game involves announcing a category and then, when you catch the ball, quickly naming an example of something from the category. For example, if the first category was COLORS, you would have to name a color before you quickly toss the ball to someone else. Family members are instructed to make eye contact with the intented recipient before tossing ball to them. To increase intensity, a time limit may added for the person to throw the ball (note that this may be contraindicated, depending on the family). Over time, increasingly personalized or emotion-laden categories may be used, such as "things that our family loves to do," "things our family really hates to do," or "things we want more [or less] of in our family." You can add to the fun by substituting a rubber chicken or other unusual object to toss.

Perspective-Taking

Family play therapy can promote perspective-taking by providing opportunities to engage, respond, and problem-solve unfamiliar tasks together. Importantly, through participating in novel, play-based activities, families have opportunities to abandon problem-saturated interactions and enter into welcoming, friendly, and enjoyable engagement with each other.

Rewriting the Script

Negative family interactions often quickly escalate, resulting in the family members feeling helpless to effect change. The purpose of this activity is to identify and deconstruct a problematic encounter by looking at and reauthoring a troublesome situation frame by frame.

Family members are asked to identify the top three problematic events of the prior week and write them on sticky notes. The therapist places all the notes on a poster board and supports the family in selecting one event to illustrate and then "rewrite" for this activity. We recommend that you help the family identify an event that is meaningful and not their family's ultimate conflict—just so they can get practice with the task.

Using an oversized film script graphic, the family collectively draws and/or writes each step of the interaction to tell the story of what occurred. Family members are then asked to think about how they might "edit" the event by rewriting the script. Each person is given a film strip graphic (figure 5.2) and redraws/rewrites the sequence to create a more satisfying encounter from their perspective. Each family member is invited to share a title for the original and rewritten scripts and tell their rewrite to the family. The therapist supports the family members telling and may offer questions, such as: What was happening before the event? What led up to the event? What surprised you about the event? What different feelings were people having? What happened immediately after? What are the long-term impacts of the interaction?

Stringing Along

This activity encourages each family member to depict and also view the relational closeness and distance in the family. Each family member has access to index cards, length of string or yarn, a marker, and a hole punch. Family members write their name and the names of their household members on index cards and are invited to reflect on how close they feel to each member. Each member cuts lengths of string to indicate the amount of closeness/distance to other family members and affixes it to their own card. Taking turns, each person places their cards on the floor and stands in the center on their own card to reflect on his/her own position in the family relationships. Next, other family members may surround the person by standing on their cards and reflecting on their relationships. Family members take turns exploring their construction of the family relationships. The family members and therapist can examine what changes in their relationships they have noticed in the past, what changes they anticipate, and what changes they wish for at this time.

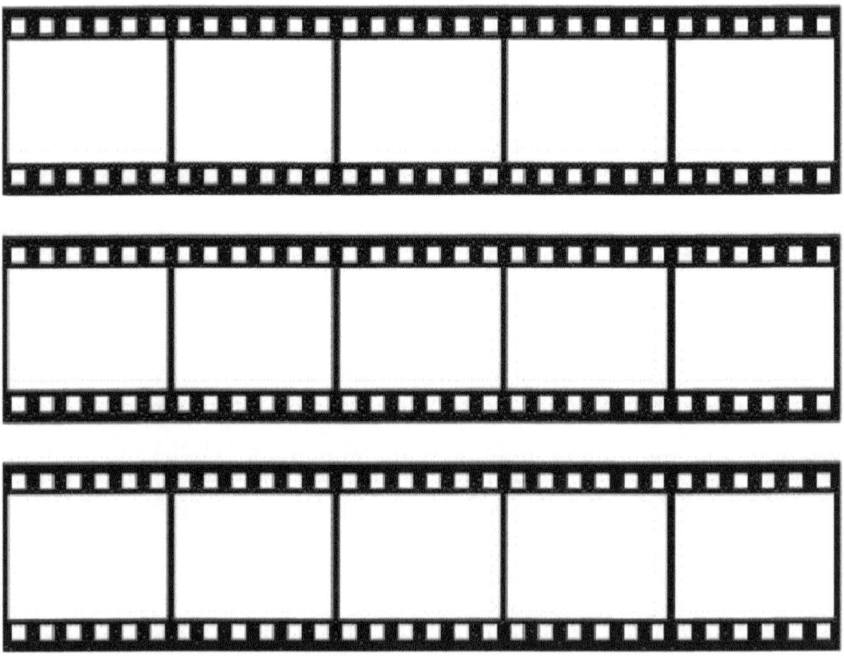

Figure 5.2. Family Film Script Graphic. Courtesy of the authors

Note to (Younger and Older) Self . . .

In this activity, family members are invited to reflect on what information, observation, or advice they might have for each other. The twist is that they are to offer the advice from the imagined perspective of being a different age. It is suggested that the parents offer advice from the perspective of being the age of their tween, and vice versa. The advice can be targeted to a specific issue or more general advice, such as elaborating on a statements like, “Here is my advice for building family trust” or “You may be surprised but here is my advice for having a happy family” or “These are the things I have found to be important keys to finding helpful solutions for the family’s problems.” Family members discuss both the content of the advice and the process of taking each other’s perspective.

Understanding the Self

Nature Family Play Genogram

The family play genogram activity invites family members to complete a genogram on poster-sized paper. A three-generation genogram usually reveals salient family themes, issues, and values. The therapist can share a legend with genogram symbol codes, such as circles for women and squares for men, and how to depict family relationships and events (divorce, death, etc.). Typically, family members then select and place miniatures to represent each person in the genogram. To illustrate, in a family with two parents and three children, there would be five miniatures on each family member’s genogram shape. The miniatures are to have attributes that correspond with perceived charactistics.

In the *nature* family play genogram, family members are asked to select items from nature that illustrate the desired characteristics, rather than using miniatures (Stewart & Green, 2014). So a tween may select a rock for her mother, sharing how she feels like talking to her mother is like talking to a stone wall. The mother may place a rose on a stem, relating how beautiful she sees her daughter and that when she approaches, she is pricked by the thorns and cannot get close. (Additional resources describing how to create genograms and corresponding symbol legends can be found online.)

Throwback Thursday

Throwback Thursday is used in social media to show past events. In this rendition, tweens and parents are asked to interview each other. The activity provides many opportunities for family members to learn about each other’s current and past interests and relationships. Here are a few sentence stems to help you get started.

When I was a tween . . .	My favorite movie was . . .	I wasn't sure about . . .
My favorite book was . . .	I was excited about . . .	My favorite band was . . .
I worried about . . .	I remember wanting to be . . .	I loved to . . .

The most important person/people in my life were . . .

Have fun creating more sentence stems with your families!

You to the Rescue

The resurgence of superhero movies can be incorporated in this family play therapy exercise. Family members are simply invited to "Draw yourself as a superhero or super heroine." Family members can name their hero and then explore the following questions together: What are your superpowers? Who are your enemies? What are your weaknesses? Do you work alone or with a league? The family can create a story or play of a quest for their superhero team (like the Avengers) to share with you.

Folding Family Poem

News reports state that tweens, now designated Generation M for their strong affiliation with social media, have between four and nine hours of screen time per day. The Folding Family Poem activity invites family members to *share* screen time by using their smartphones (or the therapist's computer) to search together for meaningful quotes. The quotes can be significant for their relevance to a given family member or descriptive of the family as a whole. Each family member selects one quote, writes it at the top of their poem paper, and passes it to the person on their left. The second person writes a sentence that adds to the first entry on the paper they received and then folds the paper so the first quote will not be visible to the next person who receives the paper (see figure 5.3). The papers are again passed to the left and the process is repeated until everyone has had the opportunity to write on one another's paper. Remember, when a person is writing they should only see the sentence before their entry. All others should be folded and hidden. At the end, everyone should have a personal poem that builds upon their first quote to share and discuss together.

CASE STUDY

The following clinical vignette illustrates the use of play therapy with a preadolescent and her family.

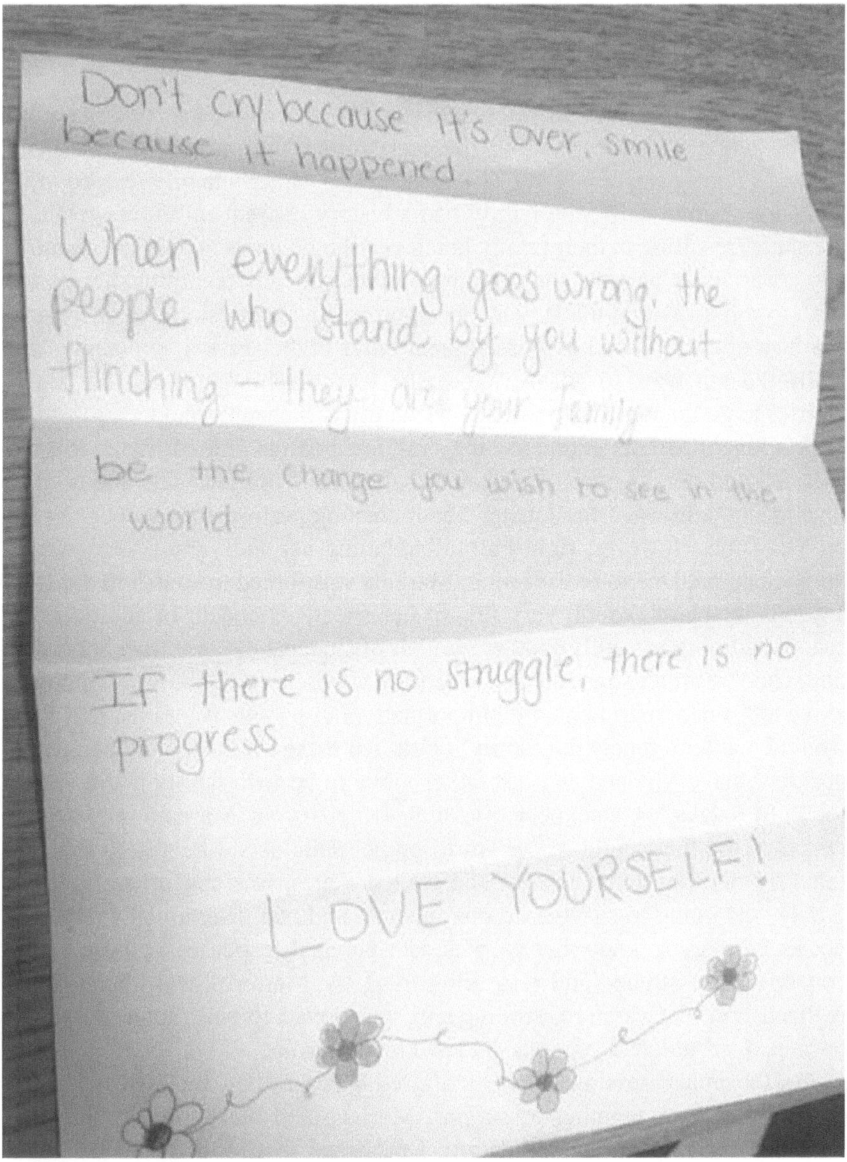

Figure 5.3. Folding Poem. Courtesy of the authors

Cast Them to the Wind: Mariana and Her Family Worries

Mariana's mother and father gazed anxiously at their slight daughter, whose eyes were cast downward. Mariana, aged eleven, and her parents came to therapy after she admitted she was thinking about running away. This confession occurred after the parents had decided that Mariana and her father would move back to El Salvador while her mother stayed in the United States for an additional year.

To explore resources for safety and support, we created a three-generation family genogram. Surprisingly, the family tree showed all of Mariana's mother's family was living in Cuba while all her father's family resided in El Salvador. Additionally, the family had a history of frequent moves while in the states, resulting in their family being very much on its own in the community. Mariana's parents showed appropriate concern regarding her stated wish to run away and made plans for appropriate supervision and check-ins. Mariana opened up and expressed great relief in the session, explaining she really did not want to go away, but she very much wanted all the family worries to go far away. She wanted her family to be happy again.

Mariana's parents explained they migrated to the United States to give Mariana and her six-year-old sister "a better life." Mariana said she used to love to sing and was "passionate" about creating performance videos to post on YouTube. However, right before beginning her sixth-grade-year, everything changed. Due to redistricting, Mariana was forced to switch to a different middle school, which very few of her friends attended. In addition, the school had a significantly smaller number of students of color than her previous school. Further stress ensued when her father lost his job, necessitating a move to a small apartment, and, importantly, her parents were unsure if they would be able to renew the family's visa. All these events led the parents to decide to have Mariana and her father move to be with family and a secure job in El Salavador. Unexpectedly, at eleven years old, Mariana felt like she was carrying the weight of the world on her shoulders. She shared that she felt very nervous about leaving the United States, was concerned how her family was going to survive on one income, and had determined she would not let her parents know her worries. Her parents' responses to these heavy concerns were attuned and reassuring. As I (A. Marrero) heard her story, I realized how the carefree, smiling girl who loved to sing, understandably became overburdened, anxious, and had lost her voice.

As the intake session ended, I offered a description for how we could continue to work together to support Mariana and the family as they approached their upcoming separation. I proposed that most meetings would include Mariana and her parents, and we would also schedule some parent consultation meetings, some whole family meetings, and occasional meetings with just Mariana and me, depending on the topics and issues to be explored. The family agreed to this format and it was determined that Mariana and I would meet together for most of the subsequent session with the parents joining us near the end for some family meeting time. I suggested this to provide time for Mariana and me to get to know each other and further assess her concerns.

At our next meeting, Mariana presented again as quiet, anxious, and seemingly unsure if she could trust me. As she looked around the room, she noticed the sand tray and asked what it was for. I invited her to use the miniatures to create a world in the sand. Her uncertain demeanor disappeared, as she thoughtfully constructed two scenes in the sand: one she entitled "Journey" and the other "Stuck" (see figures 5.4 and 5.5, respectively). In Mariana's narrative called "Stuck," a rabbit was caught inside a well and was trying to jump out while a bear watched. The rabbit wished he was bigger and stronger. Mariana said the rabbit was tired, but did not want to give up; he was going to keep trying to get out of the well, even though a bear awaited. In "Journey" two horses stood at a line in the sand facing a place that Mariana said was "far away." She created a story about father and daughter horses who were about to go on a journey to a "good place." The good place was happy and filled with kind horses that looked just like them. The journey was going to be tough and tiring. The daughter horse wanted to go, but not right now because she was scared.

Mariana was eager to share her sand tray scenes and stories with her parents. The parents joined us and together we explored the stories, staying in metaphor. The parents were curious and supportive about the characters in the scenes and everyone wondered about how the rabbit and horses might determine who or what could help and what to do next. Although we were just getting to know each other, through play, Mariana was starting to show me and her parents a more complete picture of her emotional world.

In subsequent family play therapy sessions, Mariana continued to open up and give voice to the emotions she had kept hidden. In one session, we created a web of emotions using yarn to identify and process the strong feelings the family experienced. The parents, Mariana, and I took turns writing down a number of stressful or unexpected family experiences. The events included everyday annoyances (e.g., a bad hair day) and specific trials they had survived together (e.g., had to move to a smaller apartment). All the instances were written on pieces of paper and put in a bag. Mariana, her sister, and her parents then identified the emotions that corresponded to the event. Segments of yarn were cut to illustrate the magnitude of the emotion(s) experienced and assembled into a web.

Mariana: (Picks a paper out of the bag) It says, "You find out you have to switch schools."

Therapist: Hmm . . . so you said that did happen this year.

Figure 5.4. "Journey." Sand Tray Scenes. Courtesy of the authors

Mariana: Yeah, earlier this year . . . I had to leave all my friends behind and go to this dumb, new school. It sucked.

Figure 5.5. "Stuck." Sand Tray Scenes. Courtesy of the authors

Mariana's mother: Yes, it was also hard because her little sister stayed in the other school.

Therapist: So it sounds like this was a really tough experience for the family. Mariana, do you remember what feelings you had when you first found out you were switching?

Mariana: I don't know . . . sad . . . and scared. I didn't want to go. I begged my mom to let me stay but I didn't have a choice. The next day I was in a new school surrounded by kids who didn't look like me.

Therapist: Oh, that does sound really scary. You had no control over what was happening. How big would the yarn be for this situation?

Mariana: (Grabs yarn) Yeah, I think I felt more scared and nervous than sad. I was REALLY worried about making new friends. Hmm. . . . Those two pieces of yarn should be longer than my arm. They're the biggest because I felt them a lot.

Mariana's mother: Oh Mariana, your father and I did not realize how big this change was for you—we are so sorry it happened.

During this session Mariana was able to identify and share the emotions she had not told her parents. Through therapeutic encounters, she was able to see that her parents did not need to be protected and could handle her intense emotions and were there to help her regulate them. She was beginning to express negative emotions and she discovered she did not have to suffer alone and in silence.

Identity soon became a topic in therapy for Mariana. She said that she used to proudly identify herself as half El Salvadorian and half Cuban; however, after switching schools, her identity became a source of shame. She disclosed that not only did her school have few students of color, but she was experiencing racism and microaggressions on a daily basis. She described being ignored by the White kids, but not being fully accepted by the Hispanic kids because she "acted white." To explore her identity in depth, she created an identity collage with her parents witnessing and then participating in the discussion.

Therapist: I want you to think about five identities, ways you describe yourself, that are really important to you.

Mariana: Childish, Hispanic, colorful, calm, and determined.

Therapist: So, let's talk about what each one means to you and while we are talking we can cut out pictures from magazines to represent each identity. Which one do you want to start with?

Mariana: Hispanic. I chose that one because I'm really proud of being El Salvadorian and Cuban. It's who I am.

Therapist: And what pictures would represent this part of you?

Mariana: The flags from each country. I want them big and in the center of my paper.

Therapist: Ok, great. When we think about identity, sometimes it can be difficult to figure out who we are in one place and then who we are in another place. Like in school for example.

Mariana: Yeah, I don't fit in at school. It's hard to make friends.

Therapist: I'm wondering, are there pieces of your identity that you feel aren't accepted in school? Or aren't accepted by certain people?

Mariana: Most of the kids at school look at me weird because I'm from El Salvador and speak Spanish. Not everyone is racist, but they ignore me and the other Hispanic kids.

Therapist: That sounds like it's really hurtful to have people ignore you because of your heritage.

Mariana: Yeah. It sucks. But sometimes I also get upset because some of the Hispanic kids say that I act White because I'm smart. Sometime I feel stuck in the middle, like I don't fit in any group.

During the process of creating an identity collage, Mariana was able to express some of the built-up anger and sadness she was feeling over being ashamed of her heritage. She revealed that she felt like she couldn't tell her parents about her experiences in school because they made such a big sacrifice to be in the United States and she did not want to seem ungrateful. Mariana's parents disclosed that they had also never openly discussed racism with her as she was much lighter skinned, assuming she would not be affected as they were. The experience of discussing her conflicting feelings about her identity and hearing her parents' experiences and how they connected to her experiences in school allowed Mariana to feel supported and heard by her parents.

Toward the end of our work together Mariana began reflecting on what she had learned in therapy. She used art to create an image of a tree that represented her growth across the last four months (see figure 5.6). The roots of her tree were the problems she came into therapy with: wanting to run away, significant anxiety, and withdrawing from friends. She explained that through therapy she grew tall and strong, and was able to recognize that she had a lot of people she could turn to for support. The top of the tree represented what she grew into, which she identified as stronger, hopeful, and talkative. Finally, she drew leaves falling off the tree, which represented what she was ready to let go of: wanting to run away, feeling sad, and being afraid to talk. Although she was still scared about moving back to El Salvador and changing schools again, with her parents' support, she felt more confident in her ability to cope.

Two days before Mariana and her father departed for El Salvador, we held our termination session. A major theme for Mariana had been carrying the weight of her worries alone because she was so concerned her parents couldn't handle them. Therefore, for our final family play therapy session we focused on lessening the family's worry weight; what worries were they willing to let go, and especially, how could her parents help her lessen her load? Mariana, her sister, and her parents each identified a worry that they came into therapy with, wrote it down on a piece of paper, and tied it to a helium balloon. After sharing their individual worries, they worked together to come up with a family worry they were finally ready to let go of. We walked the balloons outside and as the family prepared to let go, Mariana admitted she was scared. Her parents took her into their arms and said that they were also afraid, and were also certain the family would make it through this transition. Mariana took a deep breath and the family let go of their balloons. As she watched their worries float away, she smiled and began to sing.

INCORPORATION OF FAMILY

A tween's family is always present psychologically and in this case example, the parents and younger sister were physically present and participating in the therapeutic process as well. Tweens, like all of us, carry their families with them—in their hearts and minds. The family's beliefs and values, their expectations and histories build and rebuild the tween's psychological world.

Family play therapy materials should include domestic and wild animal family miniatures and puppet family groups, such as different sizes and colors of rabbits. It is important to have boy and girl figures with clothing, skin tones, and features representing different cultures, disabilities, and ethnic groups and (plastic) food and utensils from different cultures. In addition, assemble crayons, paints, chalk, and paper in a range of shades of brown, tan, and black. Many fun items can be found at cultural festivals, import stores, museums, cake decoration stores, and thrift shops (and from traveling friends and family). We suggest using both homemade and commercially produced items.

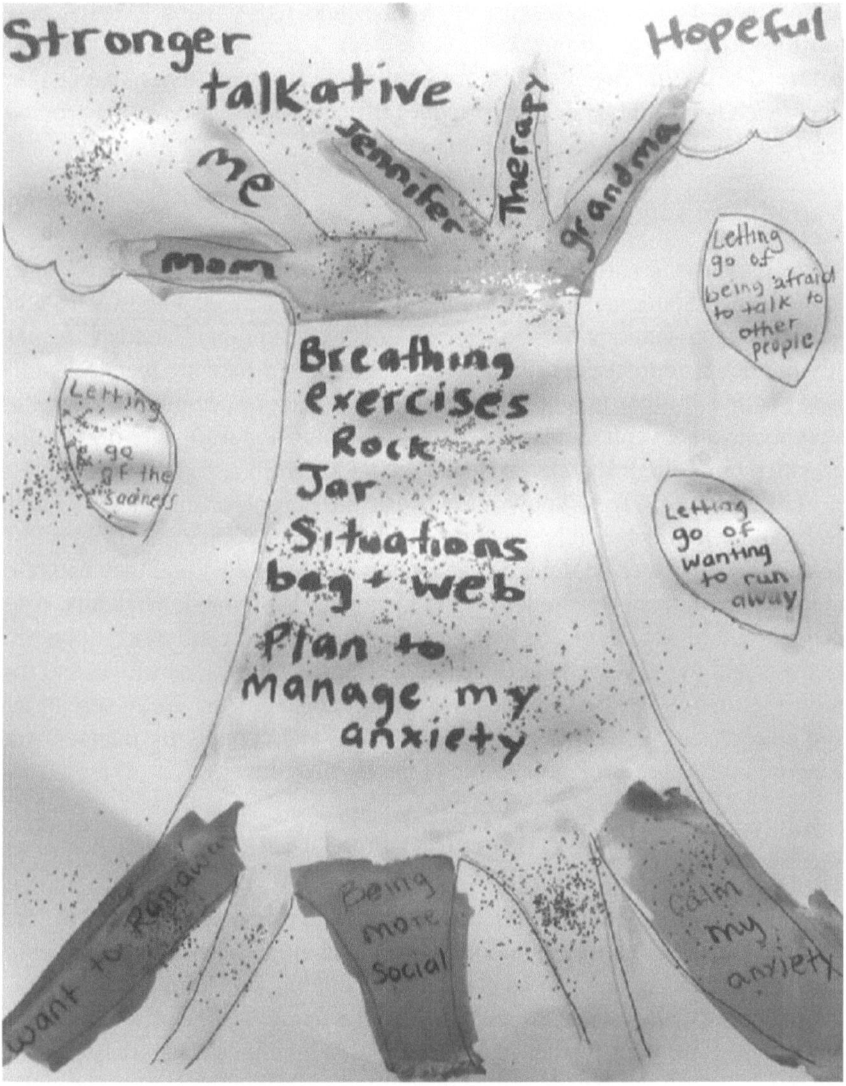

Figure 5.6. Tree Depicting Therapy Process. Courtesy of the authors

Just as you consider the tween's developmental level, you can recognize the stage of the family's development in the family life cycle. Families negotiate many developmental tasks and crises as they change and grow, resulting in a broad range of emotions. The family life cycle posits that the key emotional process for families with tweens is to increase the flexibility of the family's boundaries to support their increasing independence. You may find it helpful to reframe and "normalize" the family's concerns by telling them that it makes sense to wonder and worry—this is brand new territory for them all as they have never been a family with a XX-year-old before! The central life cycle task for families with tweens, that of navigating interdependence and autonomy, provides the context for discovering promising solutions for enhanced family connections.

Variation in Family Configurations

There are moving and dramatic changes taking place in family assemblages in the United States and throughout the world. In your work with tweens, you will encounter families that do not conform to "traditional" models. Same-sex partners, stepfamilies, single head of household parents, blended families, and many other family forms are becoming more common. In fact, the stereotypical conventional family of a married man and woman living together with their biological children is now the minority.

Tweens are ready to know more about the complex world they inhabit and will benefit from active parental (and therapist) support to explore important issues of personal growth and safety. Tweens who feel they can talk to their parent about sex are less likely to engage in high-risk behaviors, so it is important to encourage and help parents initiate conversations about bodily changes and the development of sexual feelings. Complex, sensitive, and in-the-news topics—such as sexual harassment, racism, media use/misuse, drug and alcohol use, and exposure to interpersonal and community trauma—are all compelling issues for exploration in family play therapy.

REFLECTION AND CONCLUSION

Parents who bring their tween to therapy are often overwhelmed by the tween's intense or confusing emotions and behaviors. In their search to help their child, they are likely to have difficulty noticing unhelpful and unsatisfying patterns—patterns that do not "play" to the family's strengths, to their joy and connection, their resilience and resolve. We believe a play-based, contextual view of the behavioral and emotional difficulties experienced by tweens offers unique possibilities for understanding and change. Family play therapy extends a spirited and good-natured invitation to all family members to create a more playful present and a heartwarming and hopeful future.

NOTES

1. The word *parent* is used in this chapter to represent the wide range of adult caregivers who raise children.

2. Also, see the Evidence-Based Practice for Children and Adolescents report at http://www.apa.org/practice/resources/evidence/).

3. Dabbing, or the dab, is a simple dance move in which a person drops the head into the bent crook of a slanted arm while raising the opposite arm in a parallel direction but out straight. It has been used as a gesture of triumph or playfulness. Retrieved from https://en.wikipedia.org/wiki/Dab_(dance)

REFERENCES

Bosmans, G., & Kerns, K. A. (2015). Attachment in middle childhood. Progress and perspectives. *New Directions for Child and Adolescent Development, 148,* 1–14.

Bratton, S. C., Ray, D., Rhine, T., & Jones, L. (2005). The efficacy of play therapy with children: A meta-analytic review of treatment outcomes. *Professional Psychology: Research and Practice*, *36*(4), 376–390.

Cozolino, L. (2010). *The neuroscience of psychotherapy: Healing the social brain* (2nd ed.). New York, NY: Norton.

Gil, E. (2015). *Play in family therapy*. New York, NY: Guilford Press.

Haslam, D. R., & Harris, S. M. (2011). Integrating play and family therapy methods: A survey of play therapists' attitudes in the field. *International Journal of Play Therapy*, *20*(2), 51–65.

Schaefer, C., & Carey, L. (1994). *Family play therapy*. Northvale, NJ: Jason Aronson, Inc.

Siegel, D. J. (2013). *Brainstorm: The power and purpose of the teenage brain*. New York, NY: Penguin Putnam.

Sori, C. F., & Sprenkle, D. H. (2004). Training family therapists to work with children and families: A modified Delphi study. *Journal of Marital and Family Therapy*, *30*(4), 479–495.

Stewart, A., & Green, E. (2014). *Nature-based play therapy*. Full-day workshop presented at the 4th Annual Johns Hopkins Play Therapy Institute, Johns Hopkins University, Baltimore, MD.

Chapter Six

Relational Transformation

Child-Centered Play Therapy with Pre- and Early Adolescents

Dee C. Ray and Cody Lankford

When adult and child or young person connect, as two human beings, the results can be quite memorable.—Prever, 2011, p. 11

Among the humanistic therapies, the person-centered approach stands out as arguably the most defined, explored, and researched practice in counseling today. Carl Rogers (1951) developed person-centered therapy based on his beliefs about the nature of the person as an organism naturally moving toward enhancement. Rogers's beliefs about working with people evolved over his lifetime based on his lived experiences with others, including personal and client relationships. Person-centered therapy is unique in its predication that each individual is the author and guide of his or her life. When fully engaged and present with internal processes, the individual is the person who knows best that which is self- and other-enhancing. From this philosophy of human nature derives the role of counseling/therapy, a process that serves to facilitate a person's natural inclination toward well-being. Virginia Axline (1969) further developed Rogers's approach to match the developmental level of children in her introduction of child-centered play therapy (CCPT). Axline based CCPT on the principles of person-centered therapy yet used the child's developmentally appropriate language of play to facilitate growth in clients.

A belief in each individual's ability to be aware and responsive to personal needs that lead to the betterment of self and others is juxtaposed against the common cultural understanding that children and adolescents are at the mercy of their limited cognitive ability, lack of life experience, and physical powerlessness to make a difference. Conventional wisdom regarding pre- and early adolescents is that they are in grave need of substantial guidance and direction from adults in order to navigate through turbulent years of development. Although we would concede that all children may be in need of information that they lack from general inexperience, we would contend that children are equipped with keen observational skills, a vibrant emotional life, and constructive intuition that help them determine best courses of personal action. In this chapter, we propose that pre- and early adolescents benefit from the CCPT approach that presumes the child to be the most informed guide of what is needed for individual enhancement.

LITERATURE REVIEW

The Self-Actualizing Tendency

The self-actualizing tendency as identified by Rogers (1951) is the defining cornerstone of the person-centered approach. Each person is innately endowed with the motivation to move toward self- and other enhancement. In other words, each person naturally desires to reach potential, becoming a better and more fulfilled person. Because of the positive nature of the self-actualizing tendency, the movement toward betterment of self is also related to betterment of others and relationships with others. The self-actualizing tendency is the underlying basis for the organismic valuing process (Rogers, 1951), a process that allows each person to know what is good and not good for the organism. As individuals move toward betterment (self-actualizing tendency), they use the organismic valuing process to determine direction, action, feelings, and thought that enhance the organism. When operating without interference, the organismic valuing process can be trusted to lead each person to self-enhancing decisions. Examples that support these postulates include the infant who cries when hungry, cold, or needs comfort. However, the self-actualizing tendency, along with organismic valuing processes, is often difficult to identify as children grow older and appear to have impaired functioning or make poor decisions. A concept that seemed simple enough to describe and illustrate in infancy becomes lost in the observation of persons as they grow older.

Development and Its Outcomes

To understand how children become separated from their own organismic valuing processes, Rogers offered an elegant description of development from the person-centered framework (Wilkins, 2010). Although children enter the world with everything they need to reach full potential, their interactions with the environment start to interfere with the self-actualizing tendency. When interacting with parents and family members, children receive messages that certain behaviors or ways of being are more valuable and worthy to loved ones. These messages are referred to as *conditions of worth* and are internalized by a child as being conditions that must be met to receive love and acceptance. Conditions of worth are integrated into a concept of self that is considered the self-ideal, an idea of self that typically cannot be sustained due to the pressures of meeting others' expectations that were not derived from an internal sense of self. When the way a child is and sees his or her self (self-concept) comes into conflict with the self-ideal, the child experiences incongruence. This feeling of incongruence is likely to result in emotional struggles, distorted cognitions, and negative behavior. For example, a young boy may be naturally very active and curious about the world, leading to frequent physical movement and lack of desire to sit still. His parents become frustrated with this behavior, which can be observed and felt by the boy. In addition, his parents may use punishment or withdrawal of acceptance as a way to encourage the boy to be less active and more sedentary. His school teacher also frequently uses a stern tone and disapproval as methods to influence the boy to be less active. Over time, the boy learns that what seems natural to him (movement and exploration) is an obstacle to acceptance from parents and others who are of importance to him. He develops a self-ideal that in order to be loved, he must betray what feels natural to him and become less interested in his world and his place in it. This incongruence may manifest itself as symptoms that are observed as depression (e.g., withdrawal) or anxiety (e.g., hyperactivity). Hence, by the time the boy reaches twelve or thirteen years old, he is at odds with his world and experiences a distance from his organismic valuing process. He no longer trusts his inner locus of evaluation due to the possible threat it poses to his most essential relationships.

The Antidote: Necessary Conditions for Change

Because conditions of worth serve as obstacles to activating the self-actualizing tendency, the antidote to this struggle is based on providing conditions that facilitate self-acceptance and self-trust. Rogers (1957) identified six necessary and sufficient conditions that facilitate changes toward greater adjustment. Change occurs when all six conditions are met in the therapy process. The first condition is that the therapist and child are in psychological contact, meaning that each person in the relationship acknowledges the presence of the other in their phenomenological fields. The second condition is that the client/child experiences a sense of incongruence or anxiety. As explained earlier, this feeling of incongruence is common among many children, especially those whose parents seek therapy. For the third condition, the therapist must be in a state of congruence, experiencing awareness and acceptance of self while demonstrating transparency of this awareness with the client. The fourth condition involves the therapist's experience of unconditional positive regard (UPR) for the child in which the therapist accepts and honors the person of the child while believing in the child's capacity to move toward self-enhancement. When the therapist experiences UPR for the child, the fifth condition postulates that the therapist will provide empathic understanding in which the therapist communicates deep understanding of the client's world to the client. The final condition that facilitates change is the child's ability to receive the UPR and empathic understanding provided by the therapist. Even when the therapist provides UPR and empathic understanding, some children will experience difficulty in believing in the therapist's acceptance and empathy. The sixth condition is often dependent on the child's past experiences with attachment figures and may be delayed when the child has been taught to distrust others who are responsible for providing for the child. When all six conditions are met, a child has experienced the power of unconditional acceptance and is able to access the organismic valuing process that will provide a road map for self-enhancing ways of being.

PRACTICAL INTERVENTION

Literature and research on CCPT historically supports its use with children aged three to ten years old (Ray, 2011). Processes and procedures outlined by CCPT authors (e.g., Axline, 1969; Landreth, 2012; Ray, 2011) are geared toward early to older elementary-aged children. CCPT recognizes play as the primary language of children and therefore offers materials and procedures that emphasize the nonverbal nature of childhood emotional expression. Although CCPT therapists employ play as the therapeutic language, the relationship between child and therapist serves as the most salient healing factor in therapy. In Axline's (1969) basic principles for play therapy, the therapeutic relationship is the thread that runs through all eight guidelines: (1) therapist develops a warm relationship with child; (2) therapist accepts child as is; (3) therapist establishes a feeling of permissiveness in relationship; (4) therapist is attuned and communicates the child's feelings; (5) therapist respects child's ability to solve problems; (6) therapist does not direct the child; (7) therapist does not attempt to rush therapy; and (8) therapist sets necessary limits. Axline's principles are grounded in person-centered philosophy that the child is the best decision-maker of what and how issues are addressed in therapy while the therapist serves as the facilitator of an environment that allows the child to access organismic valuing processes. Hence, although CCPT traditionally describes therapy for young children, the conditions necessary for change and the role of the therapist remain the same for older children, including adolescents. However, modifications to CCPT procedures serve to meet the developmental needs of pre- and early adolescents.

The Role of Play

For young children, play is the primary language of emotional expression. Young children struggle to connect words with experience as they acquire the language and cognitive skills to master the abstract nature of emotions. As children grow older, their language competency, as well as their understanding of feelings, also grows, resulting in greater responsiveness to verbal expression. Yet, much of their expression still occurs nonverbally through action and imaginative play. CCPT therapists recognize the need for pre- and early adolescents to express themselves verbally and nonverbally. Response categories taught for the facilitation of CCPT such as feeling and content reflections, self-esteem building, returning responsibility, reflecting on the therapeutic relationship, and limit-setting are still applicable to older children. However, CCPT therapists engage in more conversational flow with pre- and early adolescents and are flexible in following the child's nonverbal and verbal expression. For example, a thirteen-year-old girl may choose to bake cookies during her therapy session. While she bakes, she shares that her mother never allows her to bake at home because she may burn something. When she finishes baking, she asks the therapist to eat a cookie, tentatively looking at the therapist while the therapist tries the cookie. In this case, the girl is exploring her sense of competency and expressing negative feelings about self that she internalized from her interactions with her mother. Her baking, her verbal expression, and her nonverbal hesitation about the therapist's response all work together to reveal her world to the therapist. The CCPT therapist effectively responds by providing acceptance and empathic understanding through a response that addresses all the child is revealing, such as "You're not so sure about your baking because you don't get to do it much. And you're thinking your mom doesn't believe you can do it either. You're wondering if I believe that you can do it. In here, you decide if you like how you bake." Using the tenets of CCPT, the therapist reflects the child's feelings of uncertainty, reflects the child's verbal content of her mother's reaction to baking, and returns responsibility to the child through a message of UPR that the therapist believes in the child's ability to decide if she is competent. The constant flow of verbal and nonverbal expression is a hallmark of working with pre- and early adolescents.

The Playroom and Materials

Because of the particular necessity for nonverbal expression, CCPT offers a playroom in which toys and materials are designed for young children. Toys such as dolls, blocks, guns, kitchen material, and more (see Landreth [2012] for a full listing of toys recommended for CCPT) are provided in a CCPT playroom. Expressive materials such as sand, paint, crafting tools, and water are also available to children in CCPT. When CCPT is facilitated for pre- and early adolescents, materials are selected to meet changing developmental needs. In fact, we encourage CCPT therapists to modify their playrooms to more developmentally appropriate activity rooms. Activity rooms are designed to meet the needs of older children by offering materials that allow pre- or early adolescents the opportunity to create, build, and express using their growing competencies. Activity rooms are typically equipped with real-life stations for cooking, construction, and expressive arts. Materials may include a working oven/microwave; workbench with working tools for sawing, drilling, and hammering; and extensive craft/paint/sewing materials. These materials allow for the child to see themselves as older and competent in ways they see that adults are competent but additionally allow for nonverbal expression. As in traditional CCPT playrooms, activity rooms also include some toys that allow for regressed play when needed such as baby dolls, toy soldiers, guns, bats, rope, and puppets. When deciding to offer an activity room for sessions with a preadolescent, the CCPT therapist should assess the child's developmental level and ability to control impulsivity. Because materials in activity rooms can be dangerous if used unsafely, the therapist assesses the goodness of fit regarding the therapy room for each individual child.

Limit-Setting and Problem-Solving

Limit-setting is an essential component of any therapy for children due to the nature of operating in an action-oriented environment. Landreth (2012) offered the ACT method for setting limits that includes three steps: (1) acknowledge the feeling of the child; (2) communicate the definitive limit; and (3) target an alternative. For example, when a child throws paint on the wall, a therapist might respond, "You're excited about the paint but the paint is not for throwing on the wall; you can paint the paper." Although ACT is an effective method for setting limits in therapy with young children, it can often be counterproductive in working with pre- and early adolescents. When the therapist states the limit and provides an alternative, the therapist may fail to recognize the older child's ability to become aware of a limit and figure out ways in which to meet needs within appropriate boundaries. We recommend experimenting with alternative limit-setting methods with pre- and early adolescents. One alternative is for the therapist to notice a potential problem regarding limit-setting or sharing awareness of a problem, such as "I'm worried that the paint is going to spill on the floor." This example of an awareness statement allows the child to become aware of the situation and make a decision regarding whether the child wishes to change course of action, which often occurs when working with older children. Such a self-correction provides the child with a greater sense of self-efficacy and experience in self-enhancing decision-making. Awareness statements also allow the therapist to be transparent which fosters the child's ability to trust the therapist. Another alternative to traditional limit-setting with this age group is to initiate problem-solving, such as "I'm noticing the paint is about to spill on the floor, and the paint is not for going on the floor. Can you come up with another way to do what you're wanting without the paint spilling?" In this alternative, the therapist introduces the idea of problem-solving but does not pursue the child answering. The child remains the decision-maker and may choose to respond or not respond to the problem-solving prompt. Such alternatives are responsive to the growing cognitive abilities and self-control of pre- and early adolescents. In some cases, the older child may choose to not engage in responding to these alternatives to limit-setting, which may result in the therapist's decision to use the more traditional form of ACT.

The Person of the Therapist

As outlined in the necessary and sufficient conditions for therapeutic change, the attitudinal conditions provided by the therapist (i.e., congruence, UPR, and empathic understanding) are essential to the process of effective CCPT. Although provision of the attitudinal conditions is necessary with all children, pre- and early adolescents are especially sensitive to the therapist's ability to genuinely provide UPR and empathic understanding. While many younger children will often trust the genuineness of the therapist with little therapist disclosure, a pre- or early adolescent will typically seek or be sensitive to therapist immediacy and transparency. The therapist's level of congruence in acknowledging her own feelings and willingness to share these feelings when helpful will add to the therapy process. For example, if a preadolescent sits quietly through session, the therapist may feel a sense of incompetence or self-doubt, which most likely results in increased tension and anxiety in the room. An effective and congruent therapist response may be, "You're not sure what to say in here, and I guess I'm not sure what to say either." This congruent response reveals the therapist as a person who has similar feelings to the child and is willing to show and accept personal vulnerability. The sharing of personhood and vulnerability allows the child to build trust in the therapist due to revelation of what is real and felt in the room. Pre- and early adolescents are subject to intense egocentrism, self-doubt, and self-criticism. The therapist's ability to accept personal vulnerability models for the child that vulnerability is a natural part of being human and is worthy of acceptance. Working with pre- and early adolescents will frequently result in self-questioning on the therapist's side due to several factors such as child's rejection of therapist, child's withdrawn or nonverbal behaviors, or simply the therapist's connection to his or her own preadolescent experiences. The effective CCPT therapist sees him- or herself as a real person who experiences a sense of worthiness and explores moments of feeling "lesser than" or disconnected from self-worth. The CCPT therapist is continually involved in a journey toward self- and other connection in order to be in genuine, accepting, and empathic relationships with clients.

INCORPORATION OF FAMILY

Traditional CCPT with young children encourages parent consultations following every three to five play therapy sessions (Ray, 2011). In these parent consultations, young children are often not present due the therapist's need to listen to parent concerns that interfere with child's self-concept or a need to work instructionally with the parent. However, in working with pre- and early adolescents from a CCPT perspective, the therapist frequently or always includes the child in consultations. Inclusion of pre- or early adolescents in consultations is necessary for several reasons. First, the pre- or early adolescent is typically concerned about confidentiality and how much the therapist reveals to the parent. Inclusion in parent consultation ensures that the child experiences the therapist as trustworthy and an ally, not another adult who talks to his parent without consideration of child's agency. Second, inclusion in parent consultation allows the therapist to work with the family on skill-building. When working with young children, the bulk of responsibility in skill-building sits with the parent; however, older children have the ability to change and take responsibility for how they contribute to negative interactions. CCPT therapists can work with families to teach relational skills and practice those skills with each other in role-plays during parent consultations. Finally, and perhaps most important, including older children in parent consultations allows the therapist to experience the emotions and perceptions initiated from parent–child interactions, which increases the therapist's empathic understanding of the preadolescent's world.

CASE STUDY

This case study is a composite generated by the second author of this chapter in order to maintain confidentiality.

I first received notice of Lucas when his mother, Ms. Williams, called our clinic requesting assistance. Ms. Williams stated she was at a loss as to how to support her twelve-year-old son, whom she was experiencing as increasingly distant, defiant, and angry. I agreed to meet with Ms. Williams and scheduled our first parent consultation for the following week. I chose to meet with Ms. Williams without her son present in order to provide her a time to genuinely express her concerns and develop a working alliance with her. My primary goal was to establish a trusting relationship with her. Ms. Williams arrived at our scheduled meeting time a few minutes late, frantically explaining how she had encountered difficulty arranging a babysitter, and resulting in her leaving her two younger children in Lucas's care. I assured her we had plenty of time, sensing her anxiety, but made a mental note of the information she just provided me about their family.

> *Me:* "It can be a big challenge to get to an appointment by yourself when you have three kids. I really appreciate you making the time to meet with me today."

Upon noticing Ms. Williams's relief from my statement, I walked us back to a counseling room to begin. We covered the necessary processes of informed consent and signing of paperwork before transitioning to discussing Lucas's background information and a brief developmental history. I was informed Lucas was the oldest of three children, with an eight-year-old brother, Henry, and a six-year-old sister, Madison. Ms. Williams was the sole caregiver, with Lucas's father having been removed from the picture just short of two years ago, following years of physical abuse of which Lucas was the recipient. In addition, Ms. Williams reported Lucas's father often cruelly teased him and utilized humiliation as a primary method of discipline. Without any additional significant adults in his life, Lucas had not been exposed to many positive relationships with men.

When discussing major developmental milestones, Ms. Williams reported no concerns. She stated he began crawling, walking, talking, and writing at expected ages. However, she noted Lucas was small for his age, and feared this might lead to bullying. Lucas also began to encounter difficulties academically during fourth grade. His reading level was determined to be deficient, and he struggled academically with writing and math. These problems persisted into the present. Ms. Williams stated Lucas maintained slightly below average grades, and was often able to "only barely scrape by." These struggles with academic performance appeared to be influencing Lucas's self-concept, as he had made various disparaging remarks about himself over the past few years. Ms. Williams reported Lucas's most significant worry about starting seventh grade was that he was "too stupid" to learn a different language.

Ms. Williams explained that although Lucas has been a shy child ever since she could remember, he began to exhibit notable degrees of withdrawal around fifth or sixth grade. In addition, Ms. Williams recalled Lucas beginning to demonstrate noticeably heightened degrees of anger and low frustration tolerance around this time, stating he would often blow up or snap at others when things did not go the way he expected. After Lucas's father was removed from the family system, Lucas's anger, frustration, and withdrawal only seemed to increase. Lucas additionally has shown a significant lack of interest in peers his age. I immediately noted this lack of peer relationships as a strong red flag for a twelve-year-old. Ms. Williams stated she now feels she can hardly say a word to Lucas without being either ignored or verbally attacked. He appears to resent any contact from another person, and seemed to be spiraling deeper into a state of isolation and resentment.

After gathering a cohesive understanding of Lucas' circumstances and struggles, it was my turn to provide Ms. Williams an understanding of CCPT and how it may support her son. I described the process of facilitating a safe, consistent relationship with Lucas in which he would be free to engage in a self-directed process of self-exploration through the use of toys and activities, as play is the natural language of children. However, throughout our consultation process, another goal of mine was to assess Lucas's developmental functioning to determine the most appropriate environment for our therapy to take place: a traditional play room, or an activity room. It appeared to me that an activity therapy room, which at our clinic closely resemble traditional child-centered play rooms with various adjustments made to better fit the developmental needs of children ten and older, would be more appropriate. In the activity room, Lucas would have toys and materials that would allow for self-expression through play, while also having materials that would meet his growing cognitive abilities, such as a sandtray collection and a woodworking bench.

Some of my final notes to Ms. Williams were in regard to future parent consultations. Because it is common for parents to have important things to discuss with play therapists each week, I asked that we refrain from talking about Lucas in front of him, especially in the waiting room. I further requested we actually include him within our parent consultations, given his age. Ms. Williams shifted in her seat as I said this, clearly uncertain about my suggestion. Although parent consultations can provide a useful avenue through which parents feel directly heard, understood, and supported, I believe the purpose remains in supporting the child. In Lucas's case, he was at an age where including him in the process would better support his sense of trust in both his mother and me; it would reduce any fear that we were talking behind his back. Furthermore, his inclusion could both help strengthen their parent–child relationship as well as honor Lucas's growing sense of autonomy.

Our First Meeting

At the time of our first session, I observed Lucas and his mother to be sitting three chairs apart in the waiting room. Lucas had his arms crossed, head slumped, and a grim expression plastered on his face. He was sending strong messages of how he felt about being here. Ms. Williams appeared anxious, with her expression melting into a mixture of relief and urgency upon seeing me. I assumed she had things she would like to tell me before the session, but the building of my relationship with Lucas began the moment I entered the room. I was sure to acknowledge Ms. Williams, but I immediately turned my focus to Lucas, sitting down in the chair across from him, leaning forward, and introducing myself.

Me: "Hi Lucas, my name is Cody. I've been looking forward to meeting you. We will be spending some time together today in our activity room."

Lucas provided no response. He just sat in silence, head turned away from me.

Me: "You're not so sure about being here. . . ."

Me: (After a pause) "Well, Lucas, it's time for us to go back to our room. I'll show you the way."

I stood up as I said this. He initially sat frozen, determined not to provide me any feedback or response, but his mother quickly and embarrassingly leaned towards him and urged him to go with me. After shooting her an annoyed glance, Lucas obliged and reluctantly trudged behind me towards our room.

Me: "This is our activity room, Lucas. There are lots of things in here you can use and play with in many ways you would like."

Lucas stood with his back mostly to me, hardly having entered the space of the room. In the reflection of the one-way mirror, I caught a glimpse of the grimace he made in response to my statement. I wondered if perhaps it was regarding my use of the word "play." Perhaps Lucas, a now full twelve years old, perceived himself above and beyond the childish need to play. This would not necessarily be uncommon, as twelve-year-olds often experience a growing desire to be seen and treated as grown adults. I noted I would have to be intentional with my words as I worked to establish connection with him; he likely would reject any response that appeared too childlike.

Lucas continued to stand in silence while I sat down in one of the two chairs available. Lucas was sizing up the room, glancing at the various materials and toys out of the corner of his eyes. He did so with minimal effort, as if he wished to hide any degree of curiosity.

Me: "You're still just not sure about this place yet."

Lucas: *(After a long pause)* "So . . . like, I'm just supposed to randomly pick something?"

The skepticism in his voice was thick.

Me: "You can choose to do something, or you could choose not to. That'll be up to you to decide in here."

Another grimace in response. He was working hard to push back any invitation I offered for engagement. This could be anticipated, given what I knew about Lucas's history. Relationships had been unsafe for him, and a strange person in a new, strange place was threatening.

The session continued along much the same trajectory. Lucas was not yet ready to explore either the room or direct interaction with me. He instead sat at the edge of the puppet theater stage and kept his gaze on the floor. Through my responses I aimed to make contact, conveying my understanding of his experience of frustration and uncertainty with being here, while never seeking to coerce him to change or move along in any manner. I strongly desired for him to experience my acceptance of his reluctance and decision to sit silently. It was not a comfortable therapeutic hour. Lucas's anxiety was strong, and we were both actively experiencing it. However, this was an important step in him feeling free to explore. As the session progressed, I slowed the rate of my responses to match his lack of outward expression until our time was finally up.

A Slow-Building Relationship

The following three sessions unfolded somewhat similarly to the first. Lucas continued to enter the room reserved and resentful. Each time we left the waiting room he followed no less than six feet behind me. Whereas his exploration of the materials and toys in the room remained minimal throughout this time, his verbalizations increased, although they remained evaluative and rejecting in nature.

Me: "You're so frustrated your mom brought you here again."

Lucas: "You've said that before!"

Me: "You don't like it when I say things over again."

Lucas: "No. And why do you talk to me so weird?"

Me: "I do sound different—you don't like it."

Lucas: "No, I don't. I think you sound stupid. I wish you would just shut up already."

Me: "You're so annoyed with me you want me to feel bad."

Lucas: "Can't you just leave me alone?"

These sorts of exchanges were common within our beginning sessions. I would continue to try to convey my understanding and awareness of Lucas, and he continued to push back. He was unsettled by the attention and focus he received from me, and the defenses he had formulated over time were doing their work to protect him in this new relationship. He was scared of what this space offered, and it would take time for him to determine whether he could trust me. However, his increased willingness to bring his anger and frustration, one of mom's primary concerns, into the room was progress. He was directly demonstrating to me his understanding of how to relate with others.

Of course, in these moments understanding and empathizing with Lucas's process was easiest from a distance. My maintenance of the attitudinal therapeutic conditions was something I believed that Lucas needed above all else and something that I also occasionally fell short of in the moment. Although some of Lucas's behaviors were highly characteristic of a child his age, sullen and disagreeable, getting called stupid and being scoffed at multiple times in an hour can be trying. Some of his statements were more hurtful statements and evoked a negative response in me. However, I believe it was these moments, those in which Lucas so actively worked to hurt and push me away, and in response experienced my consistent strides to genuinely accept him, that perhaps mattered the most. No play therapist can perfect empathy and acceptance, certainly not with the turbulent behaviors of preadolescents, but I hoped that my efforts to return to these attitudinal conditions whenever I noticed I had strayed sent a lasting, powerful message.

Opening Up to Exploration

I noticed a shift in Lucas as I picked him up from the waiting room for our fifth session. His body posture was more relaxed and his facial expression more content than I was accustomed to. Upon entering the activity room, he began to look around.

Me: "You're curious today."

Lucas: "Eh, not really."

His behavior suggested otherwise, as he slowly made his way across the room touching a few items, but I went with it.

> *Me:* "Ah, not curious, just looking."

Lucas shot me a look, as if to convey he still did not enjoy my commentary, but he eventually sat down at the easel and poked through the paint brushes.

> *Me:* "So you've decided to paint."

Painting at the easel became a pattern for Lucas for the next few sessions. Sometimes he painted with less focus, appearing to be engrossed in the process, but often he painted with intention, re-creating a particular scene over again. Although he did not offer up details about his creations, it seemed to resemble a family of five. Painting seemed to provide him with comfort and psychological "grounding," allowing him at times to more easily engage in conversation with me, or to remain silent if he desired to. He began to offer up details and insights into his life. We talked about his favorite video games, his annoyances with his siblings, and occasionally his dislike of school. Lucas appeared to be testing out the parameters of our new relationship.

Occasionally, we still encountered road bumps. My earlier assessment of Lucas's rejection of any statements that appeared too childish proved to be true. One session, while Lucas was quietly focused on painting for a number of minutes, I found myself noticing the high degree of his concentration.

> *Me:* "You're working *really* hard on that."

> *Lucas:* "Stop saying that! I'm *really* not!"

> *Me:* "Oh, I was wrong—you don't think you're putting much effort into it."

I felt myself shrink back slightly. Did Lucas just convey to me his struggles with self-competency? After all, he had indeed appeared to be putting significant effort into what he was doing. Or, perhaps his reaction was also connected to my inflection. The emphasis I placed on "*really*" was reminiscent of the way I would often reflect encouragement to a much younger child in a playroom. In all honesty, I had reverted back to a tone that did not appropriately match Lucas developmentally, and he likely experienced it as belittling and rote. Yet, my awareness of my responses to these reactions from Lucas allowed me to take in the information Lucas had just provided me, and I sought to reengage.

Active Engagement

As we moved onward in our relationship, Lucas became more dynamic and active in the room, having branched out beyond his comfort spot with the easel and paints. His focus was more on engaging with me beyond conversation, as he now actively invited me to join him in activities. This was indeed a positive sign, as I would expect a child of his age to engage in collaborative play and dialogue, as opposed to Lucas's initial isolated behaviors.

Lucas additionally began to convey to me more of his inner world through his play. For instance, at the start of our eleventh session Lucas announced, "It is time for a show! Now go find your seat and wait while the actors get prepared." My heart warmed as I recognized just how far Lucas had come in terms of his openness to his own playful spirit and imagination.

"And now, a tale of the scary monster!" Lucas announced. Four puppets, each human, were placed on the stage. They each took turns making disparaging remarks about a fifth puppet not yet pictured, the oldest child of the family.

Mother puppet: "I just don't get it, what in the world is *wrong* with him?"

The others grumbled in agreement. Eventually, the missing character, the one I was certain represented Lucas, appeared. It was an alligator, a potent depiction of the negative messages Lucas had internalized about himself. As the scene progressed, the alligator puppet cried and pleaded.

Alligator puppet: "I don't want to be bad. . . . You just don't listen!"

Me: "He's so sad—they don't understand."

Mother puppet: "But what do you mean?"

Alligator: "It's not me! It's not me! He's the real monster, not me!"

Then, the scene changed, like the conclusion to a murder mystery novel, and the father was revealed to be the true monster. Lucas switched the puppets, the alligator now representing the father and a human boy puppet representing himself. The family's rejecting comments turned on the father alligator, and they collectively knocked him off the stage. This was the most salient moment in which Lucas represented his experience of abuse. He conveyed his feelings of confusion, fear, and isolation. His anger and frustration were clearly the work of his self-actualizing tendency, striving to make his needs heard by those around him.

Lucas and I continued individual CCPT for twenty-three sessions. Throughout that time, he further processed his experiences, feelings, and sense of self through his play. Woodworking became a method through which he explored mastery, tackling his lack of self-efficacy. His continued engagement with me supported his ability to trust and engage with others once again. Eventually, in moments in which Lucas lashed out at me, I would share my own feelings of hurt in response, in statements such as, "When you called me stupid, I felt hurt." Such opportunities allowed us to collectively experience vulnerability, followed by repair and deeper connection. Parent consultations provided additional avenues for relational repair, as I worked to support Lucas and Ms. Williams in improving communication with one another. Following Ms. Williams's reports of Lucas's decreased outbursts and isolation at home, we determined it was an appropriate time to terminate individual therapy. The next step was to consider group CCPT to foster Lucas's sense of social competency and connection with peers his age.

REFLECTION AND CONCLUSIONS

My experience of working with Lucas was deeply meaningful and brought about a sense of warmth and appreciation that extends beyond words. I was keenly aware of the potency of relationship, and the power of allowing Lucas to unfold without applying pressure for him to change in one way or another. In Lucas's case, prior to therapy, he instinctively knew that he was unsafe and engaged in behaviors that he felt would keep him safe, alternately withdrawing and lashing out at others. His self-actualizing tendency motivated behaviors and feelings to stay safe, yet the skills he developed were in reality self-destructive, and he became at odds with his environment. Lucas's mother's concerns focused on his symptoms, but Lucas intuitively knew his experiences of abuse were at the core of his isolating behaviors. In our relationship, I sought to provide Lucas with an environment in which his coping skills for safety were accepted and positively regarded as methods necessary to protect himself until he could explore other ways that would be more self-enhancing. Lucas was able to use our relationship to reconnect with another person and with his internal sense of what he really needed for his own optimal growth. This, of course, required patience and self-acceptance on my part, for being in relationship with Lucas was not always easy. Yet, it was without a doubt transformative for us both.

Preadolescents and early adolescents can be a challenging client population due to their developmental tendencies to move between verbal and nonverbal expression, as well as their intense vulnerability related to exploring identity and relationships. In addition, whereas a myriad of resources provide well-defined road maps for effectively communicating with young children in CCPT, far fewer exist for building connection with pre- and early adolescents. Engagement with pre- and early adolescents often involves a high degree of collaborative interaction and dialogue, challenging the therapist to maintain a strong sense of transparency and genuineness. Furthermore, the turbulent and sometimes rejecting attitudes of this age group present an added hurdle to the therapist's efforts, requiring strong intention to be given towards maintaining the attitudinal conditions necessary for successful therapeutic change. However, despite these challenges, CCPT intervention for this age group provides a developmentally appropriate environment of an activity room that allows for an older child to express self through multiple mediums. Most important, CCPT provides the child with a relationally focused environment in which the therapist facilitates the child's movement toward self-enhancement through offering warmth, understanding, and unconditional acceptance in a genuine, immediate way of being.

REFERENCES

Axline, V. M. (1969). *Play therapy*. New York, NY: Ballantine Books.

Landreth, G. L. (2012). *Play Therapy: The art of the relationship* (3rd ed.). New York, NY: Routledge.

Prever, M. (2010). *Counselling and supporting children and young people: A person-centred approach.* London: Sage.

Ray, D. C. (2011). *Advanced play therapy: Essential conditions, knowledge, and skills for child practice*. New York, NY: Routledge.

Rogers, C. (1951). *Client-centered therapy: Its current practice, implications and theory*. Boston, MA: Houghton Mifflin.

Rogers, C. R. (1957). The necessary and sufficient conditions of therapeutic personality change. *Journal of Consulting Psychology, 60*(6), 827–832.

Wilkins, P. (2010). *Person-centred therapy: 100 key points*. London: Routledge.

Chapter Seven

Nature-Based Play Therapy with Preadolescents

Sang Min Shin and Jacqueline M. Swank

> I go to nature to be soothed and healed, and to have my senses put in tune once more.—John Burroughs

The natural environment has healing power for many. However, children are spending less time in nature as our society becomes more technologically advanced and more children use electronic devices (e.g., tablets, cell phones) for leisure and entertainment (McCurdy, Winterbottom, Mehta, & Roberts, 2010). This is concerning because engagement in nature promotes holistic growth and development, including physical, social, emotional, and cognitive development (Revell, Duncan, & Cooper, 2014). Specifically, children are more likely to be actively engaged in physical activity when they are outside, which promotes physical health by reducing the risk for health problems such as obesity and vitamin D deficiency that can lead to long-term health issues (McCurdy et al., 2010). Additionally, a lack of engagement in the natural environment may negatively influence the mental health of children by inhibiting the development of social skills and fostering a healthy self-concept, due to sedentary behavior and limited interactions with others (Sackett, 2010). In contrast, children's engagement in nature may foster emotional and social development (Swank & Huber, 2013; Swank & Shin, 2015; Swank & Swank, 2013). Their interactions with nature may also help promote empathy for the natural environment (Feral, 1998) and reduce stress (McCurdy et al., 2010). Furthermore, researchers have found that spending time outdoors is beneficial to address specific mental health diagnoses. Kuo and Faber-Taylor (2004) found that children diagnosed with attention deficit hyperactivity disorder (ADHD) who had exposure to natural settings had decreased attention deficit symptoms. Thus, counselors may seek to integrate nature within the counseling process, viewing nature as a therapeutic partner in promoting health and wellness.

LITERATURE REVIEW

There are a variety of approaches to integrating nature within the counseling process, which at the most basic level may involve facilitating counseling sessions outside or even viewing natural scenes or listening to nature sounds during counseling sessions. Ecotherapy, specifically, involves the use of techniques to help individuals form a strong connection with nature (Burls, 2007; Reese, 2016), as there is therapeutic value in fostering these connections (Miles, 1987; Sackett, 2010). Forming a connection with nature may help individuals better understand themselves (Feral, 1998) and promote healing (Stigsdotter et al., 2010). Therefore, when integrating the natural environment in counseling, the client develops a relationship with the counselor, as well as nature. Unlike the office setting, the natural environment is not controlled or owned by the counselor and therefore this space is more neutral, allowing the counseling and client to cocreate the space (Jordan & Marshall, 2010). The natural environment is also continuously changing, unlike an indoor setting, which means that nature has an active role in the therapeutic process (Jordan & Marshall, 2010).

Other terminology that individuals use to describe the integration of nature in counseling include therapeutic gardening, wilderness therapy, adventure-based counseling, adventure therapy, nature therapy, outdoor therapy, and the integration of animals within the counseling process. However, there is controversy in referring to some of these approaches as being counseling/therapy approaches because although they include the term *therapy* in the name of the approach, some of these approaches are facilitated by individuals who are not trained as counselors (Revell, Duncan, & Cooper, 2014). In examining the helpfulness of an outdoor experience that involved "an intentional counseling/psychotherapeutic relationship," Revell et al. (2014) found that simply being outside was the most helpful aspect of the experience. The opportunity for reflection was also rated high as being a helpful component of the experience. The therapeutic relationship with the counselor was not, however, rated as high as being helpful, which the researchers hypothesized as being potentially related to many of the experiences occurring in a group setting. This seems a logical conclusion, as the relationship with group members was also rated as being more helpful than the relationship with the counselor (Revell et al., 2014).

Nature as a Metaphor

In play therapy, counselors use therapeutic toys and other play-based materials as a mechanism for children to express their thoughts and feelings, problem-solve, and work through challenging life events. Children may use play-based materials to symbolically represent or express metaphorically what they experienced or how they think and feel about themselves and others. The natural environment provides unique opportunities for children to process life situations and express themselves through the use of metaphors.

According to Piaget (1962), as preadolescents transition from the concrete operational stage (8–11 years) to the formal operational stage (11–15 years), they acquire the ability to think abstractly. Metaphorical thinking provides preadolescents with opportunities to develop insights in their life (Breen, 2005). Preadolescents may use metaphors to express their feelings by interacting with nature. For example, therapeutic gardening provides powerful metaphors for the counseling process (Courtney & Mills, 2016; Swank & Swank, 2013; Reese & Myers, 2012). Specifically, the counselor can discuss the soil as a metaphor for developing a strong life foundation. Just as plants grow when there is soil rich in minerals and nutrients, people also grow when there is a strong foundation of positive adult role models and a healthy environment. Another metaphor relates to caring for plants in order to foster their growth, and how people need care and love to foster growth. A third metaphor relates to harvesting a garden. Picking a flower or vegetable involves making a decision and after it is picked it cannot be replanted. Similarly in life, often decisions cannot be undone and they result in positive and/or negative consequences. However, individuals can learn from the decision to make similar or different decisions in the future.

The counselor can also use aspects of the natural environment as metaphors that extend beyond therapeutic gardening. For example, the change in seasons serves as a powerful metaphor for processing challenging life situations. Specifically, in working with preadolescents, the counselor can use the change in season to discuss the thoughts, feelings, and events associated with transitions. This may specifically relate to transitioning from elementary school to middle school, or transitioning between middle school grade levels. Similarly to how the natural environment goes through changes, people also go through changes and experience a variety of thoughts and feelings during that process. As preadolescents are developmentally able to conceptualize metaphorical thinking, they are encouraged to interpret the metaphors during the nature-based play therapy sessions (Milgrom, 2005). Thus, the natural setting provides a rich environment for using metaphors in counseling.

Nature and the School Environment

Children spend a significant amount of their childhood in the school environment. Therefore, school counselors and other counselors working in the school setting may consider the integration of nature within counseling in the schools. School counselors, in particular, will want to consider how to align their nature-based interventions with the American School Counselor Association's (ASCA, 2012) national model.

Swank and Swank (2013) outlined a therapeutic gardening curriculum for school counselors to use in the school environment that aligned with the ASCA (2012) national model by encompassing the academic, career, and personal/social domains of the model. The curriculum included five gardening stages, including (1) planning, (2) preparing, (3) planting, (4) maintaining, and (5) harvesting. In examining the integration of the therapeutic gardening curriculum with children with emotional and behavioral problems ($N = 31$), Swank and Shin (2015) found that the participants demonstrated improved self-esteem at the end of the gardening group. Additionally, the participants reported that they felt happier and learned to work together.

NATURE-BASED PLAY THERAPY

Nature-based play therapy involves the integration of the natural environment within the play therapy process. Nature based child-centered play therapy (NBCCPT) integrates nature specifically into child-centered play therapy (Swank, Shin, Cabrita, Cheung, & Rivers, 2015). Within NBCCPT, the playroom becomes a designated outdoor setting and the therapeutic play materials becomes natural objects (e.g., dirt, sand, sticks, leaves, rocks). Using the client-centered approach, the play therapist is nondirective and allows the child to take the lead, unless safety concerns arise that require the counselor to set limits with the child. Researchers have found promising initial results in using this approach with children individually (Swank et al., 2015) and in small groups (Swank, Cheung, Prikhidko, & Su, 2017). Scholars have examined the effectiveness of NBCCPT predominately with early elementary school children. However, within NBCCPT, children have the freedom to choose how they want to engage in the designated, natural space while having the support of the play therapist, which is beneficial for preteens as well as other older populations. In this section, we will provide strategies for play therapists to use when working with preadolescents in nature-based play therapy. In addition, we will provide recommendations for selecting a natural space and materials for nature-based play therapy interventions with preadolescents.

Preteens may think counseling, therapy, or play therapy is overwhelming, or they may feel there is a preexisting stigma about therapy (Milgrom, 2005).

Specifically, preteens may not consider playing outside or playing in nature as "cool" because of their high reliance and use of technology devices. They may not be accustomed to spending time outside in nature, without the use of electronic devices. It may take time for them to learn how to interact with the vegetation or animals/critters as well as the therapist within nature. Therefore, it is crucial for play therapists to be patient with the preteens to allow them adequate time to explore the natural space. These efforts include beginning nature-based play therapy by introducing a physical garden to them, without introducing it as "play therapy." The garden will be their space, and they can decide how to work in the garden or how to engage in this process (Milgrom, 2005). Later, the preteens may choose what they want to call the "nature-based play therapy" sessions. For example, a preteen may choose to name it after herself, calling it "Jennifer's garden," or one could name it a playful garden or backyard.

The natural environment and materials should be inviting and attractive to the preteens. However, it may still be difficult to engage this population in nature-based play therapy. When initiating nature-based play therapy with preadolescents, they might start engaging in the intervention by participating in activities that they are already familiar with (Milgrom, 2005), such as planting in the garden, listening to music, writing lyrics and poetry, and/or taking photos. Engagement in these activities may help them become more comfortable in the natural space. For example, they may become interested in taking digital photos of nature as they explore the natural spaces, or listening to their favorite song while immersing themselves in nature. The therapists show interest in the music that the preteens bring to the garden by listening to the music with them, which may help develop rapport. With time, the preteens may gradually develop an increased interest in being in nature.

Natural Space

When a play therapist considers a space designated for nature-based play therapy with preteens, it is important to find an area outside where preteens could easily interact with a variety of flora and fauna (plants and animals) in many ways (Stigsdotter et al., 2010). This type of setting distinguishes nature-based play therapy from other play therapy interventions. The outside natural space should provide preteens with ample opportunities to experience nature by using their sight, sound, smell, touch, and taste. Different species and sizes of vegetation are useful. Big trees provide preteens with shade to play under or relax while feeling the breeze, as well as offer opportunities to challenge themselves by playing or climbing on the trees (Swank & Shin, 2015). They may climb up the big trees or make a fort out of sticks that fall from the trees. They can also be adventurous by playing games (e.g., hiding, pretend camping) in bushes. Various flowers could be grown, smelled, or tasted, as they explore the area. Furthermore, vegetation brings different creatures into the nature-based play therapy area such as bugs, ants, snails, caterpillars, butterflies, and birds. Preadolescents may catch, feed, or explore these creatures. The space should have access to plenty of dirt, sand, rocks, pebbles, or water (Swank & Shin, 2015).

Materials

Materials used in nature-based play therapy are a second component that make the intervention different from traditional play therapy (Swank & Shin, 2015). Natural materials, such as cross-sectional pieces of trees, seeds, hay/straw, pine cones, rocks, pebbles, and sand, are provided in the interventions. Counselors may also include man-made materials if they facilitate interactions between the preadolescents and nature, such as gardening tools, containers, tarps, hammocks, and blowing bubbles. The materials should meet the preadolescents' developmental needs and challenge them as well. Materials are selected for nature-based play therapy by the following three guiding questions:

1. Do these materials allow preadolescents to explore their feelings?
2. Do these materials encourage preadolescents to interact with nature, and are they developmentally appropriate?
3. Are these materials natural? If not, can they be replaced with natural materials?

The first question follows Landreth's (2012) rationale of toy selection for traditional play therapy. Although nature-based play therapy is conducted outside in nature by using natural materials, the primary purpose of nature-based play therapy is the same as the one for play therapy, which allows preadolescents to explore and express their feelings. Thus, materials in nature-based play therapy should be aligned with the rationale for the traditional play therapy toy selection. The material should provide preadolescents with experiences of different feelings; with opportunities to test limits and self-control; and with development of self-understanding (Landreth, 2012). The rationale of selecting the natural materials is also to facilitate the preadolescents' exploration of their feelings while being in the natural environment, as well as playing with nature.

When selecting materials, natural ones (e.g., rocks, plants, branches, leaves, seeds, etc.) are preferred. Man-made materials should be minimized (Swank & Shin, 2015). However, some man-made materials often promote preadolescents to engage in more activities by interacting with nature in creative ways. Particularly, preadolescents have the cognitive ability to design, plan, and undertake their own projects (Breen, 2005), which may require man-made materials. For example, they may want to build a fort by using rope, big logs, and tarps. They may use the rope to tie a tarp from adjacent trees to create a roof and then surround an area with logs that are stacked together to create the fort. Others may want to make a relaxing place for themselves by using hammocks and blankets. In this case, gardening tools, tarps, hammocks, blankets, and blowing bubbles may be attractive to them and encourage preadolescents to interact more with nature. In this regard, the second question is used to determine if the man-made materials meet preadolescents' needs and challenge them enough during the nature-based play therapy sessions.

Once the second question is considered and it is determined that the man-made materials are to be included, then the play therapist considers the third question, related to whether the man-made materials can be replaced with more natural materials. For example, it is difficult to replace a camera with natural materials. Thus, a camera might be included in nature-based play therapy.

The materials in nature-based play therapy do not need to be new or high tech to be therapeutic. It is more important that the therapist creates an inviting space with functional and practical materials that encourage preadolescents to interact with nature. A sample list of materials for nature-based play therapy is provided below:

Natural Materials

Sand, leaves, rocks, pebbles, tree cross sections (large and small), logs (long/short), sticks (long/short), straws, pine cones, seeds, different species of dried moss, and different types/shapes of barks

Man-Made Materials

Gardening-related: shovels, hoes, racks, water hose, containers (various sizes), planting beds (if needed), garden sign
Camping-related: blankets, tarps, rope, threads, hammock
Other: chalk, bubbles, camera, music devices

This list can be adapted to include more materials according to the preteens' particular needs and issues.

There are several considerations in deciding on a space for nature-based play therapy, which include privacy, location, safety, size, and overall composition of flora and fauna. Like any other clinical settings, client privacy should be protected during sessions. Preadolescents should also think that their privacy is protected in the space. Unfortunately, since nature-based play therapy is usually conducted outside, we cannot guarantee their privacy unless there is a walled natural space (Greenleaf, Bryant, & Pollock, 2014).

Although it may be unrealistic to find an area outside hidden from the public like the garden in the movie *The Secret Garden* (Fuchs, Roos, Luddy, & Holland, 1993), efforts to protect client privacy should be made by finding an area isolated enough for preadolescents to feel privacy from others in public. For example, a school garden surrounded by trees and bushes and located at the end of the school building where not many people are passing by could protect their privacy. When the preadolescents play aggressive themes or make noises, it would be hard to hear or see as long as the location is isolated and naturally hidden by trees or bushes. If it is hard to find an isolated area for the sessions or if the space is adjacent to the public, the counselor should discuss privacy concerns with the child and brainstorm strategies for making the space more private, such as putting up a tarp to hide part of the view.

The space should be bigger than a typical traditional play therapy room size (12 feet by 15 feet) (Landreth, 2012). It is important that it is large enough for the preadolescents to participate in physical activities, but not so large that they feel overwhelmed. At the same time, like a traditional play therapy room, the natural space should maintain a good distance between a preadolescent and therapist even if they are outside because the relationship between them is still key in the nature-based play therapy process. The nature-based play therapy space should have easy access to water and a restroom. Preadolescents may want to water the plants or seeds they planted. Water can be another engaging play resource for preadolescents in nature-based play therapy to use in numerous ways. For example, preadolescents mix water and soil to create something out of mud/clay. Also, the client can make rainbows when spraying water in the garden. It would be convenient to have a restroom on site for preadolescents so extended time is not taken out of their session when they need to visit it.

PRACTICAL INTERVENTION: FRIENDSHIP GARDEN

Friendship Garden, adapted from a group activity presented at the American Horticultural Therapy Association Annual Conference by Meore and Ramirez (2017), is a fun group intervention for preteens to practice social skills and experience successful group work. The group members are asked to create a Friendship Garden collectively by placing different natural materials on a cross section of a tree trunk. This particular group intervention provides preteens with opportunities to collaborate with and respect others, take turns, negotiate, be assertive, and listen to each other.

Materials

This intervention requires a cross section of a tree trunk where participants create the Friendship Garden. When working with more than three group members, it is useful to use a long vertical cross section of a tree for the space. If the group consists of three members or fewer, the counselor can use a large cross section of a tree trunk. Other natural materials such as leaves, dirt, sand, pebbles, stones, twigs, pine cones, seeds, and seashells are needed for group members to create and decorate their Friendship Garden. Play therapists may obtain additional natural materials from local gardening shops, craft shops, or famer's markets, including various dried vegetation such as dried corn stalks, rye stalks, dried beeches, straws, lotus pods, cotton bolls, different species of dried moss, green moss rolls, birch roll, moss vines, Tillandsia air plants, and different types/shapes of barks. Lastly, glue is needed to secure the natural materials to the cross section of the tree trunk.

Directions

The play therapist might introduce Friendship Garden to the group in the following way: "I brought this big cross section of a tree trunk today and I am going to ask you to create a Friendship Garden with your group members by using the materials here in the garden. You can take some time to look at the materials around us. You may take a walk around our garden to find whatever materials you want to use to create your Friendship garden and bring them here." If the play therapist brought some natural materials as mentioned above, you can introduce them to the group members as well.

Once the group members are gathered together, the play therapist asks the group members to share what they brought by looking and touching while respecting everyone's materials. Then, they are asked to design and create their Friendship Garden by placing the materials on the tree cross section. While making the garden as a group, the preteen group members have an opportunity to collaborate with other members in order to create their Friendship Garden collectively. As they learn ways to communicate with each other, they engage in problem solving and negotiating.

When the garden creation is completed, the counselor guides group members to look around the cross section of the tree from various angles to gain different perspectives from above and below and from different sides. The group members are invited to share their garden with others. The play therapist may ask the following questions adapted from Allan (1998):

Tell me about your garden. (The group members are encouraged to collaboratively develop a story about the garden and share it with the therapist. Therapists should make sure that each group member has a chance to contribute to the story.)

If all of you were inside the Friendship Garden you just created, where would you be? How would you feel?

Could you tell me what you were thinking or feeling as you created this garden collectively?

What is a name for your Friendship Garden?

Then later, the therapist asks the group members the following questions (adapted from Warrick, 2008) to reflect on the process of creating the garden with group members:

How did you feel when you wanted to move someone else's objects?
How did you feel when someone moved your objects?
What is your overall reaction to the garden that your group created together?

The therapist facilitates the group discussions by asking the preteens to elaborate on their responses (Flahive & Ray, 2007). Also, the therapist should be a role model by demonstrating social skills such as listening, taking turns, and being respectful to others during the group process. At the end of session, the therapist takes a photo of the Friendship Garden and gives a copy to each individual at the end of the group.

Applications

This nature-based intervention is designed for use in a natural place with natural materials. However, not all play therapists have access to a natural place. For example, play therapists who work at urban schools and agencies may not have access to natural areas. In these situations, the play therapist can use containers of natural materials outside, even if it is on a concrete surface, or the play therapist can provide various natural materials in an inside environment. The play therapist may also use the indoor setting during weather concerns and when other situations prevent the use of an outdoor space.

The play therapist may also introduce a variety of other play-based activities in the natural space that are more directive. This may include other individual, group, or family activities, such as pressing flowers or leaves found in the space, making music using objects found in nature, or engaging in sports activities using natural materials.

CASE STUDY

Cameron (pseudonym) was a ten-year-old African American boy in fourth grade. He was referred for counseling due to his misbehaviors and angry outbursts in class. Cameron participated in weekly individual nature-based play therapy sessions for eight weeks, with each session lasting about fifty minutes. Additionally, he had participated in a nature-based counseling group with his peers prior to his individual nature-based play therapy. His individual nature-based play therapy sessions and group sessions occurred in the same natural area.

During the first two sessions of his individual nature-based play therapy, Cameron explored the garden and natural materials and was reminded of their use by his previous experiences in the garden. He threw small rocks to an empty lot and targeted trees in the distance in the garden. When he was reminded of his group garden, he carefully looked at the plants he and his peers had previously planted while he tried to remember what he had planted in specific areas of the garden. As he showed interest in packets of seeds and tools, the psychoeducation part of the sessions focused on how to use the packets of seed and tools. He watered the section that he had planted with his peers during the group counseling sessions and planted new seeds.

In the third and fourth sessions, he continued to water his group garden and planted flower seeds; there were a few sprouts coming up. He also pulled up one of the grown vegetable plants that he had planted with his peers and saw that the roots of the vegetables were very small. He was surprised that there was a carrot under the ground because it looked too small to harvest. He decided not to look at what was underneath and wait for them to grow. He wondered how much time was needed for them to fully grow and what else it needed to grow. The therapist used the metaphor that it takes time, effort, and patience to see results and reach goals in our lives.

The fifth session occurred following the classroom teacher's request. Cameron had a fight with his peers during class. When Cameron met the counselor at his classroom, he looked withdrawn and asked if the therapist could take him to the garden instead of the counselor's office. He did not say anything while walking to the garden and walking around the garden. As time passed, he slowly started looking closely at the vegetation. He noticed more sprouts grown where he planted seeds and he saw the differences in his new garden compared to his old group garden. His mood changed slowly and he gradually started talking to the counselor about the differences that he noticed in the garden. Then, he watered them and pulled out weeds in his garden as he did the week before. The therapist asked him how his mood had changed since he arrived at the garden from the classroom. He said he felt better after he went to the garden, saw the differences, and took care of the plants. The counselor talked with him about how being outside could change his mood and prevent him from having an argument with his classmates. Also, the counselor used metaphors to help provide him with insight. There were some good and bad changes in the garden, with more new sprouts, but also weeds. They talked about how he could notice how his feelings changed when he was provoked by his classmates and discussed what he could do when feeling this way.

During the sixth and seventh sessions, he continued to care for the plants, but it was not easy because in the hot weather the plants sometimes could not be watered every day. Also, some new sprouts grew too fast and died from dryness. He wondered what had happened and realized that he was not able to water them daily since he was not able to visit the garden daily. Also, the therapist added that sometimes you need to ask for help. Cameron stated that he could ask his teachers or the counselor for help when needed. During the last session, he harvested radishes and carrots from the garden. Although they were small, he was proud of what he harvested from the garden. He showed them to the school staff and teachers and took them home to cook with his family and eat.

INCORPORATION OF FAMILY

Some family members may feel there is stigma involved when they have a preadolescent family member in "therapy" (Vogel, Wester, & Larson, 2007). Nature could be a neutral medium for the family members to get involved in the preadolescent's therapeutic process to ease the stigma. There are various ways for the family members to be involved with the preteen in their nature-based play therapy. If the client wants, he or she is welcome to share with their family what they planted in the garden, or what the garden looks like by taking photos of the garden and showing them to the family members. Also, after seeds have been grown and harvested, they can take what they harvested home for family members to taste and eat. In the process of nature-based play therapy, the preteen might need help with the garden. For example, he or she might need more advanced information on planting, maintaining, and harvesting the garden. Depending on the preteen's decision, he or she could ask family members to help with them. Family members can support these preteens by being available to answer questions and offer encouragement. This opportunity provides the preteen with positive experiences with family members, which he or she may not have experienced before.

The family members could be involved in the process of therapy termination as well. It would be healthy for preteens to see that the therapist and significant others gather together to be a part of a goodbye process to celebrate what the preteen has achieved (Leben, 2008). As termination gets closer, the play therapist discusses the preteen's therapeutic journey with him or her (e.g., reason to come, initial feelings of the client, accomplishment, and current feelings) (Leben, 2008). The play therapist could also summarize the following items as well:

The preteen's favorite nature-based activities
Plants or trees that are meaningful to the preteen in the garden (e.g., those that he or she planted)
If there is any photo that the therapist took in the garden, the therapist could share them with the preteen

The client can plan and host the termination goodbye party. He or she can make a party invitation to the family and invite them to the garden. The client may share with family members at the party his or her her meaningful spots or plants in the garden and talk about their meanings.

Lastly, it is important to help the family or parents gain a better understanding of the nature-based play therapy intervention. The family may appreciate the value of using nature in therapy but may not be familiar with what to expect from their preteens in play therapy sessions outside, in nature. Thus, it is essential for play therapists to educate parents on the unique aspects of the intervention. For example, as the nature-based play therapy sessions are held outside where other people may happen to see and hear, it is difficult to guarantee the confidentiality completely. Therefore, this limit of confidentiality should be discussed with parents and addressed in the informed consent process. This limit of confidentiality should be addressed with the preadolescents as well. Play therapists also want to address safety issues with the parents and the preadolescents. Preadolescents are exposed to the benefits of nature as well as the dangers of nature. For instance, the therapist should ensure that the preadolescents are not allergic to any plants prior to taking them outside. Also, the preadolescents may accidently touch poison plants or fall on rough ground and get injured. Additionally, some preteens might need extra clothing (such as jacket, hat, and rain boots), sunblock, insect repellent, or umbrellas. Some parents might get more dirty clothes from preteens who spend their time playing in dirt or the bushes. It may be helpful to provide a list of these considerations to the family members at the start of therapy in order to develop collaborative relationships with them.

REFLECTION AND CONCLUSION

Although researchers and practitioners have explored the concept of integrating nature into the counseling process, nature-based play therapy is still a relatively new approach in play therapy. There is little guidance on how to implement nature-based play therapy. Although play therapists may have solid experiences in practicing play therapy with preadolescents, it is crucial for the play therapists to be competent in this new approach. Additionally, the play therapists should feel comfortable being in nature, as well as enjoy interacting with nature. For example, play therapists may get dirty or messy, be exposed to the sun, and sweat, like the preadolescents. It would be beneficial to the client if the nature-based play therapist were a person who appreciates the value of nature. This attitude of therapists toward nature—genuinely enjoying being in nature—would serve as a positive model for the preadolescent clients during the course of nature-based play therapy. Furthermore, it would be very useful if the play therapist were knowledgeable about different types of vegetation and animals. In addition to the therapist's competency in a natural setting, confidentiality and safety are also important parts of the process that therapists should be competent in. Compared to traditional play therapy or office counseling, therapists might experience more incidents related to confidentiality and safety in nature-based play therapy. For example, play therapists need to be prepared to address a situation in which a stranger happened to approach the therapist or the preadolescent client during a nature-based play therapy session outside. Also, safety issues should be addressed with parents and a plan should be developed before the sessions begin.

Nature-based play therapy has received attention from therapists due to the growing concerns regarding preadolescents' lack of contact with nature in this technology-driven society. It takes additional efforts for play therapists to integrate nature into play therapy practices as mentioned above. In addition, preadolescents may be reluctant to engage in nature-based play therapy. However, from our experiences, preadolescents begin to appreciate their relationships with nature as the nature-based play therapy process progresses. They begin to truly and genuinely enjoy interacting with nature. Also, because of their developmental capability, preadolescents can gain insight into their lives by connecting with nature. The role of nature-based play therapists is to build therapeutic relationships with preadolescents by supporting and encouraging their connection with nature.

REFERENCES

Allan, J. (1998). *Inscapes of the child's world: Jungian counseling in schools and clinics.* Putnam, CT: Spring Publications.

American School Counselor Association. (2012). *The ASCA National Model: A framework for school counseling programs* (3rd ed.). Alexandria, VA: Author.

Breen, D. (2005). Metaphorical thinking with adolescents. In L. Gallo-Lopez & C.E. Schaefer (Eds.), *Play therapy with adolescents* (pp. 159). Lanham, MD: Jason Aronson.

Burls, A. (2007). People and green spaces: Promoting public health and mental well-being through ecotherapy. *Journal of Public Mental Health, 6,* 24–39.

Courtney, J. A., & Mills, J. C. (2016, March). Utilizing the metaphor of naure as co-therapist in StoryPlay®. *Play Therapy, 11(1),* 18–21.

Feral, C. H. (1998). The connectedness model and optimal development: Is ecopsychology the answer to emotional well-being? *The Humanistic Psychologist, 26,* 243–274. doi:10.1080/08873267.1998.9976975

Flahive, M. W., & Ray, D. (2007). Effect of group sandtray therapy with preadolescents. *The Journal for Specialists in Group Work, 32*(4), 362–382. doi:10.1080/01933920701476706

Fuchs, F., Roos, F., Luddy, T. (Producers), & Holland, A. (Director). (1993). *The secret garden* [Motion picture]. United States: Warner Bros. Family Entertainment.

Greenleaf, A. T., Bryant, R. M., & Pollock, J. B. (2014). Nature-based counseling: Integrating the healing benefits of nature into practice. *International Journal for the Advancement of Counselling, 36,* 162–174. http://dx.doi.org/10.1007/s10447-013-9198-4

Jordan, M., & Marshall, H. (2010). Taking counselling and psychotherapy outside: Destruction or enrichment of the therapeutic frame? *European Journal of Psychotherapy & Counselling, 12,* 345–359. doi:10.1080/13642537.2010.53010

Kuo, F. E., & Faber-Taylor, A. (2004). A potential natural treatment for attention-deficit/hyperactivity disorder: Evidence from a national study. *American Journal of Public Health, 94,* 1580–1586. doi:10.2105/AJPH.94.9.1580

Landreth, G. (2012). *Play therapy: The art of the relationship.* New York, NY: Brunner-Routledge.

Leben, N. (2008). Community building sand tray. In L. Lowenstein (Ed.), *Assessment and treatment activities for children, adolescents, and families: Practitioners share their most effective techniques* (pp. 179–181). Toronto, ON: Champion Press.

McCurdy, L. E., Winterbottom, K. E., Mehta, S. S., & Roberts, J. R. (2010). Using nature and outdoor activity to improve children's health. *Current Problems in Pediatric and Adolescent Health Care, 40,* 102–117. doi:10.1016/j.cppeds.2010.02.003

Meore, A. M., & Ramirez, K. (accepted, 2017, September 9). *Horitcultural therapy & the expressive arts: The garden as a canvas.* A session was presented at the annual 2017 American Horticultural Therapy Association Conference in Burlington, Vermont.

Miles, J. (1987). Wilderness as healing place. *Journal of Experiential Education, 10*(3), 4–10. Retrieved from: http://www.aee.org/publications/jee

Milgrom, C. (2005). An introduction to play therapy with adolescents. In L. Gallo-Lopez & C. E. Schaefer (Eds.), *Play therapy with adolescents* (pp. 3–18). Lanham, MD: Jason Aronson.

Piaget, J. (1962). *Play dreams and imitation in childhood.* New York, NY: W. W. Norton & Company, Inc.

Reese, R. F. (2016). EcoWellness & guiding principles for the ethical integration of nature into counseling. *International Journal for the Advancement of Counselling 38,* 345–357. doi.org/10.1007/s10447-016-9276-5

Reese, R. F., & Myers, J. E. (2012). EcoWellness: The missing factor in holistic wellness models. *Journal of Counseling & Development, 90(4),* 400–406.

Revell, S., Duncan, E., & Cooper, M. (2014). Helpful aspects of outdoor therapy experiences: An online preliminary investigation. *Counselling and Psychotherapy Research, 14,* 28–287. doi:10.1080/14733145.2013.818159

Sackett, C. R. (2010). Ecotherapy: A counter to society's unhealthy trend? *Journal of Creativity in Mental Health, 5,* 134–141. doi:10.1080/15401383.2010.485082

Stigsdotter, U. K., Palsdottir, A. M., Burls, A., Chermaz, A., Ferrini, F., & Grahn, P. (2010). Nature-based therapeutic interventions. In K. Nilsson & M. Snagster (Eds.), *Forests, trees and human health* (pp. 309–342). New York, NY: Springer.

Swank, J. M., Cheung, C., Prikhidko, A., & Su, Y. (2017). Nature-based child-centered group play therapy and behavioral concerns: A single-case design. *International Journal of Play Therapy, 26,* 47–57. doi:10.1037/pla0000031

Swank, J. M., & Huber, P. (2013). Employment preparation and life skill development for high school students with emotional and behavioral disabilities. *The Professional Counselor 3*(2). Retrieved from http://tpcjournal.nbcc.org/employment-preparation-and-life-skill-development-initiatives-for-high-school-students-with-emotional-and-behavioral-disabilities/

Swank, J. M., & Shin, S. (2015). Garden counseling groups and self-esteem: A mixed methods study with children with emotional and behavioral problems. *The Journal for Specialists in Group Work, 40,* 315–331. doi:10.1080/01933922.2015.1056570

Swank, J. M., Shin, S., Cabrita, C., Cheung, C., & Rivers, B. (2015). Initial investigation of nature-based child-centered play therapy: A single-case design. *Journal of Counseling & Development, 93,* 440–450. doi:10.1002/jcad.12042

Swank, J. M., & Swank, D. E. (2013). Student growth within the school garden: Addressing personal/social, academic, and career development. *Journal of School Counseling, 11*(21). Retrieved from http://jsc.montana.edu/articles/v11n21.pdf

Vogel, D. L., Wester, S. R., & Larson, L. M. (2007). Avoidance of counseling: Psychological factors that inhibit seeking help. *Journal of Counseling & Development, 85*(4), 410–422.

Warrick, B.J. (2008). Community building sand tray. In L. Lowenstein (Ed.), *Assessment and treatment activities for children, adolescents, and families: Practitioners share their most effective techniques* (pp. 116–117). Toronto, ON: Champion Press.

Chapter Eight

AutPlay® Therapy with Preadolescents Affected by Autism

Robert Jason Grant

> It takes a village to raise a child. It takes a child with autism to raise the consciousness of the village.—Elaine Hall

Preadolescence can be described as a complex social, emotional, and physical developmental period for most children. Preadolescents with autism spectrum disorder (ASD) encounter many of the same challenges that their neurotypical peers are struggling with but often encounter even more challenges due to the manifestations of their ASD (Exkorn, 2005). A greater and arguably more complex peer interaction and influence system highlights the transitional period of preadolescence. For children with ASD, the transitional period of preadolescence typically presents challenges in the social, emotional, connecting evolution with peers.

Dekker, Nauta, Mulder, Timmerman, and Bildt (2014) state that preadolescents with ASD often lack the behavioral repertoire necessary to interact with others in successful ways. Deficits vary along the autism spectrum and may include lack of orientation towards social stimuli, inadequate use of eye contact, no or inadequate initiation of social interaction, difficulties in interpreting verbal and nonverbal social cues, inappropriate emotional responses, and lack of empathy for others.

The preadolescent with ASD often finds himself in a whirlwind of new and critical social navigating as well as with an increase in emotional responses, which typically are not modulated well. With the demand for an evolved skill set, the child with ASD can easily feel overwhelmed with this stage in life. This response can set a precedent for the child's ability to successfully navigate further developmental stages such as adolescence and young adulthood. Often, there is an increase in anxiety levels and a tendency to withdraw due to the new social/emotional demands. Many preadolescents with ASD will benefit from individual and group interventions that aim to help the preadolescent gain and master needed skills for maneuvering through the preadolescent years.

AutPlay® therapy is a comprehensive treatment approach designed for children, preadolescents, and adolescents with ASD and other neurodevelopmental disorders (Grant, 2016a). AutPlay® is an integration of play therapy models and behavioral therapy. Treatment protocols include structured play therapy interventions developed to increase skill acquisition in the areas of social skills, emotional regulation, and relationship connection. AutPlay® interventions can be especially promising for preadolescents with ASD who need improvement in their social functioning along with a better understanding and management of their emotional states. AutPlay® protocol is consistently promoting better relationship connection, a critical developmental issue for preadolescents. Through implementation of AutPlay® interventions, preadolescents can be expected to make significant gains in targeted skill development.

LITERATURE REVIEW

Navigating the complexities of preadolescence differs in both quality and quantity from that of neurotypically developing children. Bauminger and Solomon (2010) stated that social emotional deficits, limitations in affect-related resources, and theory of mind challenges create substantial deficits for preadolescents with ASD that neurotypical preadolescents may not struggle with. These deficits, along with other social connection struggles, appear to be some of the primary skills needed to navigate the preadolescent peer world. As children with ASD experience these skill deficits, their confidence and success in preadolescent navigation diminishes.

Dekker et al. (2014) proposed that children with ASD have a desire for more peer social interaction but do not present in appropriate ways that generate fluent social interaction with peers. Preadolescents with ASD often display substantial social relational problems when compared to neurotypically developing peers. Children with ASD have difficulty sharing affective experiences and understanding the perspective of others, which is important for social reciprocity and the development of friendships.

Solomon, Bauminger, and Rogers (2011) furthered that social impairments especially in friendships is a critical struggle area of the preadolescent development for the child with ASD. Although friendship is usually desired by children with ASD, it is often an elusive concept with little manifestation of results. Iland (2006) indicated that understanding social navigation is critical for preadolescents with ASD. To be successful involves understanding spoken and unspoken social rules, problem-solving through social challenges, and understanding the complexities of friendships both in individual and group format. Social functioning for the preadolescent with ASD involves an intricate weaving and rhythm of social skills, emotional management, and relational connection ability that does not produce instinctually or develop easily.

Huang et al. (2017) pointed to the importance of self-concept or self-image during the preadolescent years. It is critical that the preadolescent with ASD be able to measure their own perceptions of the self and their understanding of others' perceptions on themselves at a multidimensional level. When children with ASD struggle with social and emotional success, they will be less likely to engage in measuring and understanding their self accurately. This struggle can result in a negative self-concept. In many cases, the perceived failures with social/emotional success can produce what appears as a chronic hopelessness belief in preadolescents with ASD, which leads to isolation and withdrawal and lack of investment in working on skill improvement.

There are different types of interventions for children with ASD that are designed to improve social connection and emotional modulation ability. Most researched-based interventions are developed from a behavioral perspective or with a skill development emphasis (Exkorn, 2005). Several treatments have been established to address social and emotional skill improvement including applied behavioral analysis, social stories, social skill groups, autism movement therapy, parent implemented intervention, and play therapy approaches such as AutPlay® therapy.

Play therapy approaches hold many benefits for preadolescents with ASD, especially in treating social and emotional issues with which they typically struggle. Play therapy is uniquely designed for and responsive to the individual and developmental needs of each child, and recently there has been an increase in child therapy literature emphasizing play as the ideal way to treat social and emotional difficulties in children (Bratton, Ray, Rhine, & Jones, 2005; Josefi & Ryan, 2004; Grant, 2016a). Research has shown that children diagnosed with autism and participating in play therapy have gained improvement in pretend play, attachment, social interaction, self-regulation, coping with changes, emotional response, and autonomy (Josefi & Ryan, 2004; Grant, 2016a).

AutPlay® therapy is a play therapy and behavioral therapy treatment approach for working with children, preadolescents, and adolescents with ASD, developmental disabilities, or other neurodevelopmental disorders. The theoretical underpinnings of AutPlay® consist of play therapy approaches combined with behavioral therapy approaches. AutPlay® incorporates a combination of directive play techniques with behavioral and play therapy approaches to teach children skill development in three primary component areas: emotional regulation, social functioning, and relationship connection (Grant, 2015). Research (Grant, 2016a) related to AutPlay® has shown success with implementing AutPlay® protocol to children, preadolescents, and adolescents. Improvements in skill ability related to social functioning, emotional regulation, and relationship connect have been demonstrated for individuals participating in six months or longer of AutPlay® intervention (Grant, 2016a).

INTERVENTIONS

Sensory Mandala

Preadolescents with ASD often struggle with managing emotions, sensory challenges, and becoming dysregulated. Sensory Mandala is a structured AutPlay® technique designed to increase emotional regulation ability and improve sensory processing in preadolescents with ASD. I have facilitated this intervention many times with preadolescent clients with ASD who are struggling with emotional regulation. This intervention has shown great success in helping children develop a regulating coping skill. Many of the children I have implemented this intervention with have continued to create sensory mandalas on their own as they have found the process relaxing and regulating. This intervention can be implemented in any setting. The therapist will need to provide a variety of sensory materials (described below), one piece of card stock (preferable white), Sharpie markers (a variety of colors), and glue or double-sided tape.

Example materials for sensory mandalas:

Touch (tactile)—velcro, denim, burlap, ribbons, beads, buttons, foam stickers, sand paper, cotton balls, pompoms, pipe cleaners, dry pasta, bubble wrap, pieces of cloth

Sight (visual)—glitter, googly eye stickers, neon colors, glow-in-the-dark materials

Smell (olfactory)—essential oils, potpourri, scented stickers, scented markers, spices

The therapist begins the intervention by explaining to the preadolescent that they will be completing a sensory mandala. The therapist or preadolescent will draw a circle on a piece of card stock. The preadolescent can draw or color anything they want inside the circle. They will also choose some of the sensory materials to include in the mandala. The therapist should present all the sensory materials to the preadolescent and allow him or her to explore the items and choose the ones that are the most appealing. The sensory items the preadolescent chooses will be incorporated into the sensory mandala.

The preadolescent should be allowed time and space to create the sensory mandala however he or she wishes. Some children with ASD may need additional guidance in terms of what to create. For these children, the therapist will want to explain to the child that he or she can create a real scene of something or color and place objects in the mandala anyway that he or she wants. Occasionally, the abstract component of a sensory mandala can be challenging for the child with ASD. The therapist will want to monitor for this and assist the child as needed.

Once the preadolescent has completed the sensory mandala (figure 8.1), the therapist will ask the child to share about the mandala and discuss what sensory materials the child chose and why he or she chose those items. The therapist will explain that the child can collect sensory materials for home and create a sensory mandala anytime he or she needs to feel calm or relax. The child can keep any sensory mandalas that he or she creates and use them for tactile, olfactory, or visual sensory processing to practice better sensory integration and to help him or her regulate when he or she feels overwhelmed. I have discovered this intervention works well for preadolescents with ASD, ADHD, sensory processing challenges, and general regulation struggles.

Social Scales

Play therapy and play-based techniques can be appropriate interventions in working with children with ASD, especially when working with children who have little in the way of social skills navigation (Parker & O'Brien, 2011). The AutPlay® intervention Social Scales (Grant, 2016b) is designed to assist preadolescents in successfully navigating and improving social situations. The intervention provides a guide for practitioners to create specific scenarios in which a preadolescent might need help in developing better or more appropriate social responses. The social scales worksheet serves as both an assessment tool to identify what the child perceives and a practice tool to help develop more appropriate social responses. This intervention can be implemented in any setting. The therapist will need to provide a social scales worksheet and something to write with.

The therapist creates a social situations scale sheet with several situations/scales listed. The social situations should reflect social scenarios in which the preadolescent might struggle. Many of the preadolescents with whom I have completed this intervention have struggled to develop the scales on their own. Often, I will have prewritten the scales before the session with situations in which I know the child has struggled. The child is given the social scales worksheet and instructed to complete the first scale on the worksheet. The child can read the social situation and place an X on the scale where he or she believes the correct answer would be. If the child has reading difficul-

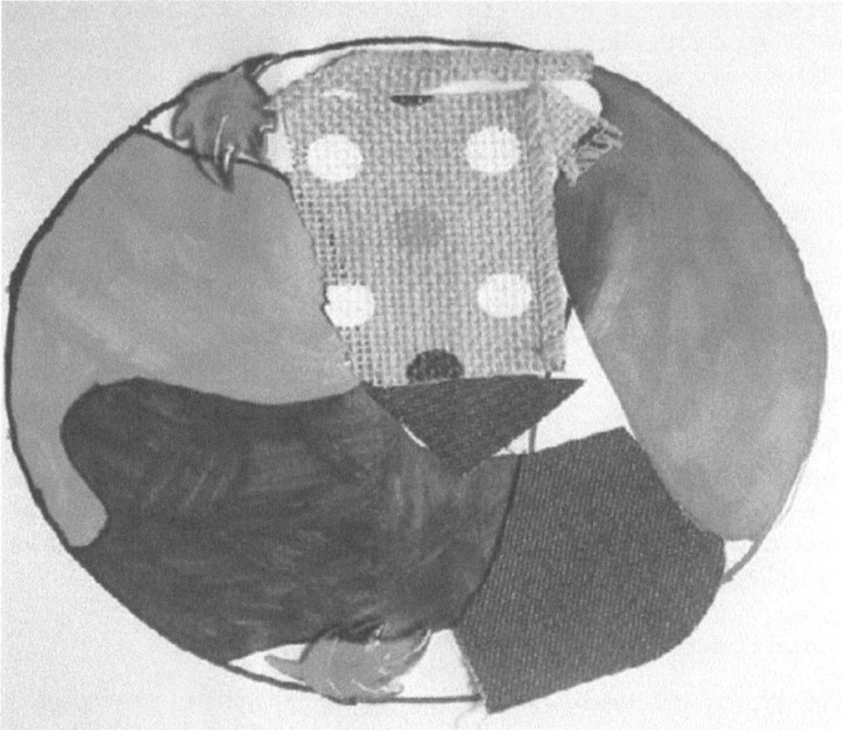

Figure 8.1. Sensory Mandala Example. Courtesy of Robert Jason Grant

ties, the therapist can read the social situation to the child. Once the child has given a response, the child's response should be processed with the therapist. The therapist should especially discuss any response that is unhealthy, unsafe, or not an appropriate social response.

An example scenario for a social scale might be "A stranger walks up to you while you are at the mall and says, 'If you come with me I can get you a free iPad.'" The child then marks on the scale where he or she thinks this would fall on the truth-to-lie scale and the safe-to-unsafe scale. The therapist and child would then discuss what the appropriate response should be and any questions the child might have.

Truth---Lie
Safe--Unsafe

This intervention can assist preadolescents in working on a variety of social skills and situations. The social scales can be directed toward identifying safety issues, giving appropriate responses, understanding concepts, and so forth. Once the child indicates what he or she believes, the therapist and child should process the response and discuss if the child responded inappropriately or if the situation might have multiple correct responses. The therapist can also role-play the scenarios with the child for further practice. I have found that I spend much of the session processing through the scenarios and the child's responses. I also make sure to spend time role-playing the scenarios that the child seems to be struggling with the most. The processing and role-playing components are vital for the preadolescent to gain better social functioning. This intervention can include parents, who can be taught this intervention to practice at home. Parents and child may even create multiple social scales at home to address new social scenarios that the child might experience.

Paper Friend

Preadolescents with ASD often desire to have friends but lack the social skills to establish and maintain friendships. Paper Friend (Grant, 2016b) is an AutPlay® intervention that helps preadolescents work on specific friendship-related skills including targeting other children to engage with and strategies to develop friendships. Friendship-related skills are one of the areas I work on the most with preadolescents with ASD. It is an area of focus that becomes not only more important during preadolescence, but also more challenging. Minimal materials are needed for this intervention; the therapist will need to provide a white piece of paper and markers.

The therapist will explain to the child that they will be working on increasing friendship skills. The therapist or child draws an outline of a person on a white piece of paper. The child identifies someone in his or her life with whom he or she would like either to be friends or to become better friends. The child designs the person outline to look like the child with whom he or she would like to be friends (typically by drawing the identified child's face

Table 8.1. Sample Social Scales Worksheet

Social Scales
You are sitting in class at school and the boy beside you starts hitting his desk. Appropriate--Not Appropriate
You are walking down the hallway at school and another student pushes you as you pass by. Bullying---Not Bullying
A student at school says your hair looks like an anime character. Funny---Not Funny
You meet a new student at school and talk for few minutes about her old school. Friend--Acquaintance

on the paper outline person). The child then writes things on the person outline that he or she could do with that person, things they could talk about, ways that he or she could be a good friend to the person, ways that he or she could initiate contact with the person, skills that help make friends, and activities that would enhance the friendship.

The therapist and child process through what the child has written, and the therapist may add additional information. The therapist and child practice the various friendship-related skills through role-play. When implementing this intervention with preadolescents with ASD, the therapist will likely have to help the child identify friendship skills. It is unlikely the child will list several things to do or even understand the most appropriate things for beginning a friendship. The therapist will likely help the child think of things to do for starting or improving a friendship.

This intervention can be taught with parents, so the parents can support the child's efforts to increase his or her friendship with another child. The parents will likely play a role in helping the child initiate some of the identified activities to develop a friendship. The parents will also want to monitor that the person the child has chosen is an appropriate person with whom the child could develop a friendship. Some children with ASD may choose a person who would not be appropriate, such as a much older adult, a much younger child, someone who lives far away, or even a fictional character. I have begun this intervention with many preadolescents who choose an inappropriate person. I always ask the child to explain who the person is before we begin writing any friendship ideas. Often, I can discern whether the person they have chosen is appropriate. If the person is not appropriate, I state this to the child and further explain that we are looking for someone currently in the child's life that is around the child's age. Parents are encouraged to role play and practice the friendship skills at home and eventually try and arrange opportunities for the child to connect with the child with whom he or she would like to become friends or another appropriate child and implement the friendship skills that have been practiced.

Feelings Key Ring

Often children with ASD struggle to identify their emotions and communicate to others what they are feeling; this is especially true when they are dysregulated. Feelings Key Ring (Grant, 2016a) is an AutPlay® intervention that provides preadolescents with a tool they can use to help identify their emotions and communicate what they are feeling. It also gives others a better understanding of what is happening with the child. This is a simple intervention that has been extremely valuable to many of the preadolescents with whom I have worked. The ability to see their emotions visually and to share what they are feeling without having to speak words has helped many pread-

Figure 8.2. Paper Friend Example. Courtesy of Robert Jason Grant

olescents improve their emotional awareness and expression. I have taught this intervention to school counselors and special education teachers who have implemented the intervention as a classroom project. This has helped the preadolescent with ASD to feel less awkward when using this tool at school as the entire class has learned about the feelings key ring and each student has created one. The therapist will need to provide several sample paint swatches, a key ring, scissors, a hole punch, and a black Sharpie marker.

The therapist explains to the child that they are going to use paint sample swatches to make a feelings key ring. The therapist gives the child several paint chip samples that have been cut into smaller sizes (or children can cut them out themselves). There should be a variety of colors available for the child from which to choose. The child is instructed to think of different feelings that he or she experiences and chooses a paint chip color to go with each feeling. The child writes the feelings on the paint chips. Once all the paint chips are completed, the child uses a hole punch on each chip and then places the chips on a key ring. The child has created a feelings key ring that he or she can keep and use to identify what he or she is feeling and to show others what he or she is feeling.

Once the feelings key ring is complete, the therapist and child review each of the feelings together and talk about times the child has felt each feeling. The therapist and child can also practice scenarios where the child might use his or her key ring. It is recommended to begin with eight to ten feelings. More feelings can be added at any time. The therapist will want to make sure that feelings the child typically struggles with are included on the key ring. Thus, the therapist may also add feelings to the key ring. When working with a preadolescent with ASD, it is possible that the child may struggle to think of feelings. In this case, the therapist will want to help the child write feelings on the paint chips.

This intervention helps work on identifying emotions, emotion expression, and managing emotions. This intervention functions as an assistive device that the preadolescent can use at home or school to help communicate to others what he or she is feeling. The child can add feelings at any time. When creating the feelings key ring, a feelings chart may be used if it would help the child to better identify feelings. It is important to make sure that feelings the child often has are represented on the swatch. Parents should be taught about the feelings key ring and instructed to encourage their child to use the key ring. Parents can help the child add feelings to the key ring and can make multiple key rings, possibly having the child keep one at school and one at home. I have had many parents report the usefulness of the feelings key ring and that they make multiple key rings for the house, car, and school.

CASE STUDY

Brooklyn (pseudonym), a ten-year-old female, was referred to see me by her school counselor. Brooklyn presented with a diagnosis of autism spectrum disorder and sensory processing disorder. I observed Brooklyn's manifestation on the autism spectrum to be in the mildly impaired category. She was intelligent and somewhat social. She seemed to produce better social skills with adults than with her peers. Overall, she presented more mature than her chronological age. The presenting issues that warranted a referral were disruptive behavior in the school setting, mainly toward peers. Brooklyn's parents also reported that she would become aggressive toward her siblings at home. Everyone seemed to agree that Brooklyn was struggling with emotional dysregulation and sensory processing issues and this was creating the behavior problems.

Figure 8.3. Feelings Key Ring Example. Courtesy of Robert Jason Grant

Therapy began with Brooklyn by implementing the first phase of treatment in AutPlay®, the intake and assessment phase. During this phase, the focus was on building relationship with Brooklyn, helping her become familiar with me and the clinic environment and conducting further assessment to determine Brooklyn's skill deficits. At the end of the intake and assessment phase, which lasted approximately four sessions, a treatment plan was established for Brooklyn. The focus of Brooklyn's treatment would be to increase emotional regulation ability and improve sensory processing struggles and thus see an improvement in her peer and sibling social interactions and a decrease in behavior issues at school and home. Brooklyn would participate in therapy with her mother and father one time a week and complete home interventions as assigned.

Once the treatment plan was established, Brooklyn began the second phase of treatment in AutPlay®, the structured intervention phase. During this phase, structured play interventions were implemented with Brooklyn and her parents during sessions and her parents were taught how to implement the interventions at home in between session dates. I had noted during the intake and assessment phase that Brooklyn enjoyed art and was drawn to the sensory materials in the playroom such as the sand tray. As often as possible during treatment, I chose structured play interventions that involved art and sensory materials to address improving emotional regulation and sensory struggles. Brooklyn was positive and cooperative throughout treatment and when participating in interventions. I noted that aligning interventions to something that Brooklyn already had a strong interest in, such as art, greatly increased her participation and her relationship with me. This is often the case with children with ASD. If the therapist can implement interventions that in some way correspond with one of the child's obsessive interests, the child will participate more fully, and session interventions will be more successful.

The beginning sessions of the structured intervention phase focused on improving emotional regulation for Brooklyn. During these early sessions Brooklyn participated in several play interventions designed to improve emotional regulation. One of the interventions completed was the Feelings Key Ring (discussed in the interventions section of this chapter). Brooklyn was especially excited about this intervention as it gave her the ability to communicate what she was feeling without having to talk. She was able to explain that when she felt dysregulated, she did not feel like talking and it was challenging for her to organize her thoughts and put them into words. She felt empowered by the idea that she could use the feelings key ring to help her identify her feeling and show others what she was feeling. Brooklyn and her parents completed two additional feelings key rings at home. Brooklyn kept one at school and one at home in her room, and Brooklyn's mother carried one with her in her purse.

After we completed this intervention, Brooklyn and her parents regularly reported to me that Brooklyn was using the feelings key ring both at school and at home with good success. Brooklyn's teachers were made aware of the key ring and Brooklyn was regularly using it to indicate to her teachers when she was experiencing a negative feeling. Brooklyn's teachers recognized this as a sign that Brooklyn needed a break and she was able to then take a break from her environment. This was already beginning to greatly reduce negative social interactions with her peers. Brooklyn's parents reported success at home but not at the same level as school. The feelings key ring was working at home to help identify and communicate feelings, but Brooklyn needed more self-regulation processes at home to help her stay calm.

The later sessions of the structured intervention phase focused on improving Brooklyn's self-regulation ability and sensory processing. I corresponded with Brooklyn's school to update her IEP to reflect receiving occupational therapy services at school to help improve sensory processing issues. Brooklyn and her parents participated with me in completing several play interventions designed to increase self-regulation and improve sensory processing challenges. Brooklyn was especially drawn to the sand tray setup in my office. Brooklyn verbalized that the sand tray felt relaxing for her. Often, when there was time left in the session after completing a structured intervention, Brooklyn would choose to play in or create a scene in the sand tray. This appeared to be both a regulating and a sensory process for her.

One of the interventions we completed was a directive sand tray. Brooklyn was instructed to create a sand tray describing what the feeling of calm meant to her. It should be noted that many children with ASD will struggle with the symbolic nature of creating in the sand tray; Brooklyn did not. I noted early in sessions that she could participate in and understand symbolism and more abstract concepts. I would not introduce a play intervention that included symbolism and abstract concepts if I was not aware that the child could participate in these types of interventions. Brooklyn was able to complete her sand tray without any assistance. Brooklyn created a scene in the tray with a little girl figure sitting on a piece of wood surrounded by water (she used several blue glass pebbles to create the water), which was surrounded by several tree miniatures. Once she had finished, I asked her to explain her sand tray to me. She discussed that the little girl miniature was her and she felt the calmest away from other people in a quiet place where other people could not easily reach her. She further explained that being alone in nature relaxed her and made her feel calm. This intervention helped me understand how to better assist Brooklyn in self-regulation ability. Working with Brooklyn's parents, we were able to set up private break times for Brooklyn and situations where she could be alone in places of nature that felt calm to her. Brooklyn's parents also invested in a sand tray set up for Brooklyn to have at home. She was able to self-regulate by having alone time to create in the sand tray any time she felt she needed to. These consistent regulation and sensory experiences begin to regulate Brooklyn at home, and negative experiences and behaviors toward her siblings decreased.

Brooklyn's presenting issues improved to a degree that she no longer needed therapeutic intervention. At this point, we entered the final phase of treatment in AutPlay®, the termination phase. I met with Brooklyn's parents to discuss ending therapy. We all agreed that treatment goals had been met, presenting issues had improved, and there were no additional goals to work on. The plan was to have two more sessions with the final session being a graduation for Brooklyn to celebrate what she had accomplished in therapy. This was explained to Brooklyn, and the termination phase proceeded and ended with Brooklyn's graduation. Brooklyn and her parents participated in thirty-one sessions, meeting once a week with me and implementing interventions at home between sessions.

INCORPORATION OF FAMILY

Treatment approaches involving parents and other family members have been a popular and beneficial model for treating ASD for many years. The merger of play therapy and family counseling as a protocol for treating children and their families affected by ASD not only supports treatment history and research but presents the most logical course for the life-long challenges that can accompany an ASD diagnosis (Grant, 2015).

AutPlay® therapy is a family play therapy approach. Parents are empowered to become co–change agents in helping their child develop and advance in skill level. The AutPlay® parent training component teaches parents how to conduct AutPlay® techniques at home. Parents learn procedures and techniques, and are shown how to implement techniques at home to increase specific skill and ability levels in their child. When possible and appropriate, AutPlay® involves the whole family, including siblings and extended family members in the treatment process.

Skill development requires repetition, a dedication to practicing until a desired skill is integrated at an acceptable level. Preadolescents with ASD will need practice to gain needed social and emotional skills. Since parents and other family members are invited into the AutPlay® process to become co–change agents with the therapist, the needed practice and repetition of AutPlay® interventions aimed at increasing the preadolescent's skill development is provided outside the therapist's office. Parents and other family members are fully trained by the AutPlay® therapist to implement AutPlay® interventions at home and are monitored by the therapist to ensure success in home implementation. Further, parents fully discuss with the therapist how to establish home intervention times and address any issues that may arise.

The home initiation of AutPlay® interventions may manifest in various forms depending on the preadolescent's needs and the configuration of the family. Consider the following examples:

Kayden and his mother establish a sensory-regulation room at home. The room is furnished with a punching bag, exercise ball, mini trampoline, balance board, and other sensory-friendly items. Kayden and his mother establish a fifteen-minute time each day for Kayden to go into the regulation room and participate in whatever activity he likes. The goal is to provide a maintenance model of sensor-regulation processing.

Christina and her parents are working on improving social skills with Christina. They have established three times a week that Christina and her parents will implement social skill interventions at home that were taught during therapy sessions. Christina's parents also reinforce social skill development by reminding Christina of social skill practice and helping her implement skills in real-life opportunities that manifest.

Joe and his family are working on improving emotional regulation for Joe. Once a week, Joe participates with his parents in an emotional regulation intervention they learned during a therapy session. A second time, the same week, Joe participates with his parents and his younger and older sibling in a family time where the whole family completes an emotional regulation intervention learned during a therapy session. Everyone in the family works with Joe and focuses on modeling appropriate emotional modulation.

Family involvement is an important component of the AutPlay® protocol. Often for preadolescents to gain needed skills, they must participate in a skill acquisition process more than once a week in a therapist's office. Parents and other family members are essential in providing additional practice time. Family involvement can include any caring adult who spends time with the preadolescent. In addition to parents and siblings, others involved could include grandparents, aunts and uncles, nannies, foster parents, case workers, residential staff, and friends. The most essential element of family involvement is having appropriate others who are willing to participate and implement interventions in the home setting.

REFLECTION AND CONCLUSION

AutPlay® therapy is a treatment approach that is based in play therapy and behavioral therapy (Grant, 2016a). It is specifically designed to meet a preadolescent where he or she is at in terms of his or her social and emotional skills level. AutPlay® helps increase needed skills and abilities, such as social, emotional, and connection skills. Further, it considers the lack of skills that may be present in a preadolescent with ASD while introducing interventions in a directive and specific manner so that children with ASD can participate and learn from the play-based techniques. Preadolescents are thoroughly assessed at the beginning of treatment to identify their skill deficits and assist the therapist in creating treatment goals and choosing directive interventions to specifically address each child's skill needs. Parents are also taught AutPlay® protocol to use at home with their child, and parents become co–change agents in the therapeutic process.

Play therapy approaches such as AutPlay® therapy are showing increasing support in the effectiveness of using play-based interventions to treat children and their families affected by ASD (Grant, 2016a). Play provides a natural and engaging element for all children, and structured play interventions, such as those found in AutPlay® protocol, provide the skill component that preadolescents need to gain in their functioning ability. The combination of play- and skill-based interventions is not only gaining in research support, but also presents a logical approach to treating children and families dealing with ASD issues. Through AutPlay® interventions we can strive to provide much needed skill acquisition for the challenging transitional period of preadolescence.

REFERENCES

Bauminger, N., & Solomon, M. (2010). Predicting friendship quality in autism spectrum disorders and typical development, *Journal of Autism and Developmental Disorders, 40,* 751–761.

Bratton, S. C., Ray, D., Rhine, T., & Jones, L. (2005). The efficacy of play therapy with children: A meta-analytic review of treatments outcomes. *Professional Psychology: Research and Practice*, 36, 376–390.

Dekker, V., Nauta, M. H., Mulder, E. J., Timmerman, M. E., & Bildt, A. (2014). A randomized controlled study of a social skills training for preadolescent children with autism spectrum disorders: Generalization of skills by training parents and teachers? *BMC Psychiatry, 14,* 189. doi: 1471-244X/14/189

Exkorn, K. S. (2005). *The autism sourcebook: Everything you need to know about diagnosis. Treatment, coping, and healing.* New York, NY: HarperCollins.

Grant, R. J. (2015). Family play counseling with children affected by autism. In E. J. Green, J. N. Baggerly, & A. C. Myrick (Eds.), *Counseling families: Play-based treatment (*109–125). Lanham, MD: Rowman & Littlefield.

Grant, R. J. (2016a). *AutPlay therapy for children and adolescents on the autism spectrum: A behavioral play-based approach.* New York, NY: Routledge.

Grant, R. J. (2016b). *Play-based interventions for autism spectrum disorders and other developmental disabilities*. New York, NY, Routledge.

Huang, A. X., Hughes, T. L., Sutton, L. R., Lawrence, M., Chen. X., Ji, Z., and Zeleke, W. (2017). Understanding the self in individuals with autism spectrum disorders (ASD): A review of literature. *Frontiers in Psychology, 8,* 1422. doi:10.3389/fpsyg.2017.01422

Iland, L. (2006). Girl to girl: Advice on friendship, bullying, and fitting in. In T/ Atwood (Ed.), *Asperger's and Girls* (pp. 33–64). Arlington, TX: Future Horizons.

Josefi, O., & Ryan, Y. (2004). Non-directive play therapy for young children with autism: A case study. *Clinical Child Psychology and Psychiatry*, 9, 533–551.

Parker, N., & O'Brien, P. (2011). Play therapy reaching the child with autism. *International Journal of Special Education*, 26, 80–87.

Solomon, M., Bauminger, N., & Rogers, S. J. (2011). Abstract reasoning and friendship in high functioning preadolescents with autism spectrum disorders. *Journal of Autism and Developmental Disorders, 41,* 32–43.

Chapter Nine

Directive Play Therapy Techniques with Preadolescents

Pam Dyson

An eleven-year-old girl walked into my play therapy room and announced, "Everybody treats me like I'm a little kid. I'm not a little kid, but they treat me like one because I'm not a teenager yet." This is a common sentiment spoken by children who are in the preadolescent stage of development. They strive for independence and want to be accepted by their peers, yet they still want and need the support of their parents. They test boundaries and rules and like to feel important and noticed.

Many preadolescents view play therapy as something for younger children, despite being developmentally appropriate for a range of youth. It is not unusual for me to show a preadolescent my playroom and have them remark, "These are baby toys. I don't see anything in here I want to play with." Over the course of my career as a play therapist, I have used a combination of both child-led and directive interventions with my clients. When working with preadolescents, I've come to appreciate that directive play therapy techniques such as games and expressive art activities are often well suited to their developmental needs, presenting problems, and individual preferences.

In this chapter, I will give examples of developmentally appropriate directive play therapy techniques that can be utilized with preadolescents to help them express their feelings, learn how to problem-solve, develop coping strategies, enhance their social skills, and build resiliency.

LITERATURE REVIEW

A review of the literature suggests that prior to beginning treatment, therapists need to consider preadolescents from a developmental lens. Many changes are occurring during the preadolescent stage of development in preparation for the shift into adolescence. Preadolescents may lack self-confidence and feel uncertain about themselves in comparison to their peers. Rapid physical growth and hormonal changes can challenge self-control. They may become more defiant, self-centered, and emotionally reactive (Davies, 2011). Though we may find these to be common developmental characteristics among preadolescents, play therapists should view them only as guidelines and be careful not to use them to label or categorize clients (Shokouhi, Limberg, & Armstrong, 2014).

The age of a preadolescent is only one aspect to consider when planning treatment interventions. Preadolescents may have different developmental abilities despite the same chronological age (Shokouhi, Limberg, & Armstrong, 2014). Stress caused by high academic demands and social expectations (Davies, 2011), as well as emotional, social, physical, or cognitive deficits, can affect the functioning for a preadolescent (Lowenstein, 1999). Thus, gathering a detailed developmental history from parents is crucial, and if the preadolescent is functioning at a younger age, treatment needs must be adjusted to reflect that level of functioning.

Once a developmental age has been determined, it is time to explore which types of directive therapy techniques are most appropriate to incorporate into the treatment plan. Practical techniques that will engage preadolescents and keep their attention can be integrated into treatment plans (Drewes, 2009). Game play, for example, especially those involving strategy rather than chance, are often enjoyed by preadolescents. Learning to play games with complicated scenarios and rules takes self-discipline and concentration. It is worth noting that the structure of these games mirrors several of the developmental tasks of preadolescence (Davies, 2011). This serves as a guideline for determining what types of game play would be appropriate for preadolescents in play therapy depending on their presenting problems and their personal preferences.

Preadolescents who are defensive and closed off may find expressive therapies to be a safe way to share thoughts and feelings they may not feel comfortable expressing verbally (Shokouhi, Limberg, & Armstrong, 2014). Expressive therapies encourage creativity and can be a source of playful enjoyment for preadolescents, while gently guiding them toward their specific presenting problems (Lowenstein, 1999). Therapists who use directive play therapy techniques need to consider the goal of an activity, the prompt or directive that will be given to help guide the preadolescent toward the goal (Leggett & Boswell, 2017), and how the activity will fit into the overall treatment plan. Therapists should be careful not to ask too many questions, as this can disrupt or slow the process, and be sure to give the client enough space and time to fully experience the activity after the initial prompt (Leggett & Boswell, 2017).

Therapists who look at their clients developmentally will be able to create play therapy treatment plans that are responsive to the emerging tasks and skills of preadolescents while engaging them in the therapeutic process (Davies, 2011). Well-timed directive play therapy interventions can be pivotal for preadolescents by helping them gain feelings of competency and self-worth.

PRACTICAL INTERVENTIONS

When using directive play therapy techniques with preadolescents, I often find myself wearing multiple hats. I'm the facilitator of the activity, but I may also be a participant. At times I may need to be an educator or a role model. I've learned to be flexible with the roles I may need to play as I shift back and forth within the same session.

Preadolescents have a strong preference for game play and are especially interested in games that involve skill and strategy. Playing games with a preadolescent engages them in the therapeutic process and helps build rapport. There are a number of commercially produced therapeutic games that are a good fit for preadolescents, but they can be expensive to purchase. I will often purchase traditional games and adapt them to have therapeutic value. Some of the games I have in my collection that preadolescents are often drawn to are Jenga®, Connect 4®, Ker Plunk!®, Trouble Game®, and Don't Break the Ice®.

I have worked with many preadolescents who enjoyed playing the game Jenga®. The game is played in the traditional way, with players taking turns by removing one block at a time from a tower of blocks and placing it on top of the tower. This creates a progressively taller and unstable structure. I add an additional step to the game, a stack of therapeutic game cards that I have created. After a block is pulled from the tower and placed on the top, the player draws one of the game cards, reads it aloud, and responds to the question (see figure 9.1). If playing the game in an initial session, I use a stack of cards with questions centered on getting to know one another. Examples of these cards might include questions about what I like to do on my birthday, my favorite holiday, and a famous person I would like to meet.

Over the years I have created multiple sets of game cards, all with a specific topic that allow me to modify this and other games in my collection to address specific presenting issues. Sets include cards about feelings' expression, anger management, social skill development, and coping with grief and loss.

I frequently create my own board games that address the issues for which preadolescents are brought to therapy. Foam board, or even a manila file folder, makes a good base for the game board. If you conduct a simple online

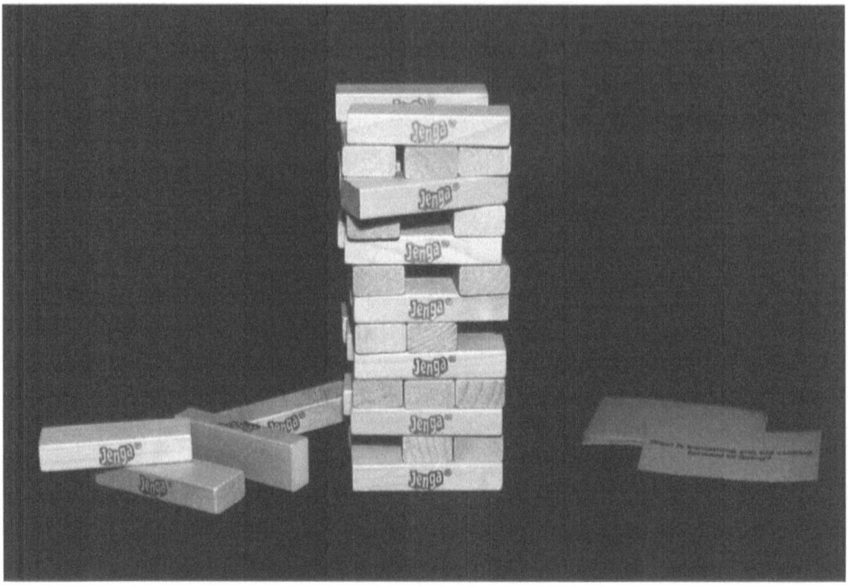

Figure 9.1. Jenga®. Courtesy of Pam Dyson

search you will be able to find a variety of printable game board templates. Templates may have a "start-to-finish" style or a "race track" style where there is not a specific ending point. My preference is for the latter, which allows the game to be played until the session time has ended or all of the game cards have been used. I sometimes add spaces to the game board where a player goes back one space, moves ahead two spaces, or loses a turn. Take a look at some of your favorite childhood board games for inspiration. You will need to add dice and game pieces, which can be borrowed from other games, along with game cards consisting of questions, prompts, or fill-in-the-blank statements similar to the ones I described using when playing Jenga®. Experience has taught me that laminating the game board and cards will ensure durability. You can also cover them with clear Con-Tact® film.

Since a large percentage of the preadolescents I see are impacted by parental divorce or separation I have created a board game I call Dealing with Divorce (see figure 9.2).

The game has three different colored spaces spread across the game board that correspond to the colors of the game cards. Players take turns rolling the dice and moving their game piece around the board. When a player lands on one of the colored spaces, they draw a card from the respective pile and respond to the question or prompt. Examples of questions or prompts on the cards include: worries I have since the divorce, something that's changed

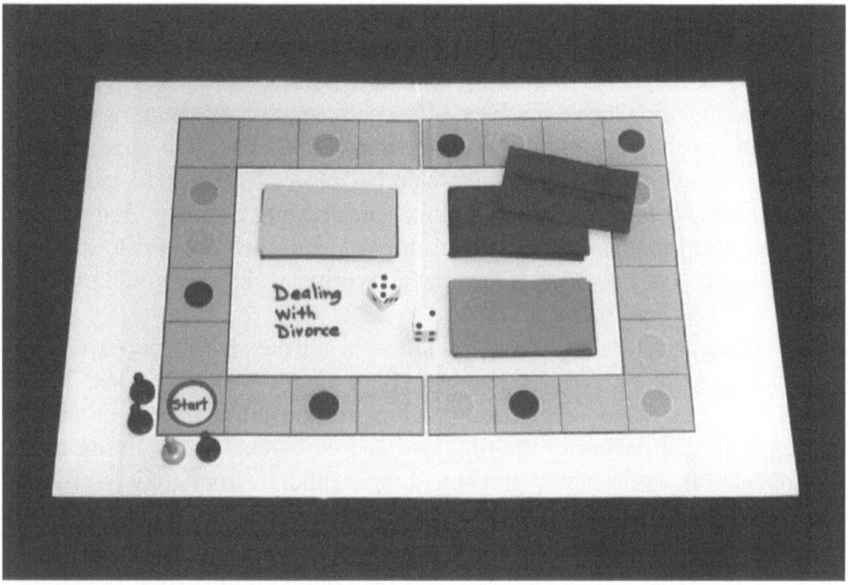

Figure 9.2. Game Courtesy of Pam Dyson

since the divorce, what I would tell a friend whose parents are getting a divorce, and something about my family that will never change.

Sand tray therapy is another intervention that preadolescents are often drawn toward. They are sometimes hesitant to create a sand tray spontaneously and will ask what they should make. In these cases, I provide them with a prompt; I may ask them to tell me about their family using animals. I have a variety of miniatures such as wild, domestic, and fantasy animals. Once preadolescents have selected an animal for each member of their families, I ask them to identify who is represented and to describe how each person is similar to the animal. I wrap up the intervention with asking them to create scenes, or tell stories, in the sand tray where the animals are doing something together. Other directive sand tray prompts include drawing a line down the middle of the tray to create two halves; I call the prompt "before and after." For example, if preadolescents experienced the death of a parent, I will prompt them to create what it was like before their parent died on one side of the tray, and on the other side of the tray what it was like after their parent died. With a follow-up prompt, I sometimes ask them to create a scene of how they think life will be in one year or five years.

Collage work offers opportunities for preadolescents to be creative and imaginative as they sort through magazine clippings picking out images and words that resonate with them. It has been my experience that when adolescents flip through old magazines searching for images and words, they are often influenced by an article or ad that contains an image. To lessen this influence, I provide a basket of images that I have previously clipped myself. In addition to magazine clippings, I provide assorted colors and textures of paper, scissors, glue, pens, markers, oil pastels, sequins, feathers, ribbon, and yarn. Some of the prompts I give for creating a collage are to create a self-portrait, a wish for the future, or a calming place. Background music can provide a serene atmosphere when clients are creating a collage, should they give me permission to play it. Instrumental and classical music are two options I offer, but I also ask if they have favorite music they would prefer to play.

A writing activity that I have found useful for preadolescents experiencing anxiety is called "What I Know, What I Don't Know" (Lyons, 2013). This activity assists preadolescents in taking responsibility over their anxiety management and decreases the time and energy parents spend trying to accommodate the environment and shield their children from anxiety-provoking stimuli. In the activity, I draw a line down the middle of a piece of paper to form two columns. I write the heading "What I Know" over the column on the left and "What I Don't Know" over the column on the right (see figure 9.3).

Let's imagine a preadolescent has just learned that their parents are filing for divorce. I will direct him to list what he knows about the divorce in the column on the left and what he doesn't know in the column on the right. For example, he might know the family will be moving, that his mother will be getting a job, and that the divorce was not his fault. The preadolescent may not know if he will be able to keep the family dog, if he will have to change schools, or when the divorce will be final. I put the list into a folder for preadolescent clients to take home and instruct them, over the course of the next week, to continue to add to the list. In addition, if they learn the answer to something they did not know, they move it over to the other column. We review the list together in our next session. This activity helps preadolescents see that they usually know more than they realized, that they cannot possibly know everything, and that they will be okay, even if they do not know exactly what will be happen. Another dimension can be added to this technique by attaching the piece of paper to a clipboard. Holding a clipboard while making a list of all the things you know can be very empowering to a preadolescent, as the person holding the clipboard in a situation is usually the one who has power or importance.

This is a small sampling of some of the directive play therapy techniques I use with preadolescents. The activities can be modified to fit the needs of each individual client. Experience has taught me that these techniques are valuable tools that can help preadolescents process experiences, work

Figure 9.3. What I Know. Courtesy of Pam Dyson

through challenges, and learn new skills in playful, creative, and engaging ways.

CASE STUDY

Christopher, a ten-year-old boy, was referred to me by his parents, Bruce and Michelle, at the suggestion of his school counselor. He was having negative interactions with peers at school that would sometimes end in physical attacks. His inability to appropriately manage his frustration and his lack of social skills were concerning, not only to his parents but to his school as well. In the past two months, Christopher's negative interactions with peers were occurring more frequently, and the school would sometimes phone his parents asking them to pick him up early. In the week before they called me, he shoved a classmate and was suspended for two days.

Bruce and Michelle came in for a consultation and shared that as an only child Christopher had few interactions with other children his own age outside of the school setting. He primarily spent his free time playing video games alone. They were not only concerned about Christopher's behaviors at school but also the amount of class time he was missing as a result of being sent out of the classroom due to his negative behaviors. Furthermore, they were not sure they could continue taking time off work to pick him up early from school. We mutually decided that I would begin seeing Christopher for weekly play therapy sessions to help him manage his frustration and learn appropriate ways to interact with peers.

In his first session, Christopher expressed interest in the sand tray, so I asked him to create a scene about something that happened at school recently. He selected a miniature for himself and one for a friend, whom he buried in the sand. He told me, "He doesn't want to be my friend." Christopher tried to rescue the friend using a helicopter but after several attempts he dropped it and said, "It didn't work." He resisted my attempts to discuss the scene any further. During his second session, he told me he was still having trouble getting his friend back. I prompted him to use the sand tray and miniatures to find another way. This time, Christopher added additional rescue figures, but he gave up easily and said nothing would work. When he entered the playroom for his third session he announced, "I got my friend back!" I asked him to show me in the sand tray and, without hesitation, he selected miniatures for himself and his friend. The miniature representing Christopher said to the miniature representing the friend, "I'm sorry I shoved you. Can we be friends again?" The friend said, "Yes," and decided to go play.

During Christopher's third session, we played a board game I had created that included game cards exploring how to handle frustrating situations. He enjoyed playing the game and his responses were thoughtful. After Christopher's three sessions, I met with Bruce and Michelle for a follow-up consultation. They were pleased to tell me that the number of incidents at school had decreased significantly, the school wasn't calling every day, and they only had to pick him up once in the past week. We scheduled three more play therapy sessions. During sessions four, five, and six, Christopher and I played board games and created more sand tray scenes depicting situations at school. The interactions between the miniatures were sometimes negative, but they usually had positive endings. I was encouraged to see that he was learning how to solve problems in a positive way and was hopeful he was implementing those strategies at school.

After Christopher's sixth session I met with Bruce and Michelle for another consultation. They told me his teacher had shared with them that she noticed a great change in his behavior, but in the past week he had hit several classmates. They were all discouraged and disappointed. I reminded his parents that sometimes progress takes more time than we would like and that it is not unusual for things to backslide before they improve. I encouraged them to try and stay focused on Christopher's ability to make changes in his behavior in order to be successful at school.

In preparation for Christopher's seventh session, I chose a set of game cards dealing with social interactions in school. I planned to use them along with Jenga®. When the session began, I dumped out the blocks and said to Christopher, "We need to build the block tower before we can play. With each row of three blocks we add, we're going to share things that we like in a friend or things we can do to be a good friend." We created a list with many ideas, including taking turns, playing what your friend wants to play, and sitting together at lunch. Once the tower was built, we took turns pulling blocks, picking a game card from a pile and responding to the situation.

I read one of my cards out loud: "A kid at school calls you a jerk. What can you do?" I paused for a moment to concentrate on an answer and noticed that Christopher was watching me very intently. I took a deep breath and replied, "You could hit him." Christopher's eyes grew wide; he leaned across the table toward me and said, "That's not a good answer." I replied, "The card didn't ask for a good answer. It just asked what you can do, so that's why I said you could hit him." Christopher rolled his eyes, shook his head, and said, "If you hit him you'll get sent to the principal's office. They'll call your parents. They'll tell your parents to pick you up and take you home. If it happens again they'll suspend you. If you get suspended a lot your parents might decide to homeschool you." Then he grinned. "Oh," I said. "You like the idea of being homeschooled." He replied, "Yea, because you could play video games all day." Then he grinned again. We continued playing the game with me asking, "What else could you do if a kid calls you a jerk?" We explored several possibilities: ignore him; take some deep breaths; tell the teacher. I helped him identify situations with peers that triggered his anger, and we worked on more effective ways of responding to those peers. I phoned Christopher's parents the next day and asked them to come in for a brief consultation. I shared with them what Christopher had told me and that I wondered if they were contemplating homeschooling. They were surprised that Christopher had mentioned it to me because they had not spoken to him about it. I told them it's not unusual for children to overhear conversations or parts of conversations and try to make sense of the information they heard. Christopher's parents asked me if it was possible that when he thought there was an option to be homeschooled, his negative behaviors increased. I agreed that it was very probable.

Christopher's parents told me they had made the decision not to homeschool. I encouraged them to sit down with Christopher to explain the situation to him and validate his wanting to be homeschooled while explaining why it was not an option for their family. I also suggested they explore possible ways for Christopher to have interactions with peers outside of the school day to have more opportunities to use his social skills. They were later able to discover events through their local recreation center and their faith community and also began scheduling play dates at their home for Christopher.

I continued to see Christopher weekly for the next two months. As his behaviors at school improved and he became involved in community activities, his parents wondered if it was time to terminate therapy. My recommendation was not to end abruptly but to gradually taper treatment having sessions every other week for two months and then one session per month for two months. After that, they could bring him back as needed for what I refer to as "maintenance sessions," similar to taking a child to the pediatrician for a well-child check. My last few sessions with Christopher were spent identifying situations with peers that were sometimes problematic and exploring appropriate ways of responding. He left my office as a preadolescent who knew how to problem solve and overcome feelings of frustration.

INCORPORATION OF FAMILY

Today's parents are under tremendous stress, and they may be experiencing a wide variety of emotions regarding the challenges of raising a preadolescent. Meeting with parents on a regular basis to discuss therapeutic progress will keep the parents involved and invested in the process. My protocol is to meet with parents after every three child therapy sessions. This gives parents an opportunity to share how their preadolescent is doing at home and at school and me the chance to offer them strategies to support their child (Dyson, 2015). I consider it crucial to acknowledge their feelings and convey empathy so they feel heard and understood. I utilize a technique I created many years ago that I call a "Parenting Metaphor Kit" (see figure 9.4).

The kit is an assortment of miniatures such as animals, a paper clip, super hero, key, compass, rubber band, a battery, sink stopper, bandage, rubber eraser, fishing bobber, battery, and a piece of rope. When I meet with parents, I display the miniature items on a tray or table top and ask them to take a few minutes to look them over and select one item that symbolizes their current parenting experiences. After they have selected one I ask them to share how that item is similar to how they feel about parenting. A parent might select a fishing bobber and say she feels like she can barely keep her head above the water. A rubber band may represent a parent who feels he is ready to snap. Selecting a compass may represent a need for direction while a battery may symbolize feeling depleted. I ask questions about the selected item such as, "How long have you been feeling this way?" or "How do you wish things were different?" The questions are structured to generate self-understanding and help with identifying parenting issues that need to be addressed. While processing the activity I reflect their feelings, validate their experiences, and express empathy. Integrating a parenting metaphor kit into parent consultation presents a concrete way of working that helps them feel heard and understood, creates a sense of connection between parents and the play therapist, and provides vital information for the play therapist.

Parents often share with me that they are reluctant to give their preadolescent more freedom or to allow them to contribute to decision making. Parents

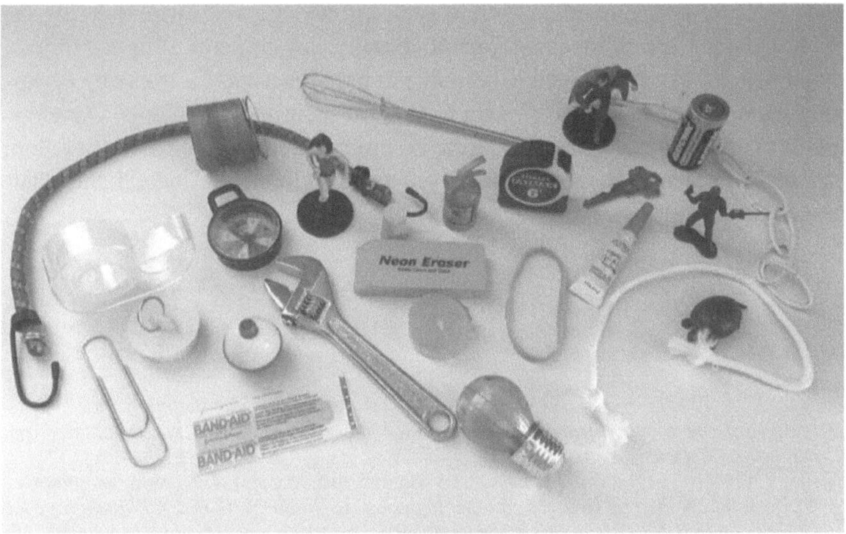

Figure 9.4. Metaphors. Courtesy of Pam Dyson

may feel threatened when their child is more interested in spending time with peers instead of with family. They may feel they are no longer as significant as they once were in the life of their child. Many parents tell me that their preadolescent argues with them about rules. They struggle with being consistent, and they are often short on patience. Even though preadolescents may appear to be able to function on their own, they need ongoing involvement from their parents. Parents who support and monitor their preadolescents help to buffer them from stress and prepare them for the transition to adolescence (Davies, 2011). Helping parents understand the typical developmental aspect of preadolescents is so important. When I share with them that other parents have similar concerns it normalizes their experience and they feel hopeful rather than helpless about the future.

REFLECTION AND CONCLUSION

Play therapy can provide a safe place for preadolescents to express their feelings and make sense of their world. When directive play therapy techniques are utilized, preadolescents can learn coping skills, discover their own strengths and resiliency, and improve their concept of self. There are many issues for play therapists to consider when working with preadolescents, as these youth often experience a wide variety of life experiences that can disrupt their developmental progress and functioning at home and school.

Play therapists who wonder what behaviors are developmentally appropriate and which ones are atypical should seek knowledge and understanding by reading books on child development. Finally, an empathic, highly trained play therapist can be a valuable resource to preadolescents' parents by equipping them with the skills they need to support their preadolescents. Developmental knowledge can and should be communicated to parents so they, too, can better understand their preadolescents' developmental needs and challenges (Dyson, 2015).

REFERENCES

Davies, D. (2011). *Child development: A practitioner's guide* (3rd ed.). New York: Guilford Press.

Drewes, A. A. (2009). Preface. In Drewes, A. A. (Ed.), *Blending play therapy with cognitive behavioral therapy: Evidence-based and other effective treatments and techniques* (pp. xvii–xx). Hoboken, NJ: John Wiley.

Dyson, P. (2015). The traumatic aftermath of parental abandonment, separation, and divorce: Play and family therapy to deal with ongoing crisis. In Webb, N. B. (Ed.), *Play therapy for children and adolescents in crisis: Practitioners share their most effective techniques* (4th ed.) (pp. 179–195). New York: Guilford Press.

Leggett, E. S. & Boswell, J. N. (2017) Directive play therapy. In E. S. Leggett & J. N. Boswell (Eds.), *Directive play therapy: Theories and techniques* (pp. 1–15) New York: Springer Publishing Company.

Lowenstein, L. (1999). *Creative interventions for troubled children and youth.* Toronto, Canada: Champion Press.

Lyons, L. (2013, Jan/Feb). Taming the wild things: Helping anxious kids and their parents. *Psychotherapy Networker, 37,* 38–45.

Shokouhi, A. M., Limberg, D., & Armstrong, S. A. (2014). Counseling preadolescents: Utilizing developmental cues to guide therapeutic approaches. *International Journal of Play Therapy, 23,* (4), 217–230. Photos by John Dyson.

Chapter Ten

Sandplay Therapy with Preteens

Audrey Punnett

Often it is necessary to clarify a vague content by giving it a visible form . . . the hands know how to solve a riddle with which the intellect has wrestled in vain.-—C. G. Jung, 1916/1957, par. 180

Sandplay promotes what Jung referred to as the transcendent function, making possible a completely new outlook on life. By bringing the unconscious and conscious together in sandplay, significant changes in the conscious attitude toward the unconscious take place. Just as in all kinds of play the symbolic process in sandplay is very natural and can act as a bridge into the psychic realm. Thus, as the above quote from Jung suggests, the use of the hands in the sand promotes a process of awareness previously unknown.

The symbols represented by miniatures in the sandplay process are thought of as tools of expression that enable our patients to reveal unconscious aspects and subtleties of their inner thoughts and feelings that speech and gestures may fail to communicate. These symbols connect our patients to unknown aspects of themselves and thus can carry the potential for transformation and healing. Since the symbols arise spontaneously from two sources, the unconscious and one's own personal experience, it is important to attend to what the symbol means personally to the patient and not jump to conclusions that are offered in symbol dictionaries. Building from the patient's personal associations, the therapist can then amplify the symbol by looking into mythological, religious, and folktale representations. Making these connections can give meaning and depth to the process.

The preteen, ages nine to twelve, is developmentally in the latter part of the period of industry versus inferiority, according to Erikson (1980), where the neighborhood and school are the main source of human relationships. The preteen is busy learning to be competent and productive using skills, tools, and intelligence to gain recognition for his or her accomplishments with a sense of effectiveness leading to industry. As a result the preteen is usually very interested in the sand.

During this developmental period, we characteristically see sequential storytelling, beginning of abstract images with the use of "knights, soldiers, horses, family constellations," as well as "mythic fantasy, dungeons and princesses" (Amatruda & Simpson, 1997, p. 54). In addition, the fighting stage continues, the world portrayed is seen as a whole, "organization of patterns and interdependence of parts is portrayed," there is "symbolic representation of towns or villages, landscapes with human settlements are common," and "animals are now represented more realistically" (Grubbs, 2005, pp. 16–17).

The case below will demonstrate how sandplay was used to promote a boy's healing and discuss the limitations his family had in addressing his emotional needs. The child therapist always must balance the needs of the child with the needs and capabilities of the parents/caregivers.

LITERATURE REVIEW

As therapists, we must be open to what occurs in the time we have and what happens in our relationship with a particular patient. C. G. Jung has summarized this by saying: "We must be able to let things happen in the psyche. For us, this is an art of which most people know nothing. Consciousness is forever interfering, helping, correcting, and negating, never leaving the psychic process to grow in peace" (Jung, 1929, CW 13, par. 20).

The symbolic is important in working with sandplay as differentiated from working with a sand tray, which does not emphasize the symbols. A word or an image becomes symbolic when it implies something more than its obvious meaning (Jung et al., 1964). The symbols point to something deep and complex that cannot be reduced to a simple verbal concept; its totality is beyond conscious grasp. At times symbols are numinous and can open up the possibility for the preteen to become acquainted with unknown aspects of the self and to reconnect with his or her authentic nature.

Dora Kalff is the founder of sandplay therapy and the founder of the International Society of Sandplay Therapy (ISST), the organization that certifies sandplay therapists in her tradition. Creating that "free and sheltered space" (Kalff, 1980, p. 29) within the therapeutic room that encourages and supports patients in using and experiencing symbols can have at least two significant benefits. First, connecting with symbols that have personal importance for a patient prompts the transcendent function. The unconscious awakens resulting in transformation and eventual healing. Second, understanding the meaning of the symbols represented in the miniatures or in how the sand is molded can help a therapist understand what the patient is communicating both consciously and unconsciously, enabling the therapist to be of greater help to the patient. That is, we understand the struggles beyond those the patient can express verbally.

It is important to maintain a metaphorical attitude when following the symbolic process, to not take so concretely what the person portrays in the sand. With this kind of attitude the patient's issues, strengths, and direction of the healing process can emerge with more clarity. In that light it is helpful when the therapist has gained a broad understanding of the language of the unconscious and is able to follow the process and help the patient establish connections to their external life situation. This is one reason why the personal process of the sandplay therapist is so important, that we experience for ourselves this deep connection to the unconscious. Then we know what it means to go to this place; we can then be sensitive to when our patients have gone there themselves.

In Jungian psychology, the suffering of the mind is seen less as a curable disturbance but more as a necessity and impulse for psychological development. Sandplay offers a way of connecting to the self and, according to Mare-Louise von Franz (Jung et al., 1964), this connection to the self allows healing, health, and the potential for fulfilling one's destiny.

We all know that playing with sand comes very naturally for children. Often as soon as I introduce the sand tray to the child as one of the possibilities they might do in the playroom, they are off and have collected a number of objects to begin their play.

A sandplay process is unique to each individual. It is not helpful to make generalizations. In sandplay we withhold judgments. We accept the uniqueness of the individual and their ways of coping and dealing with their lives. It is within this safe "space" that the healing of the inner psychological wound can occur; the self can be activated and the inner child rediscovered with all its potential for creativity and renewal.

Research in evaluating sandplay has been challenging, but qualitative phenomenological studies, mixed methods (quasi-experimental with quantitative data), and heuristic and phenomenological methods have been used to evaluate the sandplay process (Freedle, Altschul, & Freedle, 2015; Ramos & da Matta, 2008; Mandelbaum, 2008; Freedle, 2007; Reece, 2004). Parent reports of the child's progress using the Child Behavior Checklist have also been used, showing improvement in behaviors (von Gontard, 2010). An unpublished quantitative study by the author has shown improvement in positive verbalizations over the course of a sandplay process.

PRACTICAL INTERVENTION

For sandplay, the play therapy room is ideally equipped with two sand trays, one for wet sand and the other for dry sand. The dimensions for the trays are provided in Kalff's book *Sandplay: A Psychotherapeutic Approach to the Psyche* (2003). At the beginning of therapy, I usually introduce the sand trays while I am giving the child a tour of the playroom and all that it holds. I might move the sand in the tray so the child sees it has a blue bottom. Then the child is free to choose this as they would any other item in the playroom. The sandplay can be quite useful for children who have difficulty directly talking about their problems as it gives access to visually creating scenes, which may help to work out the issues.

In sandplay the therapist does not play in the sand with the child, but rather remains the observer and holder of the process. The therapist sits in a chair nearby watching; some therapists will make notes, although most children want your undivided attention. At the conclusion of the play, and if the child has not told a story along the way, the therapist might ask if they have anything they might like to say about the scene. The scene is left intact until the child leaves. After the child leaves the therapist photographs the scene.

CASE STUDY

The following case illustrates the typical stages of development through a sandplay process. Through the sandplay, this eleven-year-old boy was able to do what he needed to heal. For John (pseudonym), a maternal space or psychological womb, an emotional metaphor for the uroboric mother–child unit (Neumann, 1990), was provided.

The sandplay process usually involves a beginning that tells you the problem, a middle where the connection is made to the self, and an end in which the person is functioning better within the collective/society. We continue evolving all of our lives, but one can complete a particular phase with a therapist and when this phase has been adequately completed, both the patient and the therapist recognize this. This was the case with John.

In an ideal world we would be able to complete the process, but often our cases are interrupted by a variety of factors: moves, unforeseen stresses, and a multitude of reasons. Dora Kalff stated, "It is often very difficult for the parents of troubled children to have the necessary understanding and patience to wait for a complete cure. This is particularly true because we are dealing with the irrational events of a hidden psychic process" (Kalff, 1980, p. 139). Often the child showing improvement can lead parents to stop the treatment prematurely, as was the case with John. What do we do in these circumstances?

Therapists often experience pain observing a psyche that wants to heal and then having the therapy end suddenly or too soon. Frequently, parents see progress in behaviors, and think that's enough. This is when we must educate the caregivers, while attending to the child's needs within the family context, the family's needs, and ultimately understanding the motivation for the premature withdrawal.

The Jungian-oriented child therapist recognizes the individual psyche and that the patient is not "fixed" by the therapy, but rather has the creative resources to continue to grow and develop as an individual and as a social being within the context of family, peers, and society.

Typically we know the ending is coming when a child who often eagerly awaited his or her sessions would now rather play with their friends and sees the therapist being in the way of their daily life. The transition is made for the child to then look to the therapeutic playroom as a place they can revisit, should the need arise sometime in the future. This would be the natural progression of the therapy.

The process with John was over a sixteen-month period; there were forty sessions and fifty-one trays. It is not possible to go through each of these trays to understand the depth of what was being communicated or experienced. I will describe the first tray, one in the middle that demonstrates the activation of the self, and then a tray toward the end that shows the symbolic representation of how deeply he goes and that a healing has taken place.

Briefly, I will begin with some background history. John was referred by the international school he attended for psychological consultation. He showed negativity toward his school, difficulty taking instruction, and difficulty doing group work, which began after returning from a Christmas holiday to the States, six months after the family moved to Europe.

I met with John and recommended weekly psychotherapy. However, after I met with him and his parents, his problems at school abated and his parents elected not to follow through with my recommendation. At the beginning of the following school year, approximately five months later, his parents contacted me again when their son expressed suicidal thoughts and behaviors at a sixth-grade school retreat. John commented that he wished to die, isolated himself from the other children, and was seen by a teacher with one leg over a railing on a bridge as if he were going to jump. As a result of this incident the parents recontacted me to initiate psychotherapy.

John came from an intact family and had two younger brothers. Significant to the history was his maternal grandfather's death when John was age two years eight months; at the time John's mother was eight months pregnant with her second child. His father observed John was very sensitive to his mother's feelings at this time as she was quite upset by her father's death. John's mother was not able to go to the funeral since they were living abroad and she could not fly due to the late stage of pregnancy. There was a family history of depression on the father's side.

Pertinent to the developmental history was that John had difficulty sleeping through the night until about three years of age. He woke up every night and his mother would help him get back to sleep by lying in bed next to him until he fell asleep. He also was very orderly and would line up his toys rather than play with them.

Academically he did well and was tested in the superior range of intelligence. While attending elementary school in the States, he participated in band, had friends, but could sound like a know-it-all. The transition to a new school overseas was difficult for this fifth grader and he felt he did not fit in, there was no band, and he had no friends. He tried to logically persuade his father to return to the States stating, "I've had enough of it here." He seemed to carry the weight of the world on his shoulders and tried to make rational sense out of everything, including that other children did not like him because he was an American. He experienced that no one understood the depth of his suffering and hence his suicidal thoughts. He denied that he would have actually hurt himself and realized later how much this would have hurt his parents. He was not considered a suicidal threat and he promised he would contact me should these feelings arise again, but they did not return.

It was apparent to me that he was sensitive to his mother's feelings and that he experienced his father as emotionally distant. He seemed to have the greatest difficulty with aggressive feelings, which he handled by intellectual overcompensation, but this defense was no longer effective for him.

He complained of headaches, which came only when he was unhappy. His parents were quite rational and logical and had difficulty understanding the emotions their son displayed.

John met the criteria for major depression as manifested by depressed mood, diminished pleasure in almost all activities of the day, feelings of restlessness, loss of energy, feelings of worthlessness and guilt, and recurrent thoughts of death. These symptoms had been increasing for the past six months prior to treatment.

When I met John for the second time, he told me he was relieved to be coming to therapy. He had told his parents he felt comfortable with me and was looking forward to the sessions; I felt a comfortable cotransference had been established. He expressed guilt over his behavior at the camp and said he would never do this again.

At this time, I introduced him to the playroom and all that it contained, including the sand tray. He immediately began working in the sand and for all but one session he spontaneously used the sand tray while he talked.

John called his first tray "Times Square" (see figure 10.1), a favorite place in New York City where he stated the family would often take visitors; he then quickly erased it and made a second tray. As a result, I reconstructed the first tray after the session ended. He described this second tray as "a fight scene in a village in Warsaw in 1941" portraying the fight between good and bad, which was like the black and white reality he experienced.

To begin analyzing a tray, one generally starts with a first impression of the tray and then takes this in by using the four functions: *Sensation*—what are the facts here, what objects are used; *Thinking*—how do these things connect, use of space, organization, proportions, space, perspective, and numbers; *Feeling*—what is the emotional value of this tray and motives related to this tray; and *Intuition*—where does this tray come from, where does it go. This analysis helps one orient to the possible messages, both positive and negative.

In observing this first tray we note it is devoid of any objects. He uses the wet sand so it can be molded and shaped. He goes to the blue bottom, suggesting he goes below the surface here. This is like a map; one has a perspective view from above looking down from the top.

This is a familiar scene and one that had pleasant memories for him. He is bringing back a happy memory to what he now experiences as a life devoid

Figure 10.1. Session 1. Description: Wet sand: Six "roads" were symmetrically placed in the wet sand intersecting in the middle; the blue is exposed and there were no figures or objects. Reprinted with permission from client

of anything pleasant. He tells how his family took visitors to a very glitzy part of America; it is filled with actors and plays and is not very relational. I wonder whether this could be part of his experience of lacking emotional connection on a deeper level.

He had six roads coming together. The number six is the so-called perfect number either adding up or multiplying its divisors results in the number itself (1 + 2 + 3 = 6 and 1 x 2 x 3 = 6). Taken as a sum, the six was looked upon as the union of the 3 and the 2 representing heaven and earth added together with the original 1 representing the creative principle. Taken as the sum of 5 + 1, the six was considered as the union of the natural man with his creator, the godhead (Abt, 2005).

As 1 x 2 x 3, the 6 was understood to be composed of two triangles. The downward-facing triangle symbolizes water and the feminine; the upward facing triangle symbolizes fire and the masculine. When put together it equals a hexagram and the union of fire and water (Abt, 2005). Note how the larger triangle is the one that symbolizes water and the feminine. In addition, the number 6 is connected with Aphrodite (having 6 curls) and since she signifies beauty and love, I wondered if this foretold of his longing for connection to Eros.

Recall from the history that this was a family that valued logical reasoning, but even using logic John could not engage his father. Geometrically, the 6 is also connected to the perfect form because the radius of a circle allows exactly its own dividing up by 6.

Since the circle is the perfect form, it is a well-known symbol for totality and the godhead; the number 6 is related to the *macrocosmos* and the creator (Abt, 2005). The number 6 is related to rhythmical or circular time; it takes about 6 full circles of the moon for a year to unfold and another 6 circles to complete it. Water, the symbol for cyclical change, is also connected to the 6, namely when it is transformed to snow; the snow crystal has this basic structure.

Thus, the appearance of the number 6 in his tray could possibly point to a creative joining of the opposites in his actual life—that is, a joining of the logos, thinking function with the Eros, the emotional function.

The appearance of a map is literally showing me his experience and the possibility for change. He also made a second tray in this session, which as previously mentioned illustrated a fight between the good guys and the bad guys, a literal representation of the reality he experiences. In addition, his sense of isolation, his feelings of aggression, which he quickly projects onto others, his feelings of insecurity, and his need to be in a safe place where he can control his emotions and have an opportunity to be mirrored and not to be judged, are all crucial to the therapy. Thus, from analyzing these trays, one can ascertain the needed direction of treatment.

In the beginning phase of treatment, he continues to make trays each session. One can observe the potential for tremendous passions and emotions, which may enrich him if conducted along the proper channel, but right now there is a very one-sided development. His male ego begins to strengthen its resistance to the feminine principle—that is, to develop his own sense of self, specifically to separate from the mother (developmentally appropriate). Also during this time there is an intense transference in which he engages in giving voice to all his feelings about not being listened to or being validated by his parents and others. John would intermittently be talking to me with his shoulders back and his face within inches of my face as he loudly explained the injustices he experienced. The suffering he experienced was held within the therapeutic container. During this first phase of treatment his depression lessens as his unconscious brings together the primitive and cultural levels and shows the extreme nature of the two sides he confronts.

In this next phase of the treatment, John becomes more aware of the part he plays in developing peer and adult relationships, and this is mirrored to him so he can experience being heard and seen; with this there is increased ego strength. It was also during this time he was moved to an intellectually more challenging classroom with positive results. He is connecting his emotions and his good intellect in a more positive way, differentiating his feelings. In this middle phase of treatment, John makes a mandala scene in the wet sand, which he describes as an "old village" with a wall around it (see figure 10.2). He tells me during this session that he now has certain things he does not want to tell his mother because he does not want her to yell at him. He is figuring out which things he can handle on his own.

This is a centering, a structuring where the ego has become more differentiated and is now a constellation of his inner world and the self. This scene is a protected space where he can live, and it is a social place. Even though the walls emphasize the protection needed, perhaps his fragility, the gate allows connections to the outside in a way that can be controlled on a personal level.

For the rest of this phase of the treatment there is room to explore inner development and the ego is acquiring more structure and differentiation. He talks about difficulties in being understood by his father, who will listen but does not change. He also portrays scenes related to the mother, who does not "see" him and his struggles. He says his parents are "good parents, but they don't understand my wishes." John is now making friends and being recognized for his good sense of humor. He is more relaxed and flexible. With this improvement, the parents want to stop the therapy.

At this announcement by his parents, John thought that this particular session would be the last; it was during this session that he made ten trays, telling me a story of an old army camp that had been abandoned, how the air force buys the town and will renovate and open a base. There is a legend that a bomb is buried in the lake, but after many cycles of storms and erosion,

Figure 10.2. Session 21. Description: Wet sand: In the center of the tray is a village with a wall around it. One pathway divides the village vertically. Horizontally there is a pathway to the right with another pathway coming off this one perpendicularly; there is another horizontal pathway a little higher on the left. There are four houses in the right upper section; one house in the left upper section; two houses, one church, and two tents (blue and yellow) in the left lower section; and four houses in the right lower section, two on each side of a pathway. At the far right end of the pathway is a tunnel to the outside. The pathways are made from wooden blocks. Reprinted with permission from client

they are successful with the reconstruction and the air force rebuilds and can conduct more tests there.

John is informed that there will be more sessions after he returns from summer holiday. I have negotiated with his parents for seven more once-a-month sessions. After the seven months, I knew I would be returning to the States within a few months. When he comes back from holiday, he makes a vacant tray, just swirling his hand back and forth in the tray as he tells me about his time in the States and what he would like to do the following school year; he is glad to be back overseas. This tray evokes the emptiness, which is perhaps a state of fullness of all that is and contains infinite possibilities for "being." This could be a transition for him; it is a state where all is empty, a state that is archetypal and formless.

During this last phase of treatment, John now goes very deeply to an archetypal level. In this second-to-last tray (see figure 10.3), he states that this is a "Middle Eastern Sumerian thing with canals; this is the desert end" (pointing to the left end).

John talks about the children who annoy him at school, and he talks about the years at school that have been difficult, especially the first half of sixth grade. He thinks the headaches he had were related to stress regarding his homework. Interestingly, as he talks and is listened to and validated, his mood improves. He says he does not want to continue with therapy because "I just need to get over things."

He says his father does not understand and gets impatient but that his mother is more understanding. The mother calls, stating she thinks John has made big changes because overall he is now joining group activities and having a good time with peers outside of school; she thinks his "up and down" behavior is just him. John is showing an interest in girls and talking

Figure 10.3. Session 39. Description: Wet and dry sand: He mixes water with the sand and three-fourths of the tray is wet. The tray is divided into four parts and bounded by bricks with blue between the divisions; there is dry sand to the left and no bricks on this portion. In the center are two bricks laid flat and then one brick placed vertically on top. Reprinted with permission from client

about this with her, she thinks he is making more of a separation from her and views this as positive.

The mother does not think it is necessary to have another session with her and her husband. In fact, she tells me that even having John continue at this pace has caused conflict between them and that it must end as planned.

John's mother requests my attendance at a school meeting because John has stated he does not want to participate in some group activities at school, and the teachers are "upset." In this meeting, John stated he is feeling that he doesn't deserve anything in the world and feels that others talk about him and that he can't trust others. At this meeting, I reiterated that John have a place to decompress when he becomes upset—we agreed that he could go to his tutor's office or to the nurse's office. Since John would be stopping the therapy, the tutor would follow up on the group dynamics and assist John more directly with this.

In his second-to-last tray, John constructed the irrigation system of the Sumerians (see figure 10.3). Farming in this region depended on irrigation from the Tigris and Euphrates rivers. The irrigation system had a catch-22 aspect: if irrigation water was allowed to sit on the fields and evaporate, it left behind mineral salts; if attempts were made to drain off irrigation water and it flowed through the soil too quickly, then erosion became a problem. Some towns collapsed when the destruction of the fields by mineral salts occurred because the high concentration of mineral salts became poisonous for the plants.

He really is in a catch-22 with continuing the therapy. John knows we have one more session and he states he does not want further therapy. As painful as it is, I realize that John has done a significant piece of work and that the family dynamics are such that continuation is not possible.

John's father is not willing to consider further treatment because of the gains he has seen and his unwillingness to consider further intervention. His father's attitude has caused stress on the marriage and it is not possible at this time to intervene further with the parents. From the history, there is depression in the paternal side of the family. Thus, there is a shadow that cannot be touched at this time.

In the last session, John makes a tray he called "a park" and speaks of the death of the maternal grandfather that precipitated the depression in the mother. He says his (maternal) grandfather would be proud of this scene because he was a gardener. There something died, a loss of the person, as well as a metaphoric loss of the value of life. Given this association, one can see the value in taking a thorough history.

The park is a place to rest and to be oneself, there is the access to water, to his inner vitality as symbolized by the water, although it is a controlled access. The gardener, as one who attends to the park, may have a different attitude to nature/plants and a certain aliveness that is thinking oriented and working with the sensation function. Something got lost those years ago and now he brings it back up.

There were no people in the last tray, perhaps suggesting John is more of an introvert. He has to make the bridge to his parents, who are different from each other, and to be in both of their worlds. John has a hard time with the demanding part of his father and he needs the resources of his mother to deal with him.

The last tray to me symbolized that John would have to go forth with still more work to be done, but he completed a process in the time we had. He had to live in this family and he would have to survive. However, it is a collective scene with the possibility of interactions with others in a more natural way, in contrast to the first tray. He also has a spiritual connection as symbolized by the cross (which appeared in various trays throughout his process) that seems to be with him after his connection with the self. He has become in touch with a creative power.

John and I reviewed his progress and he was quite pleased by his gains. His mother and I talked briefly at the end of this last session. I informed her I had spoken with their pediatrician and also given the doctor the name of a colleague with whom John could work. She thanked me for all that I had done with John.

INCORPORATION OF FAMILY

I always incorporate both parents in the initial intake. This was especially important in this case as the father recalled the mother's reaction to her father's death and I was able to ascertain the impact on their son. However, the father's brother was depressed and this was difficult for the father to understand as he had compartmentalized his own problems and had little tolerance for emotions. In addition, the father's best friend had committed suicide. John's father felt that as one became closer to feelings there was opportunity for destruction/death. Therefore, as his son improved his father felt there was no need to continue. Despite attempts to have him come in to discuss this, the burden of the therapy remained on the mother, who had to balance her son's needs with those of her marriage. I had to respect her needs. John was able to learn how to manage his emotions and how to live with the father's intolerance.

REFLECTION AND CONCLUSION

John was an eleven-year-three-month-old boy at the time he was referred for treatment because of depression and a suicidal gesture. The treatment ended when he was twelve years seven months of age. There was a good cotransference from the beginning, and being two foreigners from the same country in a different culture helped this bond. His transference was intense in the beginning, and I undertook a focused sorting through of his feelings to assist him to relate to what was going on inside of him. John was helped to formulate his feelings and concepts through my mirroring and validation of his experiences. In addition, he became connected to the spiritual archetypal father as symbolized by the cross in the last tray, which allowed him to be in touch with his creative masculine energy. The *temenos* was a safe and protected space in which John connected with aspects of the self. My interventions with John's school helped facilitate the school's recognizing his strengths and his struggles so he could be seen as a human being, not a problem boy.

John's basic security was disturbed in the second year of life when his mother became depressed after the loss of her father while the family was living abroad. A healthy ego can only develop on the basis of total security between the ages of two to three. There was an estrangement from his father, who could not communicate on an emotional level with his son. Hence, John presented with identification with the patriarchal logos, which was compensating for feelings of inadequacy and insecurity and which he projected onto peers. The maternal container had been insufficient for him to freely express his feelings since his relationship with the mother had a caretaking quality to it. Specifically, he was emotionally present to his mother during the grieving for the maternal grandfather in compensation for the father's lack of expressive feelings—that is, his overly rational personality style. The mother may also have found comfort in parenting her emotionally needy child at this time, projecting what she needed. This defensive structure became overwhelming for John when the family moved to Europe and he no longer had his American peer group. In Europe, John displayed a harsh superego and incapacity to deal with his own shadow, which accounted for his paranoid tendencies—that is, that other children were intentionally being mean to him.

John made significant gains during the time he was seen, with no more suicidal thoughts, decreased depression, making friends, and participating in group activities with an improved positive attitude toward school. He could now tolerate and appreciate differences between European and American cultures. The school could view him as a child needing help, verses a problem child. His mother was empowered to become a better advocate for her son, correcting and rebalancing her relationship to him such that he was no longer in a caretaking role. This had the added benefit of facilitating his independence. Had the work continued, I would have tried to involve his father more, so he could begin to look at his contributions, but for now his mother needed to protect the marriage.

The bridge from which he attempted to jump and the bridges that were manifest in his trays became the metaphor of the meeting of opposites, the rational and emotional. John made significant gains in an imperfect world as his psyche was allowed this space and time for a natural attempt at healing.

This case illustrates the drive for the psyche to heal. Given the constraints of the family, John did a remarkable process and made considerable gains. It is important to remember the context within which we work and to honor the individual for what they can do, not what we think they should do. Fortunately, his parents were willing to concede the importance of making sure that the gains made were firmly rooted before ending the therapy. John acknowledged he was doing better and said he would have preferred twice per month, but given his father's wishes he thought once per month was fine; he did not waiver from this position.

In working with the preteen, sandplay is a worthwhile adjunct to traditional play therapy. Not only does it afford the opportunity for self-expression, it also offers independence and strategies to enhance ego strength as the therapist understands on a deeper level the workings of the psyche.

REFERENCES

Abt, T. (2005). *Introduction to picture interpretation according to C. G. Jung*. Zurich, Switzerland: Living Human Heritage Publications.

Amatruda, K., & Simpson, P. H. (1997). *Sandplay the sacred healing: A guide to symbolic process*. Taos, NM: Trance*Sand*Dance Press.

Erikson, E. H. (1980). *Identity and the life cycle: A reissue*. New York, NY: W. W. Norton & Company.

Freedle, L. R. (2007). Sandplay therapy with traumatic brain injured adults: An exploratory qualitative study. *The Journal of Sandplay Therapy, 16 , 2*, pp. 115–133.

Freedle, L. R., Altschul, D. B., & Freedle, A. (2015). The role of sandplay therapy in the treatment of adolescents and young adults with co-occurring substance use disorders and trauma. *The Journal of Sandplay Therapy, 24, 2*, pp.127–145.

Grubbs, G. (2005). The *Sandplay Categorical Checklist for Sandplay Analysis*. Woodinville, WA: Rubedo Publications.

Jung, C. G. (1953–1979). *The collected works* (Bollingen Series XX; H. Read, M. Fordham, & G. Adler, Eds.; R. F. C. Hull, Trans.). Princeton, NJ: Princeton University Press.

Jung, C. G. (1916/1957). The transcendent function. *The structure and dynamics of the psyche, CW 8*, (pp. 67–91).

Jung, C. G. (1929). Commentary on "The Secret of the Golden Flower." *Alchemical Studies, CW 13*, (pp. 1–55).

Jung, C. G., von Franz, M-L., Henderson, J. L., Jacobi, J., & Jaffe, A. (1964). (Ed. C. G. Jung). *Man and his symbols*. Garden City, NY: Doubleday & Company Inc.

Kalff, D. M. (1980). *Sandplay/A psychotherapeutic approach to the psyche*. Boston, MA: Sigo Press.

Kalff, D. M. (2003). (Ed. B. A. Turner). *Sandplay: A psychotherapeutic approach to the psyche*. Cloverdale, CA: Temonos Press.

Mandelbaum, D. (2008). The therapeutic container in sandplay therapy. *The Journal of Sandplay Therapy, 17, 1*, pp. 115–121.

Neumann, E. (1990). *The Child.* (R. Manheim, trans.). Boston, MA: Shambhala.

Ramos, D. G., & da Matta, R. M. (2008). Sandplay: A method for data analysis. *The Journal of Sandplay Therapy, 17, 2*, pp. 93–115.

Reece, S. (2004). The crucial moment in sandplay relationship: The therapist's emotive experiences. *The Journal of Sandplay Therapy, 13, 1*, pp. 131–146.

von Gontard, A. (2010). Sandplay therapy study: A prospective outcome study of sandplay therapy with children and adolescents. *The Journal of Sandplay Therapy, 19, 2*, pp. 131–140.

Chapter Eleven

Play Therapy in Middle Schools

A Cognitive-Behavioral Play Therapy (CBPT) Approach for Preadolescent Social Skills Development

Laura Fazio-Griffith

Change your thoughts and you change your world.—Norman Vincent Peale

Mental health communities, for more than a decade, have highlighted the need for effective interventions for preadolescents. The U.S. Department of Health and Human Services (2017) ignited alarm when it reported that one in five children suffered from a diagnosable mental, emotional, or behavioral disorder and about one in ten children suffered from a serious emotional disturbance, which becomes more prevalent in preadolescence. The prevalence of mental health issues displayed by children is prominent in the school environment.

Preadolescents and preteens can have great difficulty in developing and maintaining prosocial skills, such as following instructions, using self-control, responding to teasing, and avoiding fighting (Goldstein & McGinnis, 2009). These difficulties with social skills experienced by preadolescents can lead to thoughts of negative expectations and self-deprecation, physiological stress responses, dysfunctional social performance, avoidance of social situations, academic difficulties, and feelings of anxiety, isolation, and depression.

Play-based counseling approaches are needed for preadolescents in the school setting since not all preadolescents respond well to a talk-based cognitive approach (Ray, Armstrong, Balkin, & Jayne, 2015). A group cognitive behavioral play therapy approach with a focus on social skill development can prove effective for middle school students.

LITERATURE REVIEW

From childhood through adolescence, social development is one of the most critical factors in identity formation. Social skills that are taught in childhood are honed, defined, and refocused through adolescence (Feldman, 2014). Preadolescents' social skills development can alternate between superficial and intimate relationships and includes developing advanced levels of empathy, learning to accept rules, and negotiating issues of separation and dependence with their primary caregivers (Vickers, 2002). Play therapy with preadolescents in a peer-based, group setting can be an effective way to assess preadolescents' social functioning level and facilitate prosocial skills (Gallo-Lopez & Schaefer, 2005). For preadolescents with social skills deficits and behavioral concerns, group play can maximize the number of positive interactions experienced with their peers, which is often encouraged as a means of changing dysfunctional behavior patterns (Delaney, 1994). Additionally, group play therapy provides an especially effective modality for preadolescents to learn new social skills and to discover that they are capable of peer acceptance, self-control, and self-acceptance (e.g., Kayler & Sherman, 2009; Shechtman & Pastor, 2005).

The group setting provides a safe haven for preadolescents to practice social skills and explore irrational beliefs without experiencing negative consequences. Group counseling is efficient, effective, and multifaceted (Akos & Milsom, 2007; Gladding, 2012), allowing students to develop and maintain connections to others while exploring factors that influence achievement. Social skill development can be enriched by successful interactions with skillful peers, as well as appropriate interventions by teachers and school therapists. When students exhibit poor social skills it is important to provide interventions that can enhance self-concept and promote impulse control for healthy growth and development. Group counseling combined with a cognitive behavioral play therapy approach allows students to feel connected to their peers, develop life skills, and practice behaviors in the group. In turn, group members' self-esteem will increase as they provide feedback for each other and view each other as active members and resources (Kottman, 2011).

Cognitive-Behavioral Play Therapy (CBPT) Application of Prosocial Skills Groups in the Middle School Setting

Cognitive-behavioral play therapy (CBPT) incorporates theory and interventions from behavior, cognitive, and cognitive-behavioral therapies, within a play therapy paradigm (Corey, 2013; Knell, 2009). Play activities as well as verbal and nonverbal forms of communication are used to resolve problems. The general goal for the preadolescent is to increase the ability to cope with problem situations and stressors, master difficult tasks, decrease faulty thinking patterns, and/ or assist in achieving developmental milestones that have been delayed for some reason (Harrell, Mercer & DeRosier, 2008).

CBPT has six specific properties, or tenets, that provide the foundation for positive outcomes (Knell, 2009):

1. CBPT involves the child in counseling via play.
2. CBPT focuses on the child's thoughts, feelings, fantasies, and environment.
3. CBPT provides a strategy or strategies for developing more adaptive thoughts and behaviors.
4. CBPT is structured, directive, and goal-oriented, rather than open-ended.
5. CBPT incorporates empirically demonstrated techniques such as modeling and role playing.
6. CBPT allows for empirical evaluation of treatment, which can enhance the involvement of parents and stakeholders in the school environment.

Although CBPT is different from traditional play therapy approaches, the development of the relationship and communication patterns established through play are still important tenets of this approach. When combined with group therapy, CBPT focuses on the relationship with both the group leader and the group members, and within the group, concrete, objective goals are established. In sessions, the group works together towards these goals.

CBPT Techniques

The following CBPT techniques can be facilitated by therapists in a middle school group setting to help preadolescents/students develop and hone their social skills.

Modeling

Most of the techniques in CBPT are delivered by the therapist modeling prosocial skills while participants engage with a variety of expressive art materials (e.g., clay, paint). In one activity, the therapist/play therapist selects two clay creations created by members of the group, along with a social skill to focus on in that session. The therapist might say, "We are going to practice listening skills with each other today. I am going to actively listen to 'Sarah' describe her clay piece. I am facing her, providing direct eye contact, sitting with feet firmly on the floor, and acknowledging her description with nonverbal communication." Then, one student explains his or her clay piece, and a second student practices listening skills and models such skills for the rest of the group. The group provides encouragement and positive feedback to the second student, and the activity is repeated until everyone in the group has practiced their listening skills.

Behavioral Rehearsal

Behavioral rehearsal provides an opportunity for therapists to help preadolescents master difficult situations by utilizing appropriate social skills. By rehearsing, new and more functional behaviors are observed and practiced by the students. The goal of behavioral rehearsal is for students to recognize and modify social skill weaknesses by role playing a variety of alternative responses. When using behavioral rehearsal, therapists can provide immediate, concrete feedback, followed by continued rehearsal of problem situations (Knell, 2009).

Therapists can use finger puppets to teach adaptive responses to the group. In this way, social skills are first modeled for the students, and the students can rehearse the new skills. For example, the therapist chooses to focus on dealing with anger and recognizing others' anger as the targeted social skill. The puppets have a dialogue about a situation at school that has made them angry. The therapist helps the puppets express their anger in appropriate ways. The students are then given the opportunity to practice with the puppets and their fellow group members.

Behavioral Contingencies

Behavioral contingencies can be used by therapists to provide rewards in the group setting for acquiring new skills. The students will create a rewards box. Each student will be given a shoe box and asked to decorate it with construction paper, name, and art work. Students will write the different social skills on the outside of their box. The rewards the student would like to earn are written on slips of paper and placed inside the shoe box. Examples of rewards include: homework passes, selection of music to play during group, extended recess or break time during the school day. Once the students have mastered the skills, the skill will be crossed off the outside of the rewards box and rewards are given. A chart can be displayed that indicates the social skills to be mastered, each student's name, and rewards to be earned.

Coping Self-Statements

Preadolescents' ability to cope and function effectively, both socially and academically, depends not on an event that occurs but rather the way they interpret an event. Preadolescents' perception of events can negatively influence their social skill development (Knell, 2009), as negative thoughts lead to negative self-statements, which can then lead to poor decision making and interactions with peers and adults. For example, a preadolescent predicts no one will want to socialize with her at social time, a prediction supported by her negative self-statements such as, "I do not wear the right clothes," or "I always say something stupid." This negative self-talk becomes a sort of self-fulfilling prophecy, as these beliefs then lead to poor social interactions and hinder the development of positive social skills. In a group setting, therapists can help students internalize simple statements about themselves, such as, "I can contribute to the group or other groups." These positive affirmations are written on a ball. One group member throws the ball to another group member; the group member who catches the ball selects a positive affirmation and discusses the meaning of the affirmation. The ball continues to be thrown and caught until all of the affirmations are discussed. The students can apply these affirmations when learning and practicing new skills.

PRACTICAL INTERVENTION

Bibliotherapy is used to teach social skills, through a storytelling approach, to preadolescents in a group setting. Books geared towards this age group contain an abundance of social strategies in managing specific problems or traumatic events such as divorce, death, or relocation (Knell, 2009). The literature is rich with stories of compelling characters that have successfully coped with problems such as aggression, bullying, anger, and friendship. Examples of books that can be used to help preadolescents develop their social skills can be found at the end of the chapter. Therapists may use these stories or excerpts to open up a discussion about difficult topics in a less threatening way.

These CBPT techniques that were discussed above can be utilized in small groups with preadolescents who need to develop, remediate, or enhance their social skills. CBPT provides the opportunity for preadolescents to experience positive social skills in the presence of their peers through modeling, rehearsing, or learning from fictional characters in a story. This ongoing support and encouragement can be invaluable, especially for preadolescents who are struggling socially and academically in the middle school setting

CASE STUDIES

A preadolescent group met for thirty minutes each week for six weeks to focus on social skills development using the CBPT approach. The group was conducted on-site during school hours in a confidential location and was scheduled during a nonacademic period. Eight students from sixth and seventh grade were selected. The group was composed equally of males, females, Caucasian, and African American children. After obtaining parental consent, I met with each student individually to explain the purpose of the group. Then we began meeting weekly.

Session 1: Getting Acquainted, Building Rapport and Trust

Establishing group rules, developing rapport, and building trust—skills essential for forming friendships and peer groups—were the primary goals of the first group session. Group rules and norms included being respectful, talking one at a time, listening, staying in your seat, and participating in the group. The group members began getting to know one another using a modeling clay activity. Each student was asked to sculpt an item that represented something he or she wanted the group to know. I modeled this activity by sharing my clay creation and explaining, "I sculpted a beach umbrella and a beach ball, because the beach is where I love to be, especially during the summertime." Each group member followed my example by discussing his or her sculpture and how the sculpture was representative of self.

Session 2: Identification of Feelings

The second session began with check-ins; each student shared one positive interaction they had during the week at school. Then, we moved into the new skill for that group session: feelings identification. Feeling charades is a game that assists preadolescents in identifying and discussing feelings. I divided the students into dyads. I gave each dyad a sealed envelope. Inside each envelope were six feeling words: frustrated, disappointed, embarrassed, elated, worried, and discouraged. One member from each dyad was instructed to act out one of the feelings for his or her partner, without using any words. The first dyad that guessed all six feelings correctly was the winner. The prize was a homework pass for any class. After the game, group members discussed each feeling, including how the feeling can affect their thoughts and behaviors in the classroom and at home.

Session 3: Replacing Negative Self-Defeating Thoughts

The goal for the third session was to replace negative self-defeating thoughts with coping self-statements. I explained, "We are going to learn how to be positive about ourselves!" I paired the students in dyads and gave each dyad a shoe box, glue stick, glitter, markers, crayons, and yarn, along with appropriate magazines. Each pair was to create a positively positive box by cutting out pictures and words in the magazines that describe their positive qualities, things they liked, and activities they enjoyed. The goal of the activity was to develop a positive place that celebrated the students on the inside and outside. Once boxes were completed, I invited each student to share his or her part of the box and discuss the pictures and words. We also discussed how different things can look on the outside from the inside.

Session 4: Managing Anger

At the start of the fourth group, I explained that the group would end in two weeks and encouraged the group to decide on a way to celebrate its work. The group members decided to show their appreciation for each other by creating a keepsake for each group member.

The focus shifted to the goal of the group for the day, expressing anger in appropriate ways. Members created an anger montage using poster board, magazines, construction paper, glitter, yarn, paint, and markers. Each student selected pictures and words that represented anger. Once the montages were complete, I shared my anger montage. Afterwards, we discussed what I could do to effectively manage topics that made me angry. Then, each student took a turn sharing their montage and discussing ways to manage their anger. They wrote down their alternatives on construction paper and took that sheet of paper with them at the end of the group, leaving their anger montages in the room. We discussed what happens when one carries around their anger without healthy alternatives to anger expression.

Session 5: Positive Self-Image

I began the session by reminding the students that only one group remained. I positively reinforced the group members for coming to the group each week and being active participants. I introduced the skill for the week, building our self-esteem. In order to help them learn how to develop a more positive perception of self, I first asked group members to say one negative thought they have about themselves. Some examples of group members' negative thoughts were, "I am stupid," "No one talks to me during the day, I must not be a good friend," and "My dad did not pick me up this weekend for our visit and it is my fault, if only I played sports." Then, I asked each group member to approach the sand tray and to create two worlds for the group to see in the sand. I instructed the group members to "create in the sand a world that represents how you see yourself. On the other side of the sand, create a world that represents how you believe your friends, teachers, and family members see you." Each group member shared his or her two worlds, discussing the differences and similarities between them. We discussed how one's perception of self is usually very different from how others perceive them and how those two worlds influence actions at home, in school, and with peers. Finally, by integrating the new perspective, we reframed their initial negative thoughts into positive self-perceptions such as "I may have made a mistake but I can learn," "Even if no one talks to me, I can be friendly to someone," and “I am very disappointed when dad does not pick me up but even when adults have difficulties, I am still O.K. and can find something to enjoy.”

Session 6: Ending Relationships and Integrating Learned Skills

I began the final session by thanking members for their active participation and for adhering to the group rules for the past six weeks. I told the group what I appreciated about them and how I had enjoyed watching each of them grow and develop their own set of social skills. Each member created an appreciation booklet by folding paper in half to make a book. In the book, students completed the following sentences:

My proudest moment in this group was _________.
The skill I have mastered in this group is _________.
My biggest accomplishment during this group was _________.
I will leave this group with _________.

Next, students passed their booklets to the person on their right. Group members wrote one thing they appreciated about the other members in each members’ books. I gave the members time to read the appreciation notes written from fellow group members, and we each took time to reflect upon our work within the group.

CASE STUDY: ANGELA

A teacher referred Angela to the therapist’s social skills group. The teacher noticed Angela was having difficulty communicating during class and with her friends. She was spending more time isolated and presented with some anxiety in the classroom. Angela also exhibited a decline in grades, verbally disagreed with teachers, and engaged in a physical altercation with another female student when Angela forgot her gym uniform.

Angela was a twelve-year-old Caucasian female whose parents were in the process of a divorce. Angela was very close to her father and really missed him. She was angry with her mother for “allowing” her father to leave. Angela blamed her mother for the divorce, as did her father. Prior to her father leaving, Angela had been labeled as gifted and talented and was a straight-A student. Now, her grades were consistently declining, and Angela was failing to complete her homework. Angela’s mother had to take a job working afternoons and evenings, leaving Angela home in the afternoons and nights with her two brothers, ages eight and ten. Angela had the responsibility for feeding them dinner, helping with homework, and putting them to bed. During visits, her father encouraged her to “buck up and be a big girl; help Mom with the boys.” As a result of her mother’s new employment, monetary constraints, and Angela’s new responsibilities at home, Angela had to quit her extracurricular activities. Angela had begun to verbally fight with some of the girls at school for teasing her about having to take care of her brothers in the afternoon.

Angela was not very interested in the social skills group. She told the therapist during their initial meeting, "You cannot help me. I want my parents to stay married and I don't think you can make that happen by putting me in a group with other kids who have issues, so I don't want to be here." When the therapist reached out to Angela's mother to gain consent for the group participation, her mother shared, "I cannot handle any issues with her. I have enough on my plate with the boys, my new job, and my impending divorce; I need to get her support and help." Angela's father did not understand why Angela needed to participate in the group, stating, "My wife is the one with the problem. She caused all of this; she is one that needs counseling, not Angela." Nevertheless, parental consent was given.

Angela completed the six-week social skills group as an active participant. As Angela reflected upon the group process with her therapist, she noted the following as most beneficial for her: identification of feelings, managing anger, and promoting a positive self-image. Angela was able to discuss her feelings related to her parents' divorce with her mom and dad. Angela was also able to identify specific feelings related directly to her parents' impending divorce, coupled with her thoughts and behaviors. Communication between Angela and her parents improved, as Angela learned how to manage her anger more effectively and communicate more positivity. Angela felt better about herself and was able to improve her relationship with her parents, specifically her mom.

REFLECTIONS AND CONCLUSION

CBPT can be effective in the middle school setting with preadolescents who exhibit poor social skills. Many preadolescents have maladaptive social skills including poor interpersonal relationships, inability to make friends, issues with controlling emotions, negative and self-defeating thoughts, as well as ineffective anger and stress management skills. These deficiencies can negatively affect their academic, personal, social, and emotional functioning in and outside the classroom. CBPT, in a group setting, integrates the play/expressive art aspect with the progressive development of effective social skills. Through play, preadolescents learn to exhibit effective skills such as coping mechanisms, functional relationships, emotional regulation, and making appropriate choices in the middle school environment. In a CBPT group, preadolescents can learn prosocial skills and practice applying these skills to relationships in and outside the classroom.

BIBLIOTHERAPY RESOURCES FOR PROSOCIAL SKILLS DEVELOPMENT WITH PREADOLESCENTS IN THE MIDDLE SCHOOL SETTING

Albom, M. (1997). *Tuesdays with Morrie: An old man, a young man, and life's greatest lesson.* New York: Random House Publishers.
Albom, M. (2003). *The five people you meet in heaven*. New York: Hyperion.
Burnett, F. H. (1987). *The secret garden.* Boston: D. R. Godine.
Collins, S. (2010). *The hunger games*. New York: Scholastic Books. (Any in the Hunger Games series.)
Dashner, J. (212*). The maze runner.* New York: Ember.
Forman, G. (2009). *If I stay*. New York: The Penguin Group.
Frank, A. (1995). *The diary of a young girl: The definitive edition* (O. H. Frank & M. Pressler, Eds.; S. Massotty, Trans.). New York: Doubleday. (This edition, a new translation, includes material excluded from the earlier edition.)
Gaines, E. J. (1993). *A lesson before dying*. New York: Vintage Books.
Grant, M. (2008). *Gone*. New York: HarperCollins Children's Books.
Green, J. (2008). *Paper towns*. New York: The Penguin Group.
Green, J. (2012). *The fault in our stars*. New York: The Penguin Group.
L'Engle, M. (1962). *A wrinkle in time*. New York : Farrar, Straus, and Giroux.
Lowry, L. (1993). *The giver*. Boston: Houghton Mifflin.
Meyer, M. (2012). *Cinder.* Virginia: R. R. Donnelley & Sons.
Palacio, R. J. (2012). *Wonder*. New York: Random House.
Roth, V. (2011). *Divergent*. New York: HarperCollins Children's Books. (Any in the Divergent series.)
Snicket, L. (1999). *A series of unfortunate events: The bad beginning*. New York: Harper-Collins.
Zusak, M. (2005). *The book thief.* New York: Random House.

REFERENCES

Akos, P., & Milsom, A. (2007). Introduction to special issue: Group work in K-12 schools. *Journal for Specialists in Group Work, 32*(1), 5–7. doi:10.1080/01933920600977440.
Corey, G. (2013). *Theory and practice of counseling and psychotherapy* (9th ed.). New York: Brooks/ Cole Publishing Company.
Delaney, R. J. (1994). *Fostering changes: Treating attachment-disordered foster children*. Fort Collins, CO: Walter J. Corbett Publishing.
Feldman, R. S. (2014). *Development across the life span* (7th ed.). Upper Saddle River, NJ: Prentice Hall.
Gallo-Lopez, L., & Schaefer, C. E. (Eds.). (2005). *Play therapy with adolescents*. New York: Jason Aronson.
Gladding, S. T. (2012). *Counseling a group specialty* (6th ed.). Upper Saddle River, NJ: Pearson.
Goldstein, A. P., & McGinnis, E. (2009). *Skillstreaming the preadolescent: New strategies and perspectives for teaching prosocial skills*. Champaign, IL: Research Press.
Harrell, A. W., Mercer, S. H., & DeRosier, M. E. (2008). Improving the social-behavioral adjustment of adolescents: The effectiveness of a social skills group intervention. *Journal of Child and Family Studies, 18*(4), 378–387. doi:10.1007/s10826-008-9241-y
Kayler, H., & Sherman, J. (2009). At-risk ninth grade students: A psychoeducational group approach to increase study skills and grade point averages. *Professional School Counseling, 12*(6), 434–439. doi:10.5330/PSC.n.2010-12.434
Knell, S. M. (2009). *Cognitive-behavioral play therapy*. Northvale, NJ: Jason Aronson Inc.
Kottman, T. (2011). *Play therapy basics and beyond* (2nd ed.). Alexandria, VA: American Counseling Association.

Ray, D. C., Armstrong, S. A., Balkin, R. S., & Jayne, K. M. (2015). Child-centered play therapy in the schools: Review and Meta-Analysis. *Psychology in the Schools,* 52, 107–123. http://dx.doi.org/10 .1002/pits.21798 .

Shechtman, Z., & Pastor, R. (2005). Cognitive-behavioral and humanistic group treatment for children with disabilities: A comparison of outcome and process. *Journal of Counseling Psychology, 52*(3), 322–326. doi:10.1037/0022-0167.52.3.322.

U.S. Department of Health and Human Services (2017). Mental Health and Adolescents. https:/ /www.hhs.gov/ash/oah/adolescent-development/mental-health/index.html.

Vickers, B. (2002). Cognitive behaviour therapy for adolescents with psychological disorders: A group treatment programme. *Clinical Child Psychology and Psychiatry*, *7*(2), 249–262. doi:10.1177/1359104502007002011.

Chapter Twelve

Ethical Issues in Play Therapy with Preadolescents

Therapist Competence, Confidentiality, and Self-Care

Jodi Crane and Amie Myrick

Take care of yourself. You can't pour from an empty cup.—Unknown

Play therapy is a multidisciplinary field composed of professional counselors, social workers, school counselors, marriage and family therapists, and psychologists. Play therapists adhere to several ethical guidelines, including those set forth by the Association for Play Therapy (APT, 2016), primary disciplines and professional organizations, state licensing boards, and state and federal laws. We also apply the ethical principles of autonomy, beneficence, nonmaleficence, fidelity, justice, and veracity to our work with clients (Kitchener, 1984). Clients have freedom of choice, and play therapists uphold their clients' welfare, protect their clients, keep promises to clients, practice fairness, and tell the truth. Ethical decision-making involves considering legal, professional, and client-centered variables.

In this chapter, we will use the Play Therapy Practice Guidelines (Association for Play Therapy, 2016) to discuss the following ethical issues as they relate to play therapist practice with preadolescents: play therapist competence, confidentiality and its limitations, and self-care. Other ethical issues may occur, of course, but are beyond the scope of this chapter.

LITERATURE REVIEW

Clinical Competence

All ethical codes state that in order to not harm clients, one must be competent in the areas in which one practices. That is, play therapists commit to acquiring the knowledge and skills necessary to work with clients. One way a clinician can demonstrate competence in play therapy is to obtain the Registered Play Therapist (RPT) or School-Based Regsitered Play Therapist (SB-RPT) credentials. APT (Association for Play Therapy, 2017) confers these credentials to licensed mental health professionals or school counselors or school psychologists with a license or certificate from their state department of education to practice independently. Those with either credential have satisfied requirements in educational coursework, clinical experience, play therapy training, and supervised play therapy experience. Education at the master's level or higher must include coursework in child development, child and adolescent psychopathology, ethics, principles of psychotherapy, and theories of personality.

Besides education and supervised training, play therapists must self-monitor whether or not they are competent to utilize play therapy with a specific client at a particular time. Ashby, Wood, and Kilperman (2017) suggest play therapists ask themselves the following questions in determining their own competence:

1. Am I competent in working with children?
2. Am I competent to conduct play therapy?
3. Am I competent to address the presenting concern?
4. Am I competent in working with diverse clients?
5. Do I have adequate training and supervision to provide care to this client? (p. 219)

Reading one book or attending a couple of workshops does not make one competent to practice play therapy. A key component is having a play therapist supervisor who actually observes the clinician practicing play therapy (Landreth, 2012). There is no substitute for a quality supervisor. In addition, even though it may be legal in some states, it is unethical for someone who is not competent in play therapy to supervise a play therapist in training. Because of this, starting in 2020, APT (Association for Play Therapy, 2017) will count towards the RPT or SB-RPT credentials only play therapy hours that have been supervised by play therapists with the RPT-S credential.

Developmental Knowledge

Knowledge of developmental issues encountered by preadolescents, middle schoolers, and young adolescents is an important competency area for ethical practice. Typical behaviors seen at this age include:

- increased attention to physical appearance
- concern about whether one's body is developing normally
- a temporary period of extreme self-consciousness
- idealism (i.e., because things *could* be so, they *should* be so)
- invulnerability—apparent disregard for rules of safety ("I know it's not safe, but it won't happen to me.")
- the personal fable—self-dramatization and belief that their experiences are so unique that no one (especially adults) could possibly understand them
- increased argumentativeness, accompanied by what may seem to be rigid thinking, because they cannot objectively weight the merits of their own point of view against those of the person with whom they are arguing
- intense involvement with the peer group
- increased conformity to peers and concern about acceptance
- increased attention to differences between "masculine" and "feminine" gender roles and disapproval of gender-atypical behavior in others (Micucci, 1998, p. 67).

Awareness of typical preadolescent development can help play therapists normalize many preadolescent issues for clients and their parents as well as understand when a particular behavior may be cause for concern. *The Therapist's Guide to Child Development: The Extraordinarily Normal Years* (Ray, 2016) is an excellent resource in this area.

Multicultural Competence

Multicultural (or cross-cultural) competence is another necessary component of the play therapist's knowledge and skills. Play therapists are expected to practice in a way that demonstrates understanding, sensitivity, and respect to the diverse cultural backgrounds of their clients and the way in which therapists' own culture may influence their therapeutic philosophy and interventions. According to Gil (2005), this competency area entails three steps: building sensitivity, obtaining knowledge responsibly, and developing active competence. *Building sensitivity* is the introspective process of learning about one's own cultural background and being aware of one's own attitudes, values, and biases as one interacts with clients who may have different background and experiences than the play therapist. *Obtaining knowledge* responsibly concerns gaining knowledge and skills and practicing with accountability by getting feedback on one's work from more experienced colleagues and supervisors. Finally, *developing active competence* means translating one's sensitivity and awareness and cross-cultural knowledge and skills into action.

Play therapists should also have knowledge of the current culture as it pertains to preadolescents. Being aware of the latest YouTube channels, social media applications, movies, music, books, TV shows, and websites in which preadolescents are immersing themselves and are influenced by can make a qualitative difference when it comes to the therapeutic alliance and treatment success. Even though many forms of social media require the user to be at least thirteen years old, many preadolescents find ways around this. The average age of first smartphone ownership is ten, suggesting that preadolescents have far greater access to social media than some adults might realize (Chen, 2016). Play therapists can benefit from understanding the benefits, risks, and usages of as many social media platforms as possible. In order to ensure safety, the play therapist may need to educate both the preadolescent and parent on ways to safeguard privacy and protect the preadolescent from hidden dangers such as cyberbullying, sexual predators, and sexting, particularly in the form of sending nude photos of oneself over the Internet (see Myrick, 2017, chapter 4).

CONFIDENTIALITY

In addition to the usual limitations on confidentiality found in state laws and ethical codes, play therapy with preadolescents involves minors who cannot provide consent for their own treatment. Therefore, the Play Therapy Best Practices (Association for Play Therapy, 2016) states play therapists balance the preadolescent's ethical right to privacy and confidentiality with parents' or legal guardians' legal right to be informed of their child's treatment. This balance may be challenging for the play therapist, as preadolescent clients have an ethical right to know in a developmentally appropriate manner what is shared with others and why (Association for Play Therapy, 2016) while parents also have a legal right to know about their child's treatment. Parents may be intimidated by the fact that their child has a unique relationship with another adult or worry about what is being said (Martin, 2003). It is important that the play therapist develop a helpful, working relationship where parents trust the play therapist and involve parents in as much of the therapy process as possible; this may be achieved through parent consultation, filial therapy, or family play therapy.

In deciding what to disclose, play therapists should take into account the parents' reaction to the disclosure and how they may use the information (Landreth, 2012). We recommend play therapists disclose only what is in the child's best interest; this may include progress toward treatment goals, play themes, and any concerns about the preadolescent's safety or well-being. Safety concerns include suspicion of child abuse, suicidal ideation, or threats to run away or physically hurt others. In this way, play therapists can address parents' legal right to information without going into detail about what preadolescents have said, how they have played during sessions, and what toys and art material were used.

SELF-CARE

In order to connect meaningfully with clients while remaining emotionally competent and avoiding therapist impairment, it is our ethical and professional responsibility to preserve and support our well-being, monitoring ourselves for any personal impairment.

As play therapists we are prone to experience compassion fatigue, vicarious traumatization, anxiety or depression, or physical illness (Figley, 2002). We may suffer from burnout as we face physical and emotional exhaustion and fatigue, depersonalization, and a reduced sense of personal accomplishment.

Play therapists must exercise effective self-care (Bradley, Adamson, & Kress, 2013). When we exercise adequate self-care, we are able to protect ourselves from burnout, enjoy our work with clients, and provide high-quality work. Besides getting sufficient sleep, exercise, and nutrition, we must prioritize time for self-reflection or continued consultation and supervision. In addition, we can practice what we preach by using the very coping skills we recommend and teach to clients. These self-care strategies include utilizing self-compassion (Patsiopoulos & Buchanan, 2011), connecting to our spirituality (Wolf, Thompson, Thompson, & Smith-Adcock, 2014), practicing mindfulness meditation and gratitude journaling (Chlebak et al., 2013), and engaging in creativity and self-expression (Bradley et al., 2013). And, of course, we can play.

Examples of self-care strategies I (JC) have used to ensure my practice remains ethical are numerous. Besides those already listed, I journal daily about whatever is on my mind. I receive regular massages. I consult with colleagues about client issues whenever necessary. I connect to spirituality through prayer, meditation, use of a personal altar space, and yoga. I utilize my sand tray and figures to process client or personal issues. I paint with acrylics and read novels. Finally, I give and receive lots of hugs from family and friends.

CASE STUDY

Maryanne (pseudonym) was an eleven-year-old Caucasian female, referred to me (AM) by the local child advocacy center after disclosing ongoing sexual abuse at the hands of her mother's boyfriend. After Maryanne's mother, Denise, walked in on the abuse, she allowed the perpetrator to stay in the home. This resulted in Department of Social Services (DSS) removing Maryanne and her younger brother from the home and placing them with foster parents. Maryanne was distraught over the abuse and her removal from the home, and she felt great anger towards "the system." Within weeks, she was self-harming, experiencing passive suicidal ideation, having difficulty in school, and running away from her foster home. Similarly, Denise was angry, hurt, and scared. She blamed DSS for breaking up the family, refused to participate in counseling with Maryanne, and continued to have ongoing contact with Maryanne's perpetrator. She told me that Maryanne and her boyfriend had been having an affair and that "Maryanne is just as guilty as he is."

Although at this point, I felt competent in the area of treating child sexual abuse, I had never before worked with a primary caregiver who considered her child a coconspirator in her own sexual abuse. Maryanne's DSS worker was incredibly frustrated with Denise and shared as much with me. Power struggles were already evident between Denise and Maryanne's worker, and Denise was furious that DSS had given me permission to speak with Maryanne's foster mother, Sandie. Sandie was trying, unsuccessfully, to set limits with hours of the day that Denise could visit and call Maryanne. Everyone was in total crisis.

I could spend many pages here detailing the grueling, but ultimately rewarding, work that Maryanne did in therapy. I could outline later parent sessions where Denise yelled at me, tried to fire me, and told me I did not know what I was doing. I could share the power struggles I engaged in with DSS, as they tried to make reunification with this family contingent on intense trauma work, thereby putting me in the position of deciding when this child could return home. None of these topics are the reason that I chose to share this particular case in a chapter about ethics, however. I chose to share my experiences with Maryanne and her family because they taught me the value of competency and self-care when working on a difficult case.

I'll admit it, at various points in my three-year therapeutic relationship with Maryanne, I was at a loss. I was not sure how to do meaningful, healing work with her when her primary support, Denise, was sabotaging our work at every turn. I did not know if Denise would ever be able to respond appropriately to Maryanne's recounting of her sexual abuse, and I worried that Denise would not be able to recognize signs of danger and protect Maryanne in the future. For all of these reasons, I clung to my weekly supervision sessions and monthly peer consultation calls. These meetings allowed me to practice good self-care, venting my frustrations and listening to feedback from non-judging professionals. On one occasion, a colleague told me I was working too hard. "Mom is either going to be open to hearing what you have to say or not," she told me after I was lamenting about another parent session where Denise told me that I was lying about what Maryanne had told me. "You need to recognize what you have control over and what you do not. Mom is not in a place to hear that someone might know her daughter more intimately than she does. You can keep pushing, or you can let her sit with that and maybe even grieve it." Looking back, I had so clearly allowed myself to become engaged in yet another power struggle with Denise. Since this colleague was outside the dynamics, she was able to see it immediately and encouraged me to take care of myself by recognizing my limitations.

When it came to maintaining competency, I needed to consider the fact that Denise's upbringing, trauma history, and parenting style was different than my own. Additionally, Maryanne was Denise's oldest child, and therefore it was her first experience parenting a preadolescent. Taking a hard look at my expectations and potential biases towards Denise helped me determine what type of new knowledge I needed from the literature and the professionals surrounding me. I read articles and books on the effect of sexual abuse on parenting and, even more specifically, the experience of a sexually abused parent upon learning her own child had also been sexually abused. With colleagues, I discussed approaches that had worked with adults struggling with borderline personality disorder symptoms and revisited my notes on motivational interviewing. All of these pieces gave me a more comprehensive and thoughtful view of what Denise must be experiencing and what she might need to move forward with Maryanne. For example, I realized that Denise felt threatened by my close relationship with Maryanne. I considered different ways of setting limits with Denise in our sessions, and I found ways to incorporate her into Maryanne's work beyond the parenting sessions so that she felt valued and included in her role as Maryanne's mother. I realized that sharing some of Maryanne's artwork and poetry when it felt appropriate (and when Maryanne gave her permission) helped Denise feel included in the therapeutic work while still maintaining boundaries. I helped Maryanne identify some issues she wanted to address with her mother, and we began incorporating parent–child sessions into our work a couple times per month. Denise liked coming into these sessions and participated actively.

Confidentiality posed an interesting issue for me in this particular case. Maryanne was in the custody of DSS, in a therapeutic foster home, and working towards reunification with her mother. DSS wanted Denise to be as involved as possible, but at times it was unclear whether or not Denise could respond appropriately to Maryanne's unsafe behaviors and to what degree DSS wanted her to be involved. There were also legal barriers; on one occasion, DSS allowed Denise to transport Maryanne to her appointment. During this appointment, it became clear that Maryanne needed inpatient hospitalization. Denise took her directly to the hospital, only to find out that she could not do anything until DSS arrived. Throughout treatment, Maryanne's self-harm fluctuated greatly, so I had to make judgment calls, sometimes on a weekly basis, about whether or not her behaviors warranted breaking confidentiality. I utilized peer consultation and supervision heavily in these instances. Many times, I shared the self-harm with DSS first, and then the caseworker and I would discuss how best to involve Denise, if at all. As Maryanne prepared to return to Denise's custody, I kept DSS and Denise equally apprised of Maryanne's progress and any concerning behaviors.

As for my work with Maryanne, learning how to better work with Denise allowed me to prepare Maryanne for sharing her trauma narrative and details of her trauma with her mother. Overall, the session in which she shared her trauma with Denise was positive and productive. They continued in treatment with me for about six months after DSS closed its case and Maryanne and her brother returned to Denise's home. After an initial "honeymoon period" in which Maryanne seemed to be stable, her self-injurious and high-risk behaviors began anew. Denise had difficulty accepting these symptoms, as they challenged her view of herself as a "good parent." She struggled with the notion that her daughter may need increased treatment to restabilize. Unfortunately, Denise terminated Maryanne's treatment abruptly not long after I suggested hospitalization. The last contact I had with the family was Denise telling me that she had found someone else who would be able to help Maryanne as I could not. Although the way in which this treatment ended was difficult and disappointing, the self-care and work to develop useful competence that I had been utilizing for several years with this family was helpful. To this day, I feel proud of the ethical and respectful way in which I handled this case, from beginning to end, and have carried the lessons learned through to new cases and challenges in my clinical work.

REFLECTION AND CONCLUSION

Preadolescents bring with them a whole host of developmental, emotional, and intellectual challenges that are different from those of younger children and older adolescents. In order to best help them in our role as play therapist, we must consider ethical, legal, professional, and client-centered variables. Ensuring we are competent in developmental needs, the appropriateness of play and other therapies, and multicultural issues is critical if we are to assist preadolescents and their parents in managing symptoms and healing from trauma. Confidentiality and sharing information with parents becomes more nuanced as children enter preadolescence. Self-care in the form of setting limits and seeking regular supervision must be a priority in order to continue conducting effective therapy with our preadolescent clients.

REFERENCES

Ashby, J. S., Wood, L., & Kilperman, S. (2017). Ethics in play therapy consultation and supervision. In R. L. Steen (Ed.), *Emergency research in play therapy, child counseling, and consultation* (pp. 214–231). Hershey, PA: IGI Global.

Association for Play Therapy. (2016). Play therapy best practices. Retrieved from http://www.a4pt.org/?page=Research.

Association for Play Therapy. (2017). Play therapy credentials. Retrieved from http://www.a4pt.org/page/CredentialsHomepage.

Bradley, N., Adamson, N., & Kress, V. E. (2013). Creative approaches for promoting counselor self-care. *Journal of Creativity in Mental Health, 8*(4), 456–469.

Chen, B. X. (2016, July, 20). What's the right age for a child to get a smartphone? *New York Times*. Retrieved from http://www.nytimes.com.

Chlebak, C. M., James, S., Westwood, M. J., Gockel, A., Zumbo, B., & Shapiro, S. L. (2013). Mindfulness meditation and gratitude journaling: The experiences of graduate counseling psychology students. *Counselling and Spirituality, 32*(2), 79–103.

Figley, C. R. (2002). Compassion fatigue: Psychotherapists' chronic lack of self care. *Journal of Clinical Psychology, 58*(11), 1433–1441.

Gil, E. (2005). From sensitivity to competence in working across cultures. In E. Gil and A. A. Drewes (Eds.), *Cultural issues in play therapy* (pp. 3–25). New York: Guilford.

Kitchener, K. S. (1984). Intuition, critical evaluation, and ethical principles: The foundation for ethical decision in counseling psychology. *Counseling Psychologist, 12*, 43–55.

Landreth, G. L. (2012). *Play therapy: The art of the relationship* (3rd ed.). New York: Routledge.

Martin, D. G. (2003). *Clinical practice with adolescents*. Pacific Grove, CA: Brooks/Cole.

Micucci, J. A. (1998). *The adolescent in family therapy: Breaking the cycle of conflict and control.* New York: Guilford.

Myrick, A. C. (2017). *Engaging parents in adolescent therapy: Beyond the waiting room.* Lanham, MD: Rowman & Littlefield.

Patsiopoulos, A. T., & Buchanan, M. J. (2011). The practice of self-compassion in counseling: A narrative inquiry. *Professional Psychology: Research and Practice, 42*(4), 301–307.

Ray, D. (Ed.). (2016). *The therapist's guide to child development: The extraordinarily normal years.* New York: Routledge.

Wolf, C. P., Thompson, I., Thompson, E. S., & Smith-Adcock, S. (2014). Refresh your mind, rejuvenate your body, renew your spirit: A pilot wellness program for counselor education. *The Journal of Individual Psychology, 70*(1), 57–75.

Index

About the Contributors

Sarah Caprioli, LMHC, is a trauma therapist in private practice in New York's Hudson Valley. Prior to her transition to the private sector, Sarah spent approximately ten years immersed in trauma theory and treatment as a clinician and special projects coordinator with Family Services' Center for Victim Safety and Support. She provides counseling for children, adolescents, and adults impacted by trauma using a variety of therapy modalities and trauma-informed practices. Sarah is a fully trained EMDR practitioner, a DOH Certified Rape Crisis and Crime Victims Advocate, and also works as part of a certified Courthouse Facility Dog team, using service dogs to comfort and heal victims of crime. Outside of her practice Sarah provides a range of consultant services to local organizations, and additionally sits on the Board of Directors of the Dutchess County Coalition Against Sexual and Domestic Abuse (CASADA). Sarah writes and presents regularly on the topics of trauma and sexual violence.

Jodi Crane, PhD, LPCC, NCC, RPT-S, is professor in the School of Professional Counseling at Lindsey Wilson College in Columbia, Kentucky. She is past chair of the Board of Directors of the Association for Play Therapy. She sees clients through Puckett Counseling Services in Glasgow, Kentucky, and supervises clinicians working toward licensure or play therapy credential.

David A. Crenshaw, PhD, ABPP, RPT-S, is an author and clinical director of the Children's Home of Poughkeepsie. He has taught graduate courses in Play Therapy at Johns Hopkins and Columbia University.

Pam Dyson, MA, LPC-S, RPT-S, specializes in working with children three to twelve years of age at her private practice in Plano, Texas. As the founder and director of the DFW Center for Play Therapy Training she provides workshops, supervision, and consultation services. Pam was the recipient of the Association for Play Therapy 2013 Key Award for Professional Education and Training and serves on the APT Board of Directors.

Laura Fazio-Griffith, PhD, NCC, LPC-S, LMFT, and registered play therapist supervisor, is an associate professor at Southeastern Louisiana University. She is the coordinator of the play therapy program and the marriage, couple, and family counseling specialization. Her research interests include: group work, child and adolescent counseling, and supervision. Prior to coming to Southeastern, she was the clinical director at a counseling and training center, where she provided counseling for children, adolescents, and families. She has served on the Louisiana Association for Play Therapy Board for the past eight years and is the current president of LAPT.

Dr. Robert Jason Grant owns and operates the AutPlay Therapy Clinic in Springfield, Missouri. Dr. Grant is the creator of AutPlay® Therapy and is the author of several books and publications related to autism and play therapy, including "AutPlay Therapy for Children and Adolescents on the Autism Spectrum: A Behavioral Play Based Approach." For more information, visit www.robertjasongrant.com.

Cody T. Lankford, MS, LPC-Intern, NCC, is a doctoral student in the Department of Counseling and Higher Education at the University of North Texas. He has experience working with children, adolescents, adults, and parents in community-based, elementary school, college campus, and private counseling settings. Although he has worked with an array of presenting concerns, he more recently began to specialize in children with attachment disruptions. His research interests include relational depth in counseling, play therapy effectiveness, and supporting LGBTQ+ families.

Ariel D. Marrero, MS, is a doctoral student in the Combined-Integrated Clinical & School Psychology program at James Madison University. She uses her passion for play and expressive arts to fuel her work with children and families. Her background is in mental health counseling and she has worked in a variety of settings, including elementary schools, community clinics, and residential facilities.

Kristin Meany-Walen, PhD, LMHC, RPT-S, is an assistant professor of counseling at the University of North Texas. She specializes in working with children and adolescents using Adlerian play therapy. Kristin has published a number of research articles and book chapters and coauthored the third edition of *Partners in Play: An Adlerian Approach to Play Therapy.*

Clair Mellenthin, LCSW, RPT-S, holds a master's degree in social work from the University of Southern California. Throughout her career, she has focused on providing play therapy to children, teens, and their families. She is currently the director of Child & Adolescent Services at Wasatch Family Therapy. Ms. Mellenthin is a sought-after supervisor, training graduate students and interns in play therapy, and an adjunct faculty member at the University of Southern California MSW program. She is the past president of the Utah Association for Play Therapy and remains an active member on the Board of Directors. She is the author of *Play Therapy: Engaging & Powerful Techniques for the Treatment of Childhood Disorders* and the *My Many Colors of Me* workbook. In addition to being an experienced play therapist and professor, Ms. Mellenthin frequently presents professional play therapy and family therapy trainings and appears on local and national TV and radio as an expert on children and family issues.

Dr. Joseph Pellegrino received his doctorate in school and clinical psychology from the University of Virginia. He completed postdoctoral training at the Virginia Treatment Center for Children at the Medical College of Virginia, a residential treatment center for children and adolescents. His doctoral dissertation compared different approaches to diagnosing depression in children and adolescents. Dr. Pellegrino has practiced in the public schools, a university counseling center, day treatment programs, residential treatment programs, and mental health clinics. He maintains a private practice with children, adolescents, families, and adults and serves as the clinical psychologist for an intensive school-based day treatment program for children with severe emotional and behavioral disorders.

Audrey Punnett, PhD, is a licensed psychologist who holds diplomas in Adult Analytical Psychology and Child and Adolescent Analytical Psychology from the C. G. Jung Institute, Zurich. She is a Registered Play Therapist and Supervisor and Clinical and Teaching Member of Sandplay Therapists of America and the International Society of Sandplay Therapists. Currently, she is in private practice and since 1986 has been on the clinical faculty of UCSF as an associate professor. She lectures nationally and internationally on Jungian psychology and sandplay therapy. Her book, *The Orphan: A Journey to Wholeness,* published by Fisher King Press, was released in 2014; her edited book, *Jungian Child Analysis,* is due to be released in 2018.

Dee C. Ray, PhD, LPC-S, NCC, RPT-S, is a distinguished teaching professor in the Counseling Program and director of the Center for Play Therapy at the University of North Texas. Dr. Ray has published over one hundred articles, chapters, and books on play therapy, specializing in research publications examining the effects of Child Centered Play Therapy. She is author of *A Therapist's Guide to Development: The Extraordinarily Normal Years* and *Advanced Play Therapy: Essential Conditions, Knowledge, and Skills for Child Practice.*

Janine Shelby, PhD, is an associate clinical professor at the University of California, Los Angeles, in the Geffen School of Medicine, and a Guest Professor at Kobe College in Hyogo, Japan. She is the author of several publications involving developmentally sensitive, evidence-based treatments for children and adolescents. Dr. Shelby's private and forensic psychology practices are based in Torrance and Newport Beach, California. For more information, visit http://www.DrJanineShelby.com.

Sang Min Shin, PhD, is an assistant professor in the counseling program of Educational Psychology Special Service Department in the College of Education at the University of Texas at El Paso. Her research interests include play therapy, nature-based play therapy, child–parent relationship, play therapy training, and multiculturalism in child counseling. She coauthored with Jacqueline Swank, PhD, on the topics of nature-based play therapy research articles.

Anne Stewart, PhD, RPT-S, is professor of Graduate Psychology at James Madison University. She has worked in numerous postdisaster projects around the world to promote secure attachments and resilience for children. Dr. Stewart and colleagues published "Play Therapy: A Comprehensive Guide to Theory and Practice," "Becoming a Community Counselor," and "Thriving! A Manual for Students in the Helping Professions." She has coauthored book chapters and articles on attachment, resilience, and interprofessional collaboration. Anne is a member of the Association for Play Therapy Board of Directors and a playful practitioner of play and family therapy. Visit her at http://www.psyc.jmu.edu/gradpsyc/people/stewart.html.

Jacqueline M. Swank, PhD, is an associate professor of counselor education at the University of Florida. She is a licensed mental health counselor, licensed clinical social worker, and registered play therapist supervisor. Her clinical experience has focused on working with children and adolescents and their families in outpatient, day treatment, inpatient, and residential settings. Her research interests include nature and play-based interventions with children and adolescents, assessment, counselor development, and international counseling.

About the Editors

Eric Green, PhD, LPC-S, RPT-S, SP, is a faculty associate at the Johns Hopkins University School of Education in Baltimore, Maryland, as well as serving as the executive director of Better Options Initiative, a nonprofit located in Lafayette Louisiana, which focuses on protecting children from parental conflict. Dr. Green has been the author and coeditor of several recent books in child therapy, including *The Handbook of Jungian Play Therapy*, *No Child Forgotten*, *Counseling Families*, and *Integrating Expressive Arts and Play Therapy with Children and Adolescents*. He is a regularly invited keynote speaker at mental health conferences around the United States and internationally, focusing on treating childhood trauma, Jungian play therapy, sandplay, and adolescent psychotherapy. He's the author of over eighty publications and has been featured in four psychoeducational child psychology films with Alexander Street Press. For more information, visit www.drericgreen.com.

Jennifer Baggerly, PhD, LPC-S, RPT-S, is a professor of counseling and play therapy at the University of North Texas at Dallas. Dr. Baggerly also provides counseling and play therapy at Kaleidoscope Behavioral Health in Flower Mound, Texas. She served as chair of the Board of Directors for the Association for Play Therapy from 2013 to 2014 and was a member of the board from 2009 to 2015. Dr. Baggerly has taught and counseled children for over twenty years. Her published books include *Child-Centered Play Therapy Research: The Evidence Base for Effective Practice*, *Group Play Therapy: A Dynamic Approach*, and *Counseling Families: Play-Based Treatment*. Dr. Baggerly's multiple research projects and over sixty publications have led to her being recognized as a prominent expert in children's counseling. She has provided disaster response play therapy to children and adolescents impacted by the 2004 tsunami in Sri Lanka, 2005 Hurricane Katrina, numerous Florida hurricanes, 2013 tornado in Moore, Oklahoma, 2017 Hurricane Harvey in Texas, and 2017 Hurricane Maria in Puerto Rico.

Amie Myrick, MS, LCPC is the director of Education and Training at Family & Children's Services in Bel Air, Maryland, and a licensed professional counselor. She specializes in treating children, adolescents, and adults for anxiety-, mood-, and trauma-related disorders. She has been involved in trauma and play-based research for the past fifteen years with over twenty-five published peer-reviewed articles and book chapters. Her published books include *Engaging Parents in the Adolescent Therapy: Beyond the Waiting Room*, *Play Therapy with Vulnerable Populations: No Child Forgotten*, and *Counseling Families: Play-Based Treatment*.

www.ingramcontent.com/pod-product-compliance
Ingram Content Group UK Ltd.
Pitfield, Milton Keynes, MK11 3LW, UK
UKHW012040150926
475560UK00001B/96

9 781538 108604